Children's Theater

A Paradigm, Primer, and Resource

Kelly and Walter Eggers

THE SCARECROW PRESS, INC.
Lanham • Toronto • Plymouth, UK
2010

KH

Published by Scarecrow Press, Inc.
A wholly owned subsidiary of The Rowman & Littlefield Publishing Group, Inc.
4501 Forbes Boulevard, Suite 200, Lanham, Maryland 20706
http://www.scarecrowpress.com

Estover Road, Plymouth PL6 7PY, United Kingdom

British Library Cataloguing in Publication Information Available

Library of Congress Cataloging-in-Publication Data
Eggers, Kelly, 1955–
  Children's theater : a paradigm, primer, and resource / Kelly and Walter
Eggers.
     p. cm.
  Includes bibliographical references and index.
  ISBN 978-0-8108-5988-3 (cloth : alk. paper) — ISBN 978-0-8108-7292-9
(ebook)
  1. Oyster River Players (Exeter, N.H.) 2. Children's theater—New
Hampshire—Exeter—History—20th century. 3. Children's theater—New
Hampshire—Exeter—History—21st century. I. Eggers, Walter, 1943– II.
Title.
  PN3159.U6E34 2010
  792'.0226'02573dc22   2009040606

∞ ™ The paper used in this publication meets the minimum requirements of
American National Standard for Information Sciences—Permanence of Paper
for Printed Library Materials, ANSI/NISO Z39.48-1992.

Printed in the United States of America

7/5/11

Contents

Acknowledgments

This book was put together with the help of many people: generations of children who have made up the Oyster River Players, their parents and families, and other community members. They responded to every request, and their enthusiasm kept us going.

We called on children's theater producers and directors from around the world, who have been our colleagues, offering help and providing information and descriptions of their companies:

Linda M. Berg, Children's Theatre Director, The Children's Theatre of Martha's Vineyard (Island Theatre Workshop), Tisbury, Massachusetts, United States

Gregory Boris, Project Development Director, and Terri Elander, International Public Relations Director, The Missoula Children's Theatre, Missoula, Montana, United States

Pip Buining, Artistic Director, Canberra Youth Theatre, Canberra, Australia

Julia Davies, Administrative Director, Gwent Young People's Theatre, Abergavenny, Wales

Thomas Gough, Founder and Teacher, The Glenwood Shakespeare Company, Casula, Australia

Diana Green, Executive Director, The Children's Shakespeare and The Rogue Players, Palisades, New York, United States

Christian Heppinstall, Executive Director, Alaska Theatre of Youth, Anchorage, Alaska, United States

Katrina Innis, Marketing Officer, Scottish Youth Theatre, Edinburgh and Glasgow, Scotland

Jo Anne Lamun, Producer/Director, Peanut Butter Players, Lafayette, Colorado, United States

Sylvia Langworthy, Artistic Director, The Masque Youth Theatre and School, Rochester, Minnesota, United States

Albert Laveau, Artistic & Managing Director, The Children's Theatre Workshop, Belmont, Trinidad

Joyce Levinsohn, Artistic Director, National Children's Theatre, Johannesburg, South Africa

Mat Mailant, Artistic and Executive Director, Calgary Young People's Theatre, Calgary, Alberta, Canada

Karen McGrady-Parker, Associate Director, Scottish Youth Theatre, Glasgow, Scotland

Claudia Nieuwenhuizen, Educatief Medewerker, Jonna Toneelschool, Wilsele, Belgium

Heidi Rohringer, Obfrau künstlerische und pädagogische Leitung, ICH-DUWIR—Theater & Kultur, Vienna, Austria

Craig Slaight, Director, Young Conservatory, San Francisco, California, United States

Kent Suss, Theatre School Director, Manitoba Theatre for Young People, Winnipeg, Manitoba, Canada

Paul Sutton, Artistic Director, C&T (Collar & Tie Ltd), Worcester, England

Don Trotter, Board President, Children's Theatre Project, Rockford, Illinois, United States

Jenny Wake, Founder and Artistic Director, Calico Young People's Theatre, Napier, New Zealand

Directors of children's theater associations in this and other countries afforded a special broad and deep perspective:

Colin Bradie, Director, Promote YT, Edinburgh, Scotland

Orlaith McBride, Director, National Association of Youth Drama, Dublin, Ireland

Kathleen E. Taylor, Marketing Manager, and Michael Peitz, Executive Director, Educational Theatre Association, Cincinnati, Ohio, United States

Nigel Townsend, Artistic Director, Y Touring, London, England

Gillian Wells, Administrator, National Youth Dance of Wales and National Youth Theatre of Wales, Cardiff, Wales

The editors at Scarecrow Press gave us great assistance, not only in the production of this book but in reconstructions along the way.

The splendid costumes featured in the photographs were designed and built by Danuta Richards, with any help she could get, over all the years. Peggy Murray gets credit for interviewing, as for much else in support of the program. Special thanks go to David Feldman, who took charge of the photography and provided most of the shots. Photograph credits also go to Lisa Allison and to Paul Heckel, who maintains our Web site filled with pictures. Early drafts of parts of this text were read and criticized by Virginia Stuart, Eliza Hill, and others.

The original members of the company—Robert Eggers, Amanda Michaels, Nate and Nick Grondin, Natan Daskal, Mike and Megan Neal, Molly Finnegan, Ali Shaker, Sharon Bornstein, Anita Rundels, Maura Hentz, Rachel Papas, Kaitlin Owens, Ashley Tata, Jessica Richards, and many others—are still with it in spirit. Our early generation families—the Heckels, Hills, Murphys, Sloats, Rundles, and Quinns—still bolster us.

Rob, Max, and Sam, the children of the authors, inspired this book. Two people who get special thanks are Charlotte Mandell, who helped conceive this company, and Robert Houston, its godfather.

Finally, this book is dedicated to influences on Kelly's young life: her mother, Maxine Houston; Blanche Kelly; Barbara Cataldo; Mary Rawlings; Lucille Robinson; Maggie and Annie Mae Houston; Viola and Adelmo Vialpando; Margaret and Don Boyd; Carolyn and Bob Nelson; Ann and Jim Barlow; Joy and Joe Deaderick; Jane Love; Booie, Jean, and Howard Carroll; and Hans and Elaine Eugster, all of whom taught her respect and the love of young children.

Introduction: The Oyster River Players' First Production of *A Midsummer Night's Dream*

This book tries to explain a miracle: a fine full-scale production of Shakespeare's *A Midsummer Night's Dream* by children who had little experience in theater. They ranged in age between five and fifteen, and most of them were in their fourth year together as a theater company. They took classes in theater and dance, and they performed mainly musicals but also straight plays, on a seasonal schedule of four shows a year. They had never attempted such a complex or difficult production, and they succeeded.

They knew each other and their teacher-director very well, but they did have other friends and lives that were full of school, sports, and their families, even during the six weeks of rehearsals, which took place in the middle of the school year. They had no pedigrees, and their ranks were not winnowed by auditions. Anyone could join the company, and everyone got a part. The only way to account for what these children achieved was what they learned in classes and rehearsals.

They took on the challenge of Shakespeare with natural, innocent confidence. The plan was to find ways to match the play with their abilities. For their script, the text of the play would be edited, but only to cut the tangled language that would not advance the plot or show off the characters. The actors would study the language hard and deliver it loudly and clearly. The song and dance already built into this script was expanded into "numbers," because musicals were what these children knew and felt they could contribute to the play. The music would be original—specially written by one of our parents, as it happened. The music and the sets would extend the magic of many, many fairies (a whole cast of younger actors) to the audience. Differences among kinds of characters—the fairies and fairy royalty, the mechanicals, the lovers, and the others at the Athens court—would be exaggerated by costumes and makeup, and the clashes among them would be all the more comical. All the features of the production would be built on clear, simple ideas about the characters and the story.

The story was what made this show memorable for the audience. The production was complex, but the story was easy to follow and enjoy. To achieve this, rehearsals had to be hard, because the music and the choreography were ambitious and some roles were double and triple cast. But in the end a young group of actors achieved a successful production of a classic play. The production was rich for the various talents that the performers contributed, but it was also powerfully simple.

These are the aims on which this company, called Oyster River Players, was founded. The company and the classes came about as many children's theater companies do: out of school productions for children who wanted more theater, dance, and music than they were getting. Its success is based on trust and a theory of education that centers not on teaching but on students learning. Besides classes, rehearsals, and productions, the company offers young people opportunities to reflect on their values and even to change their lives by working together. It gives joy to these children and their families through hard, meaningful work.

This book builds on this example of a single small company in New Hampshire. We bring in stories of classes and productions and of the lives of the children who have been company members. We also take on the general subject of children's theater, past and present, in the United States and abroad. Most writing on the subject of children's theater is applied, "how-to" advice from teacher to teacher. This book likewise tries to be descriptive and practical, but it is also more general, describing the value of children's theater to the children themselves and to their audiences. This requires reflecting on the nature of theater and the ways children learn. In this book we offer a point of view about educating children in the arts that is supported by theoretical and critical literature.

The opening chapter is the basis for what follows. We describe different styles of learning and performing in different children's theater companies in different settings. Many of these ideas are best suited to private instruction in the arts, but they can be applied in other settings, even in public schools. We put this chapter first because some people who know and care about children and the arts consider theater impossible and even harmful when children are put on stage and given characters, actions, and lines of their own to speak. Our view is opposite. In this book, the theater we describe belongs to children, and the rest of us sit in the audience.

The subject of the second chapter is a history of children's theater companies and some of the associations they make up, not only in the United States but abroad. Children's theater is a long story: In Elizabethan England boys' companies competed with Shakespeare's, and Mark Twain sponsored a children's production company in New York's Lower East Side and got the governor to come to the show. Nowadays, children's theater is huge and growing around the world, but stories from the past have a bearing on the present. This chapter takes in the variety of children's theater companies, large and small, professional and hometown, long-standing and practically new. We also survey the associations that support them.

The last two chapters look more closely at children's theater in schools and in communities, challenging some assumptions and making the case for some changes. When theater has a place in American public schools, it is usually part of a broad curriculum, and sometimes its purposes seem confused. In most places, there is a gulf that cannot be bridged between school programs and private companies, and in the United States public support for children's theater outside the schools is thin. Children's theater sometimes carries little credit for educating or for humanizing the audience, even when the social issues it addresses are seen as critical. That is the subject of the last chapter: the important effects that children's theater has on communities around the world.

At different points in this book we use vignettes from the Oyster River Players to describe children's theater classes, rehearsals, and performances, using the words of the performers themselves when we can. Those who know children's theater firsthand will recognize these stories as similar to their own. Behind all these chapters is what theater people call a "super-objective": We try to show that as children gain artistic skills they also achieve greater confidence, deeper feelings of respect and community, and a more sensitive moral understanding. We believe that as it develops children's artistic abilities, theater has a supreme power to affect their personal and social development.

At the end of the book, as a backdrop, comes a list of children's theater associations and companies of different kinds and sizes around the world. This list will be reproduced online at http://www.childrenstheaterinfo.com, and it will continue to be revised and to grow, with the help of other teachers and directors who join in by sending us further information. Finally comes a bibliography of printed and electronic literature on the subject. A much fuller version of this file will also be posted on the Web and revised regularly.

One final point in this introduction: Calling the subject of this book "children's theater" might be confusing, as terms for this subject are varied. We try to sort this out at the end of chapter 1. In England, theater companies composed of children are usually called "youth theater," while "children's theater" applies to theater for child audiences. Those terms, defined that way, were introduced in this country years ago but did not stick. "Children's theater," as it will be used throughout this book, refers to drama performed by children.

℮⌒

This book can be read as a personal account of an ambition that overtook one family and their friends. The coauthors are wife and husband. Kelly is the teacher and director whose vision of children's theater founded and sustains Oyster River Players. Walter teaches Shakespeare and other literature to university students. Three of our children have been company members, and classes and rehearsals take place in a studio over Kelly's father's barn. This book looks out to the subject of children's theater from this vantage point. But at the center are stories of children learning theater and, in some cases, actually becoming professional actors, singers, dancers, teachers, managers, and directors. It also includes descriptions of the family and community rewards and conflicts that are part of learning. These children have been generous in allowing us to tell their stories.

1

Studio Learning and the Stage

Actors are unconventional learners. They are hands-on, practical people, focused on performing what they learn. As they learn, they have a hard time sitting still; they move and make noises even when they are memorizing. They tend to distract themselves and each other in rehearsals. They can be truly deep thinkers, but what marks them is the gift of sympathy—physical identification and commitment of the spirit. They rehearse together and collaborate, so that what they learn they can realize together in performances.

Good actors of any age are like children, learning quickly and deeply, and all children are like actors when they learn—moving, making noise, imitating, dreaming. It is no surprise that the most rambunctious schoolchildren sometimes show real promise in the theater. This means that all schoolteachers, whatever subjects they teach, should pay special attention to the kind of learning that happens on stage. Actors and directors do not usually describe rehearsals in terms of teaching, because rehearsals and performances challenge the usual ideas about learning. For this same reason, any teacher can benefit from seeing how theater directors work when children's theater succeeds.

Wise theater directors understand that the performances they want from their actors really cannot be taught, at least not directly. In trying to get everything they can out of actors, directors know that performances come from within the actors themselves, and that their job is to derive or induce, not to impose. Setting a myth—and famous examples—aside, most good directors are not controlling. They use a virtue that might not be common enough in schoolteachers: trust in what the actor knows, can do, and wants to do. This does not mean they do not exert control, but ideally control is there in only a provisional way: "Today, we will drill this for the sake of that." "Show me." This kind of teaching means sharing authority and allowing some irony, as directors themselves have to stretch their talents, and they sometimes forget and make mistakes. This is the spirit that makes a studio, and the studio is an especially good place for children to learn.

Studio learning is active and experimental in ways that most children find natural. Their first learning is everything at once—sights and sounds, language, each other, their families, stories, analyzed only afterward into parts. They enact characters in stories before they can read. They sing stories, put on costumes, and put on shows at home as they construct their own identities. They do not have illusions that are at risk or that prevent their making personal discoveries when they try things out. Children are "born actors": "They delight in playing a king, a beggar, an elephant, a dog, a robber or a prince. Sometimes they act two or three roles at the same time. Their fancy is freer than that of any poet or any lover."[1] They will explore themselves and the world around them imaginatively, every day, unless they are prevented.

In the studio, these children can be asked to take chances, sometimes ones that would feel dangerous to them personally if they were not engaged in a character and a story. On the stage, they can lose their fears in "something bigger":

> When I first joined Oyster River Players, I was very shy. It was hard for me to speak up during discussions, and the idea of acting on stage in front of a building full of people terrified me! What I learned was that you do not get rid of what scares you all at once. It happens over many experiences. At first you do improvisations in a small group, and then you go on to a small role in a play. I realized that even the littlest parts are important and have an impact on telling the story. Doing my roles well increased my confidence. I knew that I was involved in something bigger than me or anyone else in the troupe. (Pamela Benassi, ORP member)

This kind of learning cannot be achieved alone. It takes members of the cast and crew working together through rehearsals to the show.

The term "studio learning" is used by biomedical engineers, computer designers, and architects. What it means to all of them is an immediate, practical, applied kind of learning. Something is made collaboratively, and the process counts as much as the product. The *atelier* of Reggio Emilia, a compelling theory of learning for very young children in Italy, is usually translated "studio," and the paradigm for *atelier* is the performing arts, where learning means doing with others.[2] This is the kind of learning we describe and encourage for young actors in this book.

This image of a studio puts the emphasis on *doing* theater, and it applies in a natural way to children. What better way do they have to understand

themselves and the world around them than by putting on roles and inter-
acting in a story? The danger for young children is that their identities will
narrow and become fixed. Instead, what needs to be allowed—even encouraged—is the natural tendency of children to *play*, so that every role on stage
can be a personal discovery for even the youngest.

For children in theater, personal discoveries are usually made ensemble.
In musicals, the great moments are the songs and dances that take up the
stage. In the big musical numbers, even beginning students seem willing to
stretch and surprise themselves because they are together.

Solo performers who are young are brave, but traditional roles can give
them some security. Every Dorothy holding Toto, with the same braided
hair, wears the same checked dress to sing the same song. The security of
a classic role and story can enable young actors to make discoveries for
themselves and for the audience.

Whatever the role, first comes learning in the studio, and that takes high
expectations, encouragement, and trust on the teacher's part in the student's
interests and abilities. Ideally, the teacher's role is not to lay down rules for
students but to draw out feelings and understandings from within them.
Teaching of this kind depends on a student's confidence and initiative,
which can be guided, if not trained, and focuses as much on the conditions
as on the content of learning.

Sometimes there is no performance and no audience at all. Take, for
example, a dance class. First come stretches at the barre and on the floor.
The difficult part is the attention the students have to pay to each moment:
to do whole arcs of motion as a succession of movements. Then come
several small dances (fancy, repetitive footwork at the barre and on the
floor). Those at the barre get direct supervision, so everybody gets a kind
of spotlight in turn. Now they do complex rhythms, even while they are
holding themselves taut. This sometimes requires better concentration than
the children pay to their learning anywhere, even though this lesson has no

apparent content. The students are proud of what they achieve toward no single particular purpose.

In this way, teaching in the performing arts is not very different from coaching in sports. Compare actors in rehearsal (or musicians or painters in the teaching studio) with competitive swimmers doing practice laps in a pool. The swimmers receive instruction from the coach, but they are the ones who keep themselves afloat and in motion, trying out different techniques and getting stronger lap by lap. A good coach understands that learning happens within the swimmer, on the initiative of the swimmer. The conditions must be right, and the coach can shape the "curriculum" and so forth, but every bit of progress is to the swimmer's credit. It is the same in the arts. In the end, teachers have no choice but to trust their students to interpret and perform. The master painter teaching in the studio might have a huge ego, but he knows the boundaries of the teacher's role. Likewise, an effective stage director does not make the studio a schoolroom, because in the theater there is no doubt: learning happens only by the learners, and the teacher's role is limited. This is to say, an effective teacher remains a student.

> There is no better way to know that someone trusts you than to be asked to teach something. The first time I really knew that I was trusted in ORP was when I was asked to teach "Blessed Be the Tie That Binds" to the rest of the choir in *Our Town*. All the other girls were older than I was, and they had been in ORP far longer. But I was the one who had been chosen to bring the little roll-up piano into the kitchen and teach the hymn.
>
> I underestimated myself that day. Every time I went to play the piano, I thought to myself, "Why am I doing this? Why not a high-schooler?" I wished I could play the piano better. I wished I knew the song better. I wished I knew the other girls better. I wished I was a better teacher.
>
> Having done all that we could do, the other girls and I climbed the steps back into the studio to sing for the teacher. I looked around at the others when we finished singing, nervous that what we learned would not be what she wanted to hear. But she smiled and turned to me: "OK. Good!" And I knew she meant it. One of the girls held up her hand for a high five, and I slapped it with pride. I had done it: helped the company to learn something that would affect the whole play. And that is the beauty of the company. Each and every person learns, and each and every person teaches. (Lydia Beller-McKenna, ORP member)

This picture shows the accompanist now in the choir. She represents the principle that an effective children's stage director does not make the studio a schoolroom, because in the theater there is no doubt: learning happens only by the learners, and the teacher's role is limited.

The teacher plays a limited role, and yet this kind of learning depends to a great degree on the student's trust in the teacher. For a young student-actor to take the chance of exposing emotions, the teacher-director must provide a feeling of safety. This does not mean control on the teacher's part. What it means is that the student is allowed to make mistakes and even to reveal hard truths. There may be unself-conscious years in a child's development, but everyone, at every age, needs to feel safe in order to take risks.

That is why the operations of a children's theater company—in the studio and on stage—are based on trust.

"Everyone" includes the teacher. To model this behavior, the teacher puts herself on something of a par with the students, not giving over her authority and responsibility but acknowledging her limitations and even her foibles.

The teacher is part of the studio, and like all the students, she respects the others in the company. Her authority is, in one way or another, given back to her by her students trusting every day, so that she can make the studio safe and everyone can have the confidence to interpret and perform. As the studio is for the most part safe from hurts of pride, students will take chances. When they fail (as they will, sometimes) they do not feel so defeated.

Of course, some children have more experience or aptitude than others do. It is possible to draw a scale on which student-actors can be sorted out by their experience or by the thresholds they cross as they are learning. First comes the crisis of performing at all. Something enables new students to put themselves on stage when they are afraid even to learn their lines and movements, much less to be watched. Most survive. In this theater company, the door stays open and students know that they will get some part in the show if they stay this time and come back. In a later phase, after they are past the worry of memorizing lines and getting them out on time, they become interested in the audience. During the show, even when they are upstage and have no lines, they are determined to be noticed; when they do speak or move, it will be for effect. (In this stage of life, they will do anything for effect.) Finally, actors become part of the whole play. Their characters exist in relation to other characters, and their speeches are made meaningful by the broader context. Their roles have become less constrained and more complete. As they leave the studio for the stage, they have achieved the freedom to perform.

ℰ⁓

In the view of many schoolteachers and educationists, this account of studio learning and children's theater claims too much. In their view, young children cannot appreciate, much less perform, true theater. There might be exceptions, they would say, but the qualification should be set somewhere in the teen years at the earliest.[3] From that standpoint, the demands of a stage performance cannot be met by children and will be stressful, if not harmful, if imposed on them. There might be kinds of acting possible for children—upstage, silent, and still—but in that view, true independent acting requires physical and emotional maturity that children do not have. Some very strong proponents of theater for *audiences* of children—who see great value in theater *for* children—say that we should keep children off the stage altogether.

This book puts children on the stage and adults in the audience. But there are several steps between theater *for* children and theater *by* children, and all of these steps are sometimes called "children's theater." Comparing them makes our subject clearer.

First, we can set aside certain theories of child development that use the terms "children's theater" and "role-playing" as abstractions to describe socializing and maturing. These theories have no real connection with theater production. They begin with the idea that life for young children is like playacting and then use the terminology of theater to explain child development. Our interests are simpler; we are interested in the different ways children are involved in theater.

THEATER FOR YOUTH OR THEATER FOR YOUNG AUDIENCES

The terms "theater for youth" and "theater for young audiences" are used to describe plays performed by adults for children. The impulse behind this kind of theater is a natural one. There was never a time when adults did not play for children, encouraging and enjoying their responses. The profession of acting for children is worldwide in scope, and in every culture it has its own history and traditions.

In the United States, theater for children is supported by advanced academic programs with library archives and sophisticated touring companies. Brigham Young University offers an academic degree and a theater company that trains actors and directors to perform before young audiences, and the company tours nationally and internationally, recently to Southeast Asia, Yugoslavia, and Austria, performing for more than eighteen thousand children. The Theatre Education Database (TEDb) hosted by the BYU Department of Theatre and Media Arts enables teachers at every level around the world to communicate about curriculum and lesson plans. Arizona State University and the University of Wisconsin at Madison both offer doctoral degrees with specializations in theater for youth, and the ASU Child Drama Collection is "the largest American repository of manuscript materials and books documenting the history of theatre for youth throughout the world."[4] A site maintained on the Web by the University of Washington Libraries[5] identifies fifty-four such programs in American colleges and universities.

The size and extent of theater for children can be documented with statistics from the International Association of Theater for Children and Young People (ASSITEJ; called "Theater for Young Audiences" in the United States). In addition to supporting theater companies dedicated to young audiences, its mission is international exchange among eighty-one theater centers worldwide. This mission is a noble one, educating children and, as they say, even serving the cause of peace:

> Since the theatrical art is a universal expression of mankind and possesses the influence and power to link large groups of the world's people in the service of peace, and considering the role theatre can play the education of younger generations, an autonomous international organization has been formed.[6]

The Children's Theater Foundation of America, which has been allied with ASSITEJ, serves this same cause.

Most of the scripts performed by adult companies for child audiences are original, written or adapted from traditional stories by contemporary authors and composers. Advertisements for commercial sources of scripts are easy to find on the Internet. Maurice Sendak, among the best-known authors of children's stories, has produced a whole book of play scripts for young audiences, for example.[7] Different versions of the same stories are often adapted or rewritten for new audiences of children.

The printed literature and Web sites that identify most of these companies do not usually include "mission statements" because few of them feel called upon to explain or justify themselves. But many do include a sales pitch; they are self-supporting and on tour. To succeed, they have to delight their audiences of children—and they do.

READER'S THEATER

In reader's theater, children do speak, but usually sitting in place. No teacher-director is needed, and there is no "production" at all. The studio is a classroom, where students either improvise from a scenario or read a script, not for an outside audience but for themselves. The focus is on the lessons students can learn about life as they respond with drama to a narrative situation:

> Reader's theatre is a valuable tool for any classroom. It allows students to take virtually any piece of literature, analyse it and adapt it into a script. This script is then performed with a minimum of preparation, props or scenery. Reader's theatre is often defined by what it is not—no memorizing, no props, no costumes, no sets. All this makes reader's theatre wonderfully convenient. Still, convenience is not its chief asset. . . . Reader's theatre frees the performers and the audience from the physical limitations of conventional theater, letting the imagination soar.[8]

For this purpose, full-scale theater productions are useless, and, if anything, they tie the story down. In reader's theater, with no audience at all, expenses are saved, and the idea is that students can focus on something besides memorizing.

This kind of theater is effective for "increasing reading fluency and sight-word vocabulary, improving reading comprehension, providing opportunities to interpret dialogue and communicate meaning, and increasing awareness and appreciation of plays as a form of literature."[9] What more important element can there be in the education of children than learning to read and interpret stories? But the subject of this book is a different one:

children reading and appreciating drama in the studio and also performing plays.

CREATIVE DRAMATICS

Creative dramatics is its own distinct form of theater, performed by children, with stories, characters, and themes written or revised for audiences of children, if there are audiences at all. The purpose of such plays is clear in the form they take. They are dominated by familiar themes and are usually moralistic, even didactic. The child actors rehearse not to perform so much as to exercise intellectual and emotional skills, and to mature: "Creative drama is dramatic activities which have the experience of the participants as the goal. This differs from theatre classes in which preparation for a performance is the objective."[10] Usually these exercises require no costumes, makeup, or scenery, and the script or scenario is only a format, to be adapted by the teacher, who is both the director and the primary audience. Children are let in on decisions about the performance, and they are taught to work on the quality of what they produce. But the production is only instrumental, and its value is to the performers.

The first proponent of creative dramatics was Winifred Ward. Early in her career, she learned about child performers and audiences of children by taking her School of Speech students to elementary schools. She founded creative dramatics as a theatrical enactment without scripts: "[I]nstead of memorizing set speeches and acting parts in the way the teacher directs, the children develop plays out of their own thoughts and imaginations and emotions."

From this standpoint, while drama is informed by the practices of theater, it is valued mainly as a learning medium, and it is governed and validated through criteria other than aesthetics or performing skill. The script and even the scenario are secondary, and the characters and story can change along the way. Behind the looseness of these plays is a strong overriding purpose: "The child should be an *active part* of this process, not a passive observer. Observation is something they learn through other media. By doing, they are truly learning. Through performative acts, children can learn anything; imagine anything; change everything."[11] This emphasis on the performers and what they gain is part of "studio learning," as we use the term. But here there is no studio, and the drama is not "learned" for the sake of performances.

Creative dramatics is a movement in education that began as early as in the 1920s and continues in printed literature and in advanced-level education programs. It has boosted interest in the subject of children's acting, but as a method of learning and performing it is tangential in this book and will be brought in mainly for comparisons.

APPLIED THEATER

"Applied children's theater," as a technical term, refers to theater with social and psychological as well as educational purposes: "social drama (such as Theatre of the Oppressed), therapeutic applications of drama, drama for building a sense of community, and so forth. The term only emerged in the early 1990s or thereabouts, and continues to be defined."[12] The idea is that theater can change people both on stage and in the audience, and that children can be part of this process.

A program called ACT OUT!—conducted in Germany, Austria, Peru, Mexico, Colombia, and China—offers "theater of life for street kids" as "a way of de-traumatizing their lives." Theater helps young people express their feelings personally and in groups, recognizing and objectifying their lives: "They love to act their stories when they have space to exaggerate and when they can really bring out their emotions without anyone criticizing them."[13] The same stories represent different perspectives, all of them including humor. The basis of this program is the Galli Method, by which spontaneous role-playing is used as the basis for conflict resolution and personal development.[14]

There is no doubt that the personal powers of theater can have a deep effect on children:

> [D]ramatic play is the "work" of childhood, and it is the precursor to higher cognitive and psychological functioning. However, when there are emotional, developmental, or behavioral issues at play, this natural, intrinsic process may become stalled. Children with these issues, whether they be transient due to outside forces (i.e., divorce, death, difficulties at school) or long term (due to a developmental or mental disability) need a structured, goal-oriented approach to help them. Drama therapy offers this structure, and is a natural, fun way for a child to work through issues and find resolution.[15]

The idea of drama therapy is an insight into how every play works, and we can apply it more broadly than to the clinic. Children do not need "issues" to benefit from engaging in characters, enacting stories, and affecting an audience. We can take this description of drama therapy as a tribute to the power of theater—and hold that idea aside, for our purposes in this book.

CHILDREN'S THEATER OR YOUTH THEATER

Here is the subject of this book: children's theater or "youth theater," as it is called in England, in which children perform and an audience enjoys the play. It requires a stage and a script, sometimes a score and choreography, and usually costumes, makeup, lights, and sound. It can be turned to many special purposes on behalf of children, like remediation, personal and social therapy, and instruction in literature, history, language, and speech. But these purposes are secondary, from the standpoint of this book. Here we watch children learning in the studio and performing on stage, and we applaud.

What we call "children's theater" is sometimes disparaged. In a book on theater for child audiences, Moses Goldberg offers the term "recreational drama" for productions by children. In his view, we should not call them "theater" at all, because in children's productions, "the development and experience of the performers is more important than the aesthetic enjoyment of the audience."[16] He believes that we should not expect or demand too much of children on stage—but sincerely he means no slight, as he defines the term "recreation" grandly, as "an activity that re-creates the self." (By this definition, adults should call their own best plays "recreational"!)

Lowell Swortzell published a monumental, worldwide survey of theater companies that involve children. He distinguishes between "children's theatre" and "educational theatre," but either way, in his view, when children perform on stage it is for their education, not for the entertainment of the audience. His introduction sketches a history of theater for and by children, and he shows that children have produced professional plays in the past—and notably, in different cultures (see chapters 2 and 4 in this book). But he ties the future to ASSITEJ, dedicated to theater for young *audiences*.[17] The bulk of his book is lists of adult companies performing for audiences of children, organized by countries around the world, and in these lists companies with child actors are almost altogether excluded. The section on the United States mentions only a single "exceptional" company of children on stage, which went out of existence in the late fifties.[18]

Our focus is on companies of children. The studio and the stage where they learn and perform drama can be immensely important places in their lives. We have seen that theater gives them whatever they are willing to take: abilities in voice and movement; powers of sensitivity, reflection, and expression; concepts of human character and moral judgment; the capacity to enjoy and learn from stories; and more. The youngest children exercise and refine these abilities as they undertake a play, learning their scripts and blocking, practicing, and performing.

Moving from the studio to the stage, trust extends, and they offer these skills and insights to the audience (including proud parents and friends). And what they create, when they succeed, is in fact the art of drama.

Now that we have the children on stage, in the next chapter, our focus shifts from learning to the production itself: the history of children's theater companies in different cultures and the support they get from children's theater associations.

NOTES

1. Balawanta Gāragī, *Theatre in India* (New York: Theatre Arts Books, 1962), 213.

2. See Lella Gandini, Lynn Hill, Louise Caldwell, and Charles Schwall, eds., *In the Spirit of the Studio: Learning from the Atelier of Reggio Emilia* (New York: Teacher's College Press, 2005).

3. The rules spelled out on a Northwestern University Web site are that audiences should be younger than performers and performers should be younger than eighth grade, "because of the demands of effective drama leadership" ("The Drama/Theatre Continuum," http://faculty-web.at.northwestern.edu/theater/tya/continuum.html). See likewise Vera Mowry Roberts, "Theatre Education in the United States," *Educational Theatre Journal* 20 (1968): 308–10. There, children's theater is divided into creative dramatics, theater for children, and teen theater. Matt Buchanan, playwright and drama teacher, says, "left to my own devices, I would almost never do Theatre by Children and Youth with kids much younger than Middle School" ("Definitions and Discussion of Important Terms," http://www.childdrama.com/def.html#tcy).

4. "The manuscript collection fills over 1,000 linear feet of shelf space. Included are: collections for individuals, theatre companies and publishing houses; audio-visual media; pre-print materials; production materials; posters; typescripts; oral histories; musical scores; study guides; teaching aids; correspondence; curricula and lesson plans; photographs; slides; theses and dissertations. Many of these items are unique, the only ones in existence. In 2002, there were over 2,000 books and over 3,000 playscripts" ("Child Drama Collection," ASU Libraries, http://www.asu.edu/lib/speccoll/drama/collections.htm).

5. "Youth Theatre and Theatre Education Programs," http://www.lib.washington.edu/Drama/childram.

6. ASSITEJ International, http://www.assitej-international.org/english/documents/constitution.aspx.

7. Coleman A. Jennings, ed., *Theatre for Young Audiences: 20 Great Plays for Children* (New York: St. Martin's Press, 1998). Sendak helped to found Night Kitchen, intended to be a national theater for children.

8. Lois Walker, "Readers Theatre in the Elementary Classroom" and "Strategies for Reading: Readers Theatre in the Middle School," excerpted by Karen McCormick in "Reader's Theatre Basics," http://bms.westport.k12.ct.us/mccormick/rt/whatrt.htm.

9. Lila Carrick, "Internet Resources for Conducting Readers Theatre," *Reading Online*, http://www.readingonline.org/electronic/elec_index.asp?HREF=/electronic/carrick/. Jennifer O. Prescott titles a very helpful essay, "The Power of Reader's Theater: An Easy Way to Make Dramatic Changes in Kids' Fluency, Writing, Listening, and Social Skills," in *Scholastic Instructor*, http://teacher.scholastic.com/products/instructor/readerstheater.htm.

10. Janine Moyer Buesgen, "Creative Drama," *Creative Drama & Theatre Education Resource Site*, http://www.creativedrama.com/creative.htm. An extensive book of essays on creative dramatics is edited by Geraldine Brain Siks and Hazel Brain Dunnington: *Children's Theatre and Creative Dramatics* (Seattle: University of Washington Press, 1961).

11. Charles E. Combs, "Theatre and Drama in Education: A Laboratory for Actual, Virtual or Vicarious Experience," *Youth Theatre Journal* 2 (1988): 9. See also Gregory D. Freeman, Katherine Sullivan, and C. Ray Fulton, "Effects of Creative Drama on Self-Concept, Social Skills, and Problem Behavior," *Journal of Educational Research* 96 (2003): 131–39.

12. Adam Blatner and Daniel Wiener, eds. *Interactive & Improvisational Drama: Varieties of Applied Theatre and Performance* (Lincoln, NE: iUniverse, 2007).

13. "ACT OUT—Theatre of Life," http://www.act-out.org/pages/act_out_frameset .html.

14. See the Galli Group, "Association for Theatre for Social Change," http:// www.galli-group.com/pageID_6124577.html.

15. Creative Therapy and Learning Center, http://creativetherapykids.com/_wsn/ page2.html. See Helen Nicholson, *Applied Drama: The Gift of Theater* (New York: Palgrave Macmillan, 2005).

16. Moses Goldberg, *Children's Theatre: A Philosophy and a Method* (Englewood Cliffs, NJ: Prentice Hall, 1974).

17. Lowell Swortzell, *International Guide to Children's Theatre and Educational Theatre: A Historical and Geographical Source Book* (New York: Greenwood, 1990), xviii–xxx. Likewise, in 1955, Geraldine Brain Siks described "children's theater" in various countries around the world, but references to children performing are few: "Theatre for Youth: An International Report," *Educational Theatre Journal* 7 (1955): 306–14.

18. Swortzell, *International Guide*, 337.

2

The Story of Children's Theater

[T]here is, sir, an eyrie of children, little eyases, that cry out on the top of question, and are most tyrannically clapped for't. These are now the fashion, and . . . berattle the common stages.

—*Hamlet*, 2.2

If I were going to begin life over again I would have a children's theater and watch it, and work for it, and see it grow and blossom and bear its rich moral and intellectual fruitage; and I should get more pleasure and a saner and healthier profit out of my vocation than I should ever be able to get out of any other, constituted as I am.

—Mark Twain[1]

The enterprise of children's theater has grown enormously over the past twenty years. There have always been school and community plays of one kind and another, and there are more every year. Today, in the United States and around the world, almost anyone can find an independent children's theater program within driving distance of home. Between school and private companies, there might be no other activity in the arts that involves more young people on a continuing basis. Many students take music lessons and then perform together in bands and orchestras, mainly at school. But in theater, private classes and productions supplement school programs, not only during the school year but also in the summer when school is out. In small, remote towns, community theaters—including children's theaters—are sometimes the only public arts activity around.

At the other end of the spectrum, usually in large towns and cities, are fully professional children's theater companies with teachers, directors, and production assistants, all of them adults. Tickets are printed and seats assigned—and prices might seem high. These companies sometimes have their own permanent theaters with sophisticated machinery. Costumes and sets are very elaborate. Singing and dancing might be accompanied by a special orchestra. The children in the company audition for their roles: To be cast, they show how well they can interpret and represent, and they are trained in elocution and poise. Only one best performer is cast per part. Rehearsals go long. Opening night is reviewed.

The range between professional and hometown children's theaters is wide, with most companies falling somewhere in between. This book tries to represent this wide world in various ways. We sketch the history of children's theater and also survey the present scene, not only in the United States but abroad. There are city agencies that recruit and train child actors for professional audiences. There are children's theater companies with outright political or religious motives. Some companies offer special programs in script writing or in the technology of production, in film as well as on stage. There is children's street theater, and there are children's companies that tour. Many independent companies are affiliated with private and public schools. Most companies require tuition, but many give assistance to those who need or especially merit it. The appendices to this book describe programs of every kind, and this chapter offers a context.

$$\mathcal{C}\!\sim$$

In the modern "legitimate" adult theater, children play the roles of children— sometimes important roles, but rarely leading roles. But there was a time in this culture when children were independent and professional, and children's theater competed with adult theater for dominance on stage. During the Elizabethan period in England, children's theater companies performed new plays that were as substantial and successful as most of the plays performed by adults. Boy actors were not only popular, but they were respected as professionals by adult audiences. In no drama since the Elizabethan period have child actors had such prominence. On these grounds, the Elizabethan drama claims some special attention from us.

Boys' companies competed with Shakespeare himself, and you can hear his frustration about how successful they were in *Hamlet*, where there is a jab at professional children actors. They are "little eyases" (nasty young hawks) who seem to be drawing the audience away:

ROSENCRANTZ
[T]here is, sir, an eyrie of children, little eyases, that cry out on the top of question, and are most tyrannically clapped for't. These are now the fashion, and . . . berattle the common stages. . . .

HAMLET
What, are they children? Who maintains 'em? How are they escoted? Will they pursue the quality no longer than they can sing? (2.2.326–33)

Audiences enjoyed the competition between adult and child acting companies, and there was nothing surprising in Shakespeare's theater about jokes like this. Except for a spell in the 1590s when boys' companies were in effect banned from popular stages in London, they drew large audiences and had privilege to perform in great houses and at court. Hamlet's complaint about the competition from children's theater was sincere.

The best proof of the talents of Elizabethan child actors is what Shakespeare himself did with them in his own plays: There were no women performers, and the parts of girls were acted by boys before their natural voices completely changed. Those parts dominate Shakespeare's romantic comedies, and think also of Juliet, Ophelia, Desdemona, and Cordelia. Take these roles as evidence of what child actors might still achieve.

The tenor of Elizabethan drama was different from what we now expect. The most sophisticated professional plays—Shakespeare's included—were recognized as plays even at their most engaging moments. That might have put less strain on boy actors to play female roles realistically. But their skills on the stage were refined. They competed with the best of adult actors, and they were as well known. There were child stars in leading roles, carrying the audience's loyalty and capable of a high level of professional performance.

Michael Shapiro, the scholar who has best helped us understand the importance of child actors in Shakespeare's day, seems to believe that these days, other children—or at least his own children, in their hometown theater company—are not capable of truly professional work. He describes parents' "ritual of obligation" to attend their children's shows: "[W]e smile condescendingly at the inaudible diction and uncertain movements, all the while longing for the relief of the final curtain." Thinking about Elizabethan boy theaters and female parts, he remarks that "it was not always so," and he implies that it can never again be.[2] The argument of this book is that we should always expect more, even these days.

The boys' companies were eclipsed in England not long after Shakespeare's career ended, and since that time there has been no other such dominant professional children's theater. But another example from history points up the social and educational value of children's theater, as well as its special pleasure for audiences.

In 1907 the Children's Theater of the Jewish Educational Alliance was adopted, in effect, by Mark Twain. This company was made up of poor children from Manhattan's Lower East Side, and while its audiences consisted mainly of other children, Twain was able to interest his own adult admirers, for a period of time, in attending their shows and supporting this company financially. He allowed the text of his *The Prince and the Pauper* to be adapted as a script for this company in April, and he organized a benefit performance in November. This was one of the greatest New York social gatherings of the day, including the governor, the president of Harvard University, Andrew Carnegie, and Samuel Guggenheim.

Twain idealized the purposes of children's theater, not only as a way to educate children and their audiences but also as a potential way to change society. He believed that children who perform drama learn that "the true motives of life are to reach for the highest ideals," because they see that they can "act for themselves and think for themselves."[3] In a speech to the audience between the acts at that show, Twain declared that children's theater should be "part of every public school in the land."[4] He even suggested that for immigrant children theater could serve as a partial *substitute* for public schools! In a letter to Amelia Dunne Hookway, he declared that "a children's theatre is easily the most valuable adjunct that any educational institution for the young can have," and "that no otherwise good school is complete without it." Theater can teach morals and revive history because it "never bores the pupil, but always leaves him sorry when the lesson is over."[5]

Finally, in the same letter, Twain describes the practical artistry theater requires of any children who are involved in productions:

> Our young folks do everything that is needed by the theatre, with their own hands: scene-designing, scene-painting, gas-fitting, electric work, costume designing—costume making, everything and all things indeed—and their orchestra and its leader are from their own ranks.

The motive here is just as much practical as ethical, and this kind of learning is also a benefit to the students and to the audience, just as children's theater directors will tell you today.

In 1911 Charles W. Eliot, the president of Harvard who attended that gala show, contributed an introduction to a book written by the woman who conceived this children's theater company and who directed it, Alice Minnie Herts. He idealizes what her theater represents: "[A] strong educational force, for the most part unutilized in American schools, can be exercised through the wise training of the strong dramatic instinct in children."[6] Eliot points to Herts's prophecy in her own words, at the end of the book:

> The wise man who would build the endowed drama on a rock should turn his attention and his resources to Children's Educational Theatres, and the rain of moving-picture theatres may descend, and the floods of vaudeville come, and the winds of perverted problem plays blow and beat upon these houses, but they will not fall, for they will be founded upon a rock.

There was a strong ethic in Herts, aimed at the social class difference her students felt. But she also fought on behalf of children's theater as *theater*, with the belief that it could transform any child's life: "Through proper cultivation it may be made a force of education so far reaching that under its organized impulse the entire character may be developed, mind quickened, sympathies broadened, ambitions ennobled, and bodies lifted and remade."[7]

Herts's book is extraordinary: a long and detailed emotional description and argument for the cause of children's theater. Her fifteen chapters include excerpts from lectures by well-known academics entitled "The Dramatic Instinct of the Young Child," "Poetic Drama," and "The Drama in Its Relation to Education." Two years before, in 1909, Jane Addams had published *The Spirit of Youth and the City Streets*, which includes an account of children who found a kind of salvation in the "magic power" of the stage:

[E]very settlement in which dramatics have been systematically fostered can . . . testify to a surprisingly quick response to this form of art on the part of young people. The Hull-House Theater is constantly besieged by children clamoring to "take part" in the plays of Schiller, Shakespeare, and Molière, although they know it means weeks of rehearsal and the complete memorizing of "stiff" lines. The audiences sit enthralled by the final rendition. . . . Even when still more is required from the young actors, research into the special historic period, copying costumes from old plates, hours of labor that the "th" may be restored to its proper place in English speech, their enthusiasm is unquenched. But quite aside from its educational possibilities one never ceases to marvel at the power of even a mimic stage to afford to the young a magic space in which life may be lived in efflorescence, where manners may be courtly and elaborate without exciting ridicule, where the sequence of events is impressive and comprehensible. Order and beauty of life is what the adolescent youth craves above all else as the younger child indefatigably demands his story.[8]

Order, beauty, and hard work. And what the theater especially offered children was a truly appreciative audience. These were settlement children who had little other access to the arts, and they took on sophisticated literature that transformed them, at least for the duration of the show. The critical movement for children in American theater is usually reckoned as beginning in the 1930s and 1940s. But Herts's and Addams's books come much earlier, and they are impressive tributes to what theater can do for child performers and for an audience.

Over the years in the United States, most children's theater companies have risen out of public schools. Among private, independent companies, the Children's Theatre of Maine might be the oldest in the United States, dating back to 1923. But on the schools side, the first chapter of the National Thespians, later to become American Educational Theatre Association, was founded in 1929, in Casper, Wyoming. There is no telling how much local theater activity lay behind this event across the country, but by the end of that school year seventy-one troupes had been chartered as chapters.[9]

℮⁓

Since the early twentieth century, other national and international children's theater associations have been founded and continue to grow. The broadest is the International Drama, Theatre and Education Association (IDEA), which advocates theater education in countries around the world through workshops, publications, and conferences. Founded in 1992, IDEA has grown to represent more than ninety countries, meeting in periodic "world congresses" where "thousands of drama and theatre education teachers, grassroots activists, scholars and artists from across the world [meet] to exchange and celebrate workshop techniques, case studies, pedagogical theories, new curricula and performances, united by a deep respect for difference and a shared vision: to develop our creative, empathetic and analytical intelligences through drama/theatre and education to nurture a just and peaceful world."[10]

This mission includes "twinning" more and less economically advantaged national programs in collaborative projects. IDEA also sponsors international "solidarity and healing" in practical domains like AIDS and even peace education. Its practices are unified in three broad aims:

> (a) to demonstrate and advocate drama/theatre education as part of a full human education, particularly through international project collaborations; (b) to promote international dialogue and research around the practice and theory of drama/theatre and education; and (c) to support the practice of drama/theatre and education to achieve human rights and peace throughout the world, particularly for young people, children and excluded communities threatened by violence.[11]

In this mission, IDEA is affiliated with the International Society for Education through Art (InSEA). These associations are often involved in sponsoring international tours and competitions of individual children's theater companies.

The International Amateur Theatre Association (AITA/IATA) maintains a Standing Committee for Children and Youth and offers an annual World Festival of Children's Theatre, begun in 1991. This festival is held every four years in Lingen, Germany, and on a two-year cycle in other countries around the world. Children are at the center of these festivals, as producers, actors, and audience, discussing what they learn from what they see.

Especially broad-scale networking among national associations supporting children's theater was established between the Riksorganisationen Auktoriserade Dramapedagoger (RAD, National Organization of Professional Drama Teachers) and the Eastern Africa Theatre Institute (EATI), in 1999. The Web site Dramatool (http://www.dramatool.org) includes an international forum for exchange among children's theater companies in East Africa, Latin America, and Sweden, through the agency of the University of Högskolan Väst.

The benefits of cross-national connections like these have grown through meetings, exchanges, and festivals. National associations that focus internally usually emphasize a segment of companies—public or private schools, or independent communities. The primary focus of any children's theater company is local, and most companies have no formal affiliation at all. But a broad survey of nations shows that children's theater is becoming more and more interconnected, even cosmopolitan. The survey that follows is incomplete, but it shows the variety of children's theater associations that have developed around the world.

U.S. NATIONAL ASSOCIATIONS

The Educational Theatre Association (EdTA) dates from 1929, and over the decades its mission and membership have expanded steadily to include American state and international chapters and to provide new incentives to education. It is oriented toward theater in the schools, school-based educators, and students preparing to teach in the schools: "[T]he Association . . . serves as the eyes, ears, and voice of the school theatre community, advocating a stronger role for theatre education in the curriculum."[12] There are international association members (from Australia and Canada, according to the latest listing), but the calendar and locations of meetings are designed to accommodate mainly the American membership. State-based associations are affiliated through the EdTA, and the International Thespian Society, the student division of the EdTA, is the world's largest honor society for students engaged in theater.

The total number of teacher and student members and member institutions in EdTA is huge: more than four thousand professional association members, about 3,400 North American high school chapters with over two million members, more than 350 additional middle school chapters of "junior thespians," as well as "pre-professional" members. Formal conferences and festivals are organized by states and nationally, including the annual Thespian Festival. They include international connections and affiliated state-based programs.

The mission of the EdTA is basic and comprehensive. It has assumed leadership in shaping the theater curriculum and advocating for professional and community support:

We strive, alongside educators, advocates, and artists, to make theatre an instrument of lifelong learning. The Association also serves as the eyes, ears, and voice of the school theatre community, advocating a stronger role for theatre education in the curriculum. We are the professional association for theatre education.[13]

This mission includes publications for theater students and teachers: *Dramatics*, which includes a script index, and *Teaching Theatre*, a quarterly journal for theater educators. Separate branches of the EdTA serve high schools and middle schools.

An American association with an enormous mission and little public funding has to be concerned with membership and revenues—fees and dues, souvenirs, and ads in publications. A point system for members and graduation from one membership level to the next give students goals and help keep them loyal and on track. The scope of the EdTA has broadened over the years to include charity and community support, but the focus is the theater education of its student members through member schools.

While the orientation of the EdTA is to the American high school year, summer is also on the calendar. Two issues of *Dramatics* print directories of college and summer theater programs nationally and internationally. Also, each summer EdTA offers a weeklong International Thespian Festival in Lincoln, Nebraska: "the best week of high school theatre in the country," including about twenty-five hundred students. Many well-known theater professionals came up through early training in EdTA and endorse it, and it reaches out to all interested students, whose interest in theater will carry through later in life, whether on stage or in the audience. But there is no real attention in EdTA to all the private children's theater companies in the same communities, working around high school terms and vacations and flourishing in the summers.

A smaller national association, the American Alliance for Theatre & Education (AATE), embraces theater "for and by" children. AATE creates accessible, targeted ways for those interested or involved in theater and education to meet and interact with others of similar interests, background, and work experience. AATE offers the umbrella for ten different networks which exchange, develop, and put ideas to work, providing professional development and advocacy. In addition, it connects members to other arts education organizations, from local to international. Network areas are co-ordinated by involved practitioners and include: PreK–8, High School, College/University/Research, New Guard, Youth Theatre, Professional Theatre, Theatre in Education (TIE), Playwriting, and International. Other areas of service include advocacy, including a national campaign to support theater arts in the curriculum. Encouraging the continuing artistic development of its network, AATE keeps updated a directory of published and in-progress plays by members.[14]

U.S. STATE AND REGIONAL ASSOCIATIONS

At the level of states and regions in the United States, children's theater associations are almost all public and are built on systems of public schools. Some are affiliated with the EdTA, while others cut across the other arts and community organizations.

The South Carolina Theatre Association, for example, incorporates professional theater but also includes secondary and children's divisions, and young students are recruited through schoolteachers. The Tennessee Educational Theatre Association is a chapter of the EdTA; it offers a statewide conference during the school year to students and teachers in public and some private schools. In turn, the ten-state Southeastern Theatre Conference, "the largest and most active regional theatre organization in the country,"[15] affiliates and supports state associations, offers an adult K–12 Institute for teachers, and provides a competition for high school playwrights.

In the northeast, the Connecticut Drama Association claims to be one of the oldest children's theater associations in the country, beginning with a spring drama festival in 1936. Affiliated with the EdTA, it organizes high school students with annual festivals and contests. At the regional level, the New England Drama Council sponsors an annual festival comprising the two winners of each of New England's respective state drama festivals. Regional associations in the United States typically offer annual conventions and programs during the school year.

The New York State Theatre Education Association (NYSTEA) is made up of ten regional chapters. They cooperate in annual student and teacher conferences, publish a newsletter, and present awards to students, teachers, and programs. The mission of NYSTEA is embodied in a code that claims just about every educational and social benefit there is:

> Theatre is a powerful tool for understanding the human condition. The future of theatre in our society is dependent upon theatre education. Students of theatre acquire personal resources and life skills through intellectual, aesthetic, physical and emotional development. Drama/theatre instruction is an essential part of a K–12 education for all students. Opportunities for drama/theatre instruction and educational theatre instruction are essential at the college and university level. A strong statewide organization is necessary to advocate drama/theatre education in New York State. Theatre educators benefit from networking and sharing resources. Theatre flourishes in a society where it is supported in the schools.[16]

NYSTEA advocates for theater at both the state and local levels to both schools and communities, and it takes on curriculum, assessment, standards, and certification through conferences, awards, and a quarterly newsletter.

The state of Texas is proud of its claim to be "the first state to provide for secondary school drama teacher certification and accreditation and to establish drama as a separate subject in a fine arts program in junior and senior high school curricula."[17] Theater teachers at every level, elementary through college, constitute the Texas Educational Theatre Association. There are two sections of the association—kindergarten through grade 12, and college/university—and they work together to set standards of education: "advocacy, scholarships, auditions, workshops, and the encouragement of scholarly research and publication." Membership in TETA is "open to all who work or teach in the non-commercial theatre of Texas," but its orientation is toward the schools. It publishes a quarterly newsletter, *Texas Theatre Notes*, with practical value for teachers. A professional journal called *Texas Theatre Journal* includes K–12 pedagogy in its range of subjects.

A position paper adopted by the California Educational Theatre Association (CETA) might be the strongest and most detailed argument for formal theater education in American public schools. The focus is on public school teachers and curriculum requirements, and at the center are critiques and recommendations set out for the profession. The paper is political and practical: It argues that too many theater teachers lack specific credentials in teaching theater, and that students' natural interests and abilities are neglected. What students need is "credentialed theatre educators" and "standards-based theatre arts curriculum and instructional strategies."[18] This will require changes in policies and attitudes.

There has been a motive in California's legislature to recognize theater as a real subject, fit for public schools. In 1983 the legislature required a year of either arts or languages in high school; in 2003 California public colleges and universities started to require one year of visual or performing arts for entering students. The California Senate adopted "content standards" for teaching visual and performing arts in high schools in 2001. Still, in California as throughout the country, theater and dance rank far below art and music in the numbers of high school students who participate. The banner of the teachers is that "every child in every school every day should have the opportunity to be involved in theatre arts in the classroom." But it is hard to see that goal, even on the horizon.

CETA's document pushes for a sequence of theater education in the schools: "creative drama" in elementary school, an emphasis on the "process" of drama in middle school, and full-fledged instruction in all of the elements of theater embodied in high school productions. Such a full and complete program, year to year, will require a commitment on the part of schools and districts that the teachers themselves say that they seldom see in public school systems. They are determined—but also frustrated.

Their frustration is heard in public schools across the United States. There might be no more determined group of American schoolteachers than those in the EdTA. They work hard to win support that the other, related disciplines—art and music—have in the curriculum. But they complain that they do not get the respect for theater and the backing they need. This is a theme for later in the book, but in this context, closer affiliations between public school and private children's theater companies might be a benefit all around, not only for frustrated schoolteachers but also for children who have to suspend their education in theater for the summer or find another place to learn and practice their art. This would require affiliation among children's theater programs of different kinds and at different levels. (See chapter 3.)

NATIONAL AND INTERNATIONAL ASSOCIATIONS AROUND THE WORLD

Children's theater associations can be found around the world. They communicate and sometimes cooperate in particular projects, often within the domain of IDEA, described above. In some countries, as in the United States, companies that are not affiliated through school systems connect only in incidental and accidental ways.

Drama Australia is an especially strong national organization with seven regional associations, each with its own bylaws. It has its own constitution and an administrative board that takes on national issues in drama education and advocates, even negotiates, on behalf of the member regions. Membership is increasing overseas, with companies that subscribe to guidelines that have to do with working conditions, for example. Drama Australia puts out its own publications, *NJ—The Journal of Drama Australia* and *ADEM—Australian Drama Education Magazine*.

The primary children's theater association in England, the National Association of Youth Theatres (NAYT), founded in 1982, is expressly "outside of formal education." It claims to include only England and Wales within its territory (with about seven hundred programs), but it reaches out internationally. And its philosophy and practices have great value to anyone interested in our subject. Its Web site is filled with good advice about teaching and also about theater production, and clearly members of the association are eager to share what they learn. Summer is high season for the theater companies that are part of the NAYT, but most operate year-round. They meet at local, regional, and national levels, and their main agenda is education: They discuss practical matters and issues, which evolve from season to season. The NAYT Web site is huge and growing, providing not only communication among members but also a magazine and a sounding board. This site also reflects concerns with social issues like children with disabilities.

A great advantage for the NAYT is its public support. It is a registered charity, and its board members are trustees. The staff can be small, because it does not need to concentrate on expanding membership and fundraising. Also, the programs it sponsors are not exclusive to members, and dues and fees for meetings and advertising in the newsletter are modest, only meeting expenses.

The encompassing term for the enterprise of the NAYT is "youth theatre": "'Youth theatre' is a broad term used to describe a wide variety of organisations and approaches engaging young people in theatre related activities. Youth theatre takes place outside of formal education, is adult led and based on the voluntary participation of young people."[19] The NAYT elaborates upon this definition in describing its principles. The emphasis is on the difference that theater can make to the lives of children, as a test and proof of their "bravery": "If you can't be brave when you're young, then when can you?" What makes this principle compelling is that it is focused on the students themselves, on "making a difference to a young person's life."

The NAYT sponsors a number of special programs, such as regional and national mentoring and such special programs as ARTiculation, which gives "vulnerable and excluded" children "the opportunity to do drama—often the preserve of the middle class."[20] The NAYT also helps to fuse theater with the other arts.

In Finland, the Finnish Drama/Theatre Education Association (FIDEA) is affiliated with IDEA. Its membership is especially broad, including teachers, consultants, students, and professionals in drama and education. In 2003 FIDEA hosted an international conference, sponsored by UNESCO, that focused on how the interrelationship of the arts can achieve broad social purposes. The mission of the conference was "especially to find new ways to benefit and learn from the peaceful coexistence with the different artistic and cultural backgrounds and knowledge that are presented by refugees and immigrants."[21] This is not the only claim made by children's theater to promote peace and world culture.

The purpose of theater is the production of good plays, but it has intrinsic social and educational dimensions as well. The German association Bundesarbeitsgemeinschaft Spiel und Theater (BAG) extends this principle interculturally. It sponsors children's theater projects with Morocco and Turkey and a forum that includes representation from Bolivia, Ghana, India, Thailand, and the United States. It looks to companies that achieve both artistic excellence and social importance. BAG also functions as a nationwide umbrella organization for sixteen associations and publishes *Zeitschrift für Theaterpädagogik*, a magazine for children's theater teachers. Another German association, Bundesverband Theaterpädagogik (BuT), supports theater teachers at various levels.

The Hungarian Drama and Theatre in Education Association (HUDEA) was founded in 1988 to support independent children's theater and to improve drama education available in schools. Its major activity is the annual National Children's Theatre Festival, which draws together local productions organized in six regions; about ten thousand young people between the ages of seven and fourteen participate nationwide. The festival also serves as a forum for critical discussions. HUDEA is constructed on the purpose that makes children's theater distinctive in the arts and education:

> Children's and youth theatre activities in Hungary are based on the principles and methodology of drama in education, i.e., practitioners place the emphasis not on copying "adult theatre" but on the step-by-step development of group activities, involving the participants' creative initiatives. Improvisation, developing communication skills and group cohesion are therefore the hallmarks of these activities.[22]

In addition to its annual calendar of competitions and celebration, HUDEA is responsible for school and private youth theater within the Hungarian National Core Curriculum, established by the National Education Act of 1995. In this context, teachers at every level are trained through conferences and examinations. Finally, HUDEA coordinates the publication of printed materials and films.

The National Association of Youth Drama (NAYD) is at the heart of children's theater in Ireland, with a program that includes festivals, publications, research, and training. More than fifty companies are supported locally, and they connect with social service and cultural agencies and institutions. The NAYD extends support for the schools and independent companies by cooperating with the National Youth Arts Programme and the college-based Association for Drama in Education in Ireland. Its program includes national and regional festivals of youth theaters, commissions for new writing, publications, resources, training, and other services, as well as research and policy development.

The structure of the NAYD is democratic, and it focuses on local programs, involving them in planning and administration committees. Its own strategic plan involves all of the stakeholders. It produces an exceptionally handsome and rich magazine, *Youth Drama in Ireland*.

In Scotland, Promote YT sponsored its first national festival in 2005 and launched its Web site—http://www.promoteyt.co.uk—in 2006. A three-year plan, *SKILL-UP 2006*, has advanced children's theater in Scotland through a "youth board," a "youth web," and the first "networking and skills event" for young people. The relationship among the member companies is loose—affiliation rather than organization—partly because Promote YT is young and still underfunded but also because a loose structure and independent board of directors can be strengths.

Member programs are not school based or curricular: The mission is not the formal teaching of drama or the training of teachers. But the emphasis is equally on the process of rehearsals as on the finished show. Enrollment in member programs is increasing rapidly, as is public and private funding. The Scottish Arts Council has conducted reviews and awarded several grants to Promote YT since its founding.

The National Youth Theatre of Wales (NYTW), founded in 1976, centers around an annual summer project, organizing a company that mounts a production to tour Wales. The company is competitive and includes technical and design students as well as actors aged sixteen to twenty-one. A new dimension of the NYTW is identifying and supporting young dramatists.

℮∽

The appendices to this book list about nine hundred children's theater companies from around the world. This list was made up from a broad variety of sources, and each entry offers a brief description of the company, in most cases derived from its current Web site. Some companies without Web sites of their own are linked through other sources. There is no telling how many companies are left out. Certain geographical sites are much better represented than others, and parts of the world are beyond our reach. We plan to continue expanding and correcting this list, and we will maintain it at http://www.childrenstheaterinfo.com. We welcome any information we receive at ctsurvey2@aol.com. The purpose of this list is to provide the basis for a broad network among colleagues. They will decide what purposes this list will serve, but we hope to encourage communications and even collaborations, near and far ranging.

NOTES

1. A letter to Mrs. Amelia Dunne Hookway, quoted by Albert Bigelow Paine in *Mark Twain: A Biography*, http://etext.library.adelaide.edu.au/t/twain/mark/paine/chapter261.html#fn183.

2. Michael Shapiro, *Children of the Revels: The Boy Companies of Shakespeare's Time and Their Plays* (New York: Columbia University Press, 1977), 31.

3. Mark Twain, "True Patriotism at the Children's Theater" (1907). See "Mark Twain's Anti-Imperialism," http://users.erols.com/kmdavis/gb2a.html.

4. "Uptown Audience at Children's Play," *New York Times*, November 20, 1907, http://www.twainquotes.com/19071120.html.

5. See *Mark Twain's Letters 1907–1910*, reprinted in http://www.mark-twain.classic-literature.co.uk/mark-twains-letters-1907-1910.

6. Charles W. Eliot, introduction to *The Children's Educational Theatre* (New York: Harper & Brothers, 1911).

7. "'TO MAKE GOOD CITIZENS—THE THEATRE FOR CHILDREN'; Miss Alice Minnie Herts Outlines Interesting Plan for a Permanent Institution of National Scope," *New York Times*, November 12, 1911, http://query.nytimes.com/mem/archive-free/pdf?res=9F05E3DD1E31E233A25751C1A9679D946096D6CF. In a related article on Herts's company, J. Garfield Moses predicts that "this Children's Theatre will grow from more to more. In its very nature it is not a local institution or a mere adjunct of settlement work. It should reach children of all classes and conditions." See "The Children's Theatre," *Charities and the Commons* 18 (1907), reprinted in *The Children's Educational Theater: Supplement,* http://www.boondocksnet.com/editions/herts/theater_cc0704.html.

8. Jane Addams, *The Spirit of Youth and the City Streets* (New York: Macmillan, 1909), 89–90.

9. For an account of the beginnings of the "National Thespians," see Jo Anne Lough, "A Legacy: Cause and Effect," *Fairmont State College Occasional Papers*, no. 5, 8–10, http://www.fairmontstate.edu/publications/o_papers/05_lough.pdf.

10. "Congreso Mundial de IDEA: 1992–2010," http://www.idea-org.net/es/articles/Congreso_Mundial_de_IDEA_:_1992–2010.

11. "IDEA home—Members," http://www.idea-org.net/en/articles/IDEA_home__Members.

12. "How to Join EdTA/ITS," Educational Theatre Association, http://www.edta.org/membership/join/default.aspx. For an engaging history of the EdTA, see Glenn Becker, "Our Story: A Short History of the Educational Theatre Association," *Dramatics* (1984), http://www.edta.org/about_us/our_story/default.aspx.

13. "How to Join EdTA/ITS."

14. "Designing the Arts Learning Community," http://handbook.laartsed.org/models/index.ashx?md=37.

15. "Who We Are," http://www.setc.org/about/index.php.

16. "About," http://nystea.org/?page_id=4.

17. "Our History," Texas Educational Theatre Association, http://www.tetatx.com/history.php.

18. "CETA Position Paper," CETA, http://www.cetoweb.org/pdf/CETA_Position_Paper.pdf.

19. "What Is Youth Theatre?" National Association of Youth Theatres, http://www.nayt.org.uk/support/whatisyouththeatre.htm.

20. "ARTiculation," National Association of Youth Theatres, http://www.nayt.org.uk/events/archive/articulation/index.htm.

21. "International," Finnish Drama and Theatre Education Association, http://www.fideahomepage.org/eng/int_eng.htm.

22. Hungarian Drama and Theatre in Education Association, http://www.drama.hu/mdt.pl?ID=en&VALUE=0&GUID=0.

3

Children's Theater
and American Schools

A children's theatre is easily the most valuable adjunct that any educational institution for the young can have, and . . . no otherwise good school is complete without it.

—Mark Twain[1]

Two Oyster River Players in the same seventh-grade English class were told by their teacher that their in-class performance of the lines they learned for an ORP production could not "count" for credit. It took an angry visit by their parents to the principal to get the credit validated, on principle. The schoolteacher's assignment had been to memorize lines out of a play, and these children had performed their lines beautifully in class as well as in the production. But the teacher wanted to disqualify these speeches because they were first learned outside of school—and because, after all, young children cannot appreciate Shakespeare.

This example poses some important questions about the arts in the schools. What *should* count for academic credit? What constitutes learning in the theater, and what is it worth? If we want students to learn more from drama than how to memorize speeches, what is that subject and where and how should it be learned? Is Shakespeare beyond them? If theater is more than sport and entertainment—if it can be part of children's education—who are the teachers, and can we accredit their instruction?

There is no doubt that theater is dangerous for children in school. It can be chaotic. It undermines authority. It often attracts students whose behavior is unusual or whose intelligence, if it is recognized, is sometimes written off at school. Although the learning involved in theater is very practical, because it builds toward something concrete and effective, it can also seem

33

frivolous—you can say it has come to nothing when the play is over. Learning in the arts is difficult to understand and control.

For reasons like these, the arts in general and theater in particular take a secondary place in most American public schools. Instruction in music and the visual arts, recitals, and exhibitions are offered in all or most high schools, but "serious" young musicians and artists usually identify themselves with instruction outside of school. As for theater, it is rare in elementary schools and slighted in secondary schools. Theater productions do not usually carry academic credit, as bands and chorales usually do; when there are theater courses, they are not always related to productions. Productions are an after-school activity, like sports. This should not be surprising, taking a practical view. Professional, full-time theater teachers are a major investment, and full-scale theater productions are very expensive in a school setting if they require an expert teacher, a dedicated theater facility, licensed scripts and music, rented costumes, and so forth.

These high costs might be enough to explain fewer courses and productions than we wish for, but there are additional social factors that put some schools ahead of others: "In general, large schools, schools in the Northeast (especially at the secondary level), schools with low minority enrollments, and schools with low poverty concentrations tend . . . to show more activity in arts education."[2] If public school enrollments in the arts are skewed to advantage in some places and populations, like these, then others must be below average. Taken together, these numbers show that the arts—and theater in particular—are neglected in most American public schools. Many young students, whose imaginations might never be more receptive to the drama, have to wait or find other outlets.

Private primary and secondary schools that are not constrained in the same way can devote more of the curriculum and course offerings to the arts. In part to attract students, some of them advertise specialties in the arts, theater included. These schools, as some public schools, are exceptional, and later in this chapter we will return to examples of how well they work. But first we will look more closely at the suitability of children's theater mainly in American public schools. This chapter will compare instruction in the arts in different settings, and we will argue that achieving theater in the schools requires a shift in basic public attitudes toward the arts, their relationships to other subject areas, and their potential effects on students.

$$\mathcal{C}\!\sim$$

American public school budgets are never adequate, most parents of public school students agree, and the subjects that suffer most are usually the arts. Local attitudes often put the arts outside the academic curriculum, at least as far outside as sports, and fund them no better—and sometimes not as well. They are often disregarded and even disparaged. While American state accrediting agencies acknowledge the importance of the arts to young children, their descriptions tend to be abstract or pontifical, and they usually do not have much influence on local school districts. About drama in particular, the policy is not uncommon at the local level that plays that are worth studying: the "classics," like Shakespeare, should be read and understood as literature and history, not as theater.

Young children do not sort their experiences this way. They have an especially good time watching film or television drama, as well as stage plays. We might think of children as naive, but they certainly know how to laugh when something is funny to them, and their sympathies and fears can be acute. They are capable of what might seem to be sophisticated responses, like recognizing fiction as fiction, giving themselves over to characters and to the story but staying detached enough to see the story as a story. Then, over the next decade, children usually spend much more time with the drama in movies and television than with stories they read. That is for good or for ill, but to the extent that it is true, we should take what they learn through the drama seriously.

Here is a personal example. In nursery school, our son Robert decided to produce "Conan the Barbarian" with his classmates: He provided costumes; cast his blond, wavy-haired girlfriend as Valeria; and rigged their plastic slide as a mountain. This is recognizing a story as such and using it, for enjoyment and for meaning. Conan is embedded in Robert's memory. He will never have the shoulders to audition for that role, but now he is a professional in theater and film—and it should be on his résumé. His performance showed that a child is capable of creating a world through his imagination. That capacity grows in all children, and with encouragement they can actually become sophisticated with scripts even before they learn to read well.

Children's own personas—like their heights, their voices, and their shapes—change quickly and continuously, and their teachers can never keep up with how they identify themselves in stories. Stories change in significance for children because their expectations change, and we have to try to keep up. This is not to ask parents and teachers to give over their authority or their broader, deeper understandings. But we need to recognize that children can develop an expertise in drama at an early age. This means that we can trust children's interests and abilities, and they can learn. But not many children are encouraged to pursue this interest in school, and not many schools answer to students' interest in drama.

The formal accreditation of public schools should ensure the quality of instruction in theater as in every other subject area, and in recent years there have been efforts in the context of public school curriculum assessment to reset the standards in the arts, including theater. The National Standards for Arts Education, developed by the Consortium of National Arts Education

Associations, set parameters for young Americans for education in the arts. On this basis, the National Assessment of Educational Progress (NAEP) in 1997 defined a full-scale set of goals, to be developed at the level of states. The hope was that students would achieve these goals in at least one discipline, but as one of the state public school commissions explains about arts courses, they are always elective and "the fact is that few students are able to have . . . a consistent and comprehensive experience in any area [of art]."[3] About theater in particular, the overriding problem, as it is described at the beginning of the NAEP Arts Report Card, is that "many students receive little exposure to theatre in school. Those students who do engage in theatre-related activities in school do so primarily by reading the texts of plays in literature classes, and attending occasional school performances."[4]

The NAEP Report Card goes on to explain that its own findings about theater programs might be unreliable—and that reality might be even worse than its findings—because so many schools refused to participate in the study in theater and so many students made themselves unavailable for the survey or withdrew their responses afterward. No such problems were encountered in music or the visual arts. Speaking broadly, if the arts in general are neglected in the public schools, theater is sometimes forgotten altogether: "The problem is that drama/theatre instruction has generally not been a part of arts education in our schools. In fact, by many administrators, teachers, and parents, arts education is viewed as music and visual arts."[5]

Similar findings are reported around the world. According to a United Nations report on arts education in Asia, "[T]he situation is, in fact, fairly good with music and visual arts, as they are officially printed in most school curriculum. But there are still many countries, where drama and dance are not at all taught in the school. If drama exists, it is either as a part of mother tongue lessons or volunteer theatre clubs after school."[6] The situation of theater education in Canadian public schools seems no better: "[I]t is now virtually impossible to discuss in general terms primary and secondary school theater education for the reason that it is now tenuous or non-existent in most cases. . . . Schools change their theatre programs as budgets change. . . . Programs which usually suffer first, when negative decisions are made, are the arts courses." The best conclusion is a general one: "Grade-school teaching has always (and will likely continue) to rely on an individual teacher's love of theatre."[7]

Typically, schools in the United States stage performances of plays but have no serious theater curriculum. If there are theater courses, they are taught to small numbers of students, and the credits do not satisfy arts requirements. Secondary schools offer only about half the coursework in theater that they do in the other arts.[8] If there is a theater facility, it belongs as much to concerts or student assemblies as to theater productions, and theater rehearsals and productions are an after-school activity. The job of directing theater productions often goes to English teachers by default, even though they themselves might never have been backstage. In schools that are accredited, directors carry teaching credentials—but not always in theater. Directing is often a part-time teaching job requiring only a secondary qualification.[9]

Some exceptions to this rule are regional associations of schools cooperating in special theater programs, like the Cappies, founded in the Virginia suburbs of Washington, D.C., and now spread across the United States with local programs and a national affiliation.[10] If theater competitions among regional public schools were modeled after athletic conferences, across regions, would the competition be more intense?[11]

The hope for children's theater, looking at public schools in the United States, is the Educational Theater Association (described in chapter 2). It has a deep claim on school communities across the country, and its large membership will continue to grow. Teachers, student teachers, and students are all active members; college teachers whose subject is children's theater are members who can sit on the board. The national association includes state chapters and also chapters outside the United States. But from an external perspective, the EdTA seems confined. It admits as affiliates into the association only high schools, middle schools, and junior high schools with active theater arts programs. And "non-traditional schools (e.g., home school groups) . . . must be organized and under the administrative and financial control of a public school district or the private school equivalent."[12] This also means that the EdTA will not consider private, independent children's theater companies for membership. Because it is tied to public schools, you could say it does not officially recognize summer, except for its national meeting. Students go away and come back in the fall, no worse for what happens in a private summer company—but no better? The high season for American private children's theater companies is summer, when they recruit veterans from schools, but many companies continue through the year, separately, on the other side of town. Some students and teachers lead a double life, working on both sides year-round. Because private U.S. companies have no national association of their own, negotiations between schools and private companies seem hopeless.

Some other national associations (described in chapter 2) are the opposite, based on private companies. There, school programs take second place, but likewise with little communication. Either way, divisions between school and private companies are a loss for the children. A clear benefit to students, wherever they learn and practice theater, would be a melding of public school and private programs.

Public schools in the United States have become more stringent over the years about formal teaching certification in the arts, but only twelve states expect prospective high school teachers to be specially qualified to teach in theater; seven states ask elementary or "multiple subject" classroom teachers to demonstrate knowledge or ability in drama or theater. Some other states include theater in "arts" certification, but usually "arts" means visual arts and music. Sometimes theater counts in a tacit way. In New Jersey a certified elementary teacher can teach up to 50 percent time in the visual and performing arts without special certification.[13] Connecticut has recently formulated state-level requirements in teaching theater for credit, but points out that visiting "guest artists or contracted artist-consultants" can be allowed for enrichment programs or enhancements; and certification is not required "to direct after-school drama productions that are not offered for credit."[14] What all the states require of all these teachers is credentials in teaching, whatever the subject matter.

At the same time, in particular in the cities, some U.S. public schools now do specialize in the arts. The Houston High School for the Performing and Visual Arts in Texas claims to be "the first public high school in the nation to correlate an academic program with concentrated training in the arts." To be accredited as a public school, the curriculum and graduation requirements must be the same as at all Texas public schools, but at HSPVA the theater department "provides a pre-professional program, which reflects the traditions and working relationship of all professional theatres."[15] "Charter schools" operate free from the regulations that ordinarily govern the curriculum. They are public schools "of choice," answerable to a local authority for meeting their educational objectives, which can include a specialty in theater. The Center for Education Reform publishes the online National Charter School Directory,[16] which provides contact information and profiles of charter schools nationwide. An example of a charter school that includes a special focus on theater is the Lehigh Valley Charter High School for the Performing Arts in Pennsylvania, which admits theater students based on competitive auditions, essays, and interviews. While the school satisfies standard academic requirements, half the day is devoted to education and training in theater. In New York City, nine "special" public high schools include the famous Fiorello H. LaGuardia High School of Music & Art and Performing Arts, the model for the movie and television series *Fame*. These are not "charter" schools, but they receive special funding from the city or (in the case of this school only) from the state. By these examples, a public school can be a professional academy that provides general education but does not charge tuition.[17]

Magnet schools, from a movement in U.S. history related to racial desegregation, likewise allow students to cross geographical district boundaries, sometimes to attend schools with a particular academic focus. The original emphasis on social diversity seems, in many cases, to have been replaced by an academic specialty, which can be in the arts. This makes them hard to distinguish from charter schools. Corresponding public high schools in England and Wales are called "specialist schools"; among them, by current count, are 408 "arts colleges," many of them with particular programs in theater.[18]

Many or most American *private* secondary schools do not require formal teaching certification of faculty in the arts. State education departments are more stringent than ever with regulations that govern certification for public school teachers, but private schools are not governed by these regulations, and few of them hire arts teachers on this basis. This gives them a freedom that they can turn to their advantage, if they will and can.

As a private school, the Adda Clevenger Junior Prep & Theater School in San Francisco claims the freedom to mount an extensive professional training program on top of a high school curriculum, but its Web site assures prospective students that the school day and year are longer than standard, so that both the professional program and the academic program can be complete.[19]

The Baltimore Actors' Theatre includes the Conservatory, a full-scale, accredited academy for students in preschool through grade 12. It offers professional training in music, drama, and dance; at the same time, the Maryland State Department of Education has distinguished it as a "model college preparatory school." Its scope of affiliations—not only programs and tours, but diplomas—is international. In addition, it offers a theater program that runs through the summer. Here we have a private theater school making broad claims for education in the arts. Capable students are no doubt the better for carrying a serious purpose of some kind through their general education.

The determination of a young artist can carry over naturally into academics as an asset to learning, and a focus in the arts can be sharpened through the humanities and the sciences, as the wide world is the context for whatever we create on stage. Students in the arts carry strong purposes with them, and that can boost their determination to learn. They are also not often enough credited with the intellectual abilities that can advantage them academically:

> There is a growing realization and acceptance that performance in the arts is not simply expressions of feelings, but cognitive in nature—providing the tools of thought needed to improve understanding across academic subjects as well as the imaginative, creative thinking capacities rapidly becoming societal necessities.[20]

This philosophy is embodied in Walnut Hill School, an independent secondary school for the arts in Natick, Massachusetts, that trains students intensively in ballet, creative writing, music, theater, and visual arts. The focus is the arts, but students are also offered a comprehensive and rigorous academic curriculum, and what makes this program work is the young artist's disposition to hard work: "[E]ach student arrives at Walnut Hill motivated by an internal passion equipped with a strong work ethic."[21]

There are many more examples of private schools distinguished in the arts.[22] They challenge the idea that it takes formal teaching credentials to educate in theater. But if there are certified schoolteachers who lack the credentials of experience, there are also teachers in private schools and private companies with no apparent qualifications at all. It takes nothing more than an ad or a sign to put a children's theater company into business, and certificates can be store-bought.

Most private companies, operating during the summer or year-round, can be described as being not full-scale academies but offering only classes and productions. The appendices to this book list hundreds of these companies—but only the portion of those that can be located through the Internet. While in the United States these companies typically have little to do with one another, in other countries they make up the recognized associations of children's theaters. (Many of these are described in chapter 2.) There, the private companies have the advantage of learning from one another. They have national meetings and contests that reinforce their solidarity.

The subject of private theater companies takes us away from this chapter, but it makes an important point that has come up before. This book argues that there is a need for cooperation between public and private education in children's theater. In this country, most public schools close down for the summer and students disappear until September. If they find a private company to join for the summer, well, no harm.

What would it take to connect private children's theater companies with public schools? As we have seen, there are magnet and charter public schools that put a focus on the arts, and some private schools combine the virtues of the standard curriculum and studio education. But for them, the model is urban, large school systems. What can happen in, say, Montana?

In June 2008 the *Missoulian* announced that "[t]he founder of Missoula Children's Theatre stunned a committee of Missoula County Public Schools trustees . . . with a proposal to partner a resident drama school with the city's high school program." This local school board believed that theater might bring in new, out-of-town students who would pay tuition, but they were also proud that this program would educate capable students especially well. This company has always been innovative. Its well-known Little Red Truck travels from town to town, setting up its theater out of what the truck can carry and recruiting and training local children to produce a play:

> The Missoula Children's Theatre provides a week-long residency "starring" 50–60 . . . local students in a full-scale musical. MCT has been touring for

more than 30 years. Annually, MCT visits nearly 1,200 communities in all 50 states, 4 Canadian Provinces and overseas. Our mission is the development of life skills in children through participation in the performing arts. Creativity, social skills, goal achievement, communication skills and self-esteem are all characteristics that are attained through participation in this unique and educational project.[23]

Direct, authorized collaboration with local schools is the next step in Missoula. Here is an outstanding example for communities that want to encourage children to pursue their interests and abilities.

Another example of cooperative programming between private companies and public schools is the First Stage Children's Theater in Milwaukee, Wisconsin, which offers students at different ages and levels of ability exercises, workshops, and ongoing programs in school classrooms and in the studio. First Stage Academy bridges the gulf between public schools and private programs—and between summer and winter—for students who want to learn theater year-round.

From the college side of theater education is the issue of how high school credits in theater should be received. The Association for Theatre in Higher Education (ATHE) is urging colleges and universities to award advanced placement credits in theater to students through College Board Advanced Placement tests. Advanced placement in music and art are available to high school graduates this way. Can an equivalent exam in theater be devised?

While most disciplines, including music, offer an AP exam to high school seniors, theatre is not yet accepted as a subject worthy of such an exam. . . . If administrators of high school and college continue to view theatre purely as an extracurricular subject and theatre remains marginalized as non-codifiable, then the discipline will maintain its position as outside the quantifiable and acceptable subjects of the school curriculum. University professors must be willing to concede one introductory course in order to gain both a larger contingent of student applicants and a legitimacy for the field of theatre.[24]

The subject of the AP exam in music is music theory, and it is difficult to imagine a parallel exam in theater. The AP exam in studio art might model an AP exam in theater performance: Students could send forward audition tapes, following AP instructions about what they contain, just as the art students do in assembling their portfolios. Performances on these tapes might not seem "codifiable" and "quantifiable," but they could be evaluated in a credible, professional way. The trouble is, the acting course that students might bypass does not come first in many college theater curricula. Often the basic course is a combination of theater history and rudimentary acting instruction, satisfying a general education requirement and not providing a gateway to the major. It is hard to find an equivalent course in the other arts programs in the same colleges.

An evaluation examination in theater, whether or not it carried AP credit, would put the focus on students' abilities, no matter where they were discovered or developed. Entrance auditions for actors into professional schools work the same way: not "How many credits have you earned?" but "What can you do?" and "How well can you do it?"

ℯ⌒

This chapter has spanned a full range of education in children's theater, from schoolrooms to studios, from Saturday classes to professional training. These differences accommodate children with different interests and ambitions, but it is too bad there is no closer interrelation among them. The archives of the Ohio Theater Alliance include the following statement of purpose from when it was founded in 1973:

> [T]o bring together all levels of theater (professional, community, college/ university, secondary school, and children's theater), to promote communication and understanding, and to take action on matters of mutual concern. . . . The state, regional, and national associations presented a united front to the academic, professional, social and cultural entities of society which positively affected the dramatic arts.[25]

The Ohio Theater Alliance is now much more tightly focused, and currently no organization, local, national, or international, connects education in children's theater as broadly as this. Let that be a resolution of this book: All of us engaged in children's theater should regard our subject as broad and deep, and on that basis better learn from one another.

NOTES

1. "Mark Twain's Letters 1907-1910 (to Amelia Dunne Hookway)," http://mark-twain.classic-literature.co.uk/mark-twains-letters-1907-1910/ebook-page-08.asp

2. "Arts Education in Public Elementary and Secondary Schools: 1999–2000," National Center for Education Statistics, http://nces.ed.gov/surveys/frss/publications/2002131/index.asp?sectionid=6. See also "Arts Education in Public Schools," Americans for the Arts: Online Resource Center, http://www.artsusa.org/information_services/arts_education_community.

3. "North Carolina Standard Course of Study: Preface," Public Schools of North Carolina, http://www.ncpublicschools.org/curriculum/artsed/scos/intro/preface.

4. "Creating/Performing and Responding in Theatre: A Close Look at the NAEP 1997 Theatre Assessment," NAEP 1997 Arts Report Card, http://nces.ed.gov/nations reportcard/pdf/main1997/1999486d.pdf. See also National Endowment for the Arts, *Toward Civilization: A Report on Arts Education* (Washington, DC: United States Government Printing Office, 1988).

5. Lin Wright, "But Are They Implemented? The Promise and Reality of National Theatre Standards," *Arts Education Policy Review* 102 (2000): 11. See also his "Preparing Teachers to Put Drama in the Classroom," *Theory into Practice* 24 (1985): 205–11. Shifra Schonmann offers a "wake-up call, reclaiming the place of the artistic and the aesthetic in theatre and drama education as its core experience." "'Master' versus 'Servant': Contradictions in Drama and Theatre Education," *Journal of Aesthetic Education* 39 (2005): 31–39.

6. Tintti Karppinen, "Measuring the Impact of Arts in Education" (paper presented at the UNESCO Expert Symposium on Arts Education in Asia, Hong Kong, SAR China, 9–11 January 2004), http://www.unescobkk.org/fileadmin/user_upload/culture/Arts_Education/HKPresent/Session%203%20-Tintti%20Karppinen%20-%20Paper.pdf.

7. *Canadian Theatre Encyclopedia*, http://www.canadiantheatre.com/dict.pl?term=Education.

8. National Center for Education Statistics, "Surveys and Programs," http://nces.ed.gov/surveys/.

9. "[A] whole lot of schools simply dump directing responsibilities on whomever they can find among their faculties to volunteer." "High School Drama Help," The Aggregating Educator: Exploring and Reviewing Resources for Teachers, http://aggregatingeducator.blogspot.com/2006/12/high-school-drama-help.html.

10. See Bill Strauss and Judy Bowns, "The Cappies: Celebrating High School Theater Like Never Before," New Horizons for Learning, http://www.newhorizons.org/strategies/arts/strauss.htm.

11. The Virginia High School League includes theater, forensics, and debate among athletic team competitions during the school year. See "Virginia High School League: Building Better Citizens," http://www.vhsl.org.

12. Educational Theatre Association, "Membership Policy of Educational Theatre Association," http://www.edta.org/pdf_archive/membership_policy2672007115430.pdf.

13. See Arts Education Partnership, "Arts Education State Policy Database: New Jersey," http://www.aep-arts.org/database/results2.htm?select_state_id=25.

14. Connecticut State Department of Education, "Theatre Arts Teacher Certification in Connecticut: Information for Administrators and Prospective Teachers," http://www.sde.ct.gov/sde/lib/sde/Word_Docs/Curriculum/artccl/Theatre_Arts_Certification_General_Information_03_19_08.doc.

15. High School for the Performing and Visual Arts, "Theatre Department," http://hspva.org/departments/index.cfm?DepartmentID=10.

16. Center for Education Reform, "National Charter School Directory," http://www.edreform.com/charter_directory/searchresults.cfm?start=1&groupsize=all.

17. See the account of the re-created Bronx Theatre High School: "Lights! Camera! Build The Theatre Action!" Talk Bronx, June 20, 2008, http://www.talkbx.com/tag/bronx-theatre-high-school.

18. See Department for Children, Schools and Families, "Arts," http://www.standards.dfes.gov.uk/specialistschools/what_are/arts/.

19. Adda Clevenger Junior Preparatory & Theater School for Children, http://www.addaclevenger.org/page2/index.html.

20. The National Arts and Learning Collaborative at Walnut Hill, a nonprofit organization affiliated with Walnut Hill School, has the mission to "transform schools by providing students with opportunities to learn in and through the arts" (http://www.artslearning.org).

21. Walnut Hill School, "Educational Philosophy," http://www.walnuthillarts .org/school/philosophy.html.

22. See Private School Review: Private Elementary Day Schools & High Schools, "Schools for the Arts," http://www.privateschoolreview.com/articles/47.

23. Rob Chaney, "Children's Theater Founder Proposes Drama School in Missoula, *Missoulian* June 15, 2008, http://www.missoulian.com/news/local/article_ 29311536-5171-597a-be54-186aff12042e.html.   See also the follow-up, "Arts School Proposal Gains Support," June 26, 2008, http://www.missoulian.com/news/ local/article_88382e9e-756a-594a-afe4-61575da51995.html.

24. Karen Berman, "Why the AP Exam in Theatre Is Important to ATHE," Association for Theatre in Higher Education, http://www.athe.org/resources/ATHENews/ 071126/apexam.

25. "Ohio Theatre Alliance," Special Collections and Archives, Paul Laurence Dunbar Library, Wright State University, http://www.libraries.wright.edu/special/ manuscripts/ms95.html.

4

The Promise of Children's Theater

The most powerful force of the future [is] summoned up in children by the theater.

—Walter Benjamin[1]

The audience makes theater special among the arts. Experiencing a play is not solitary, like reading a novel or visiting an art museum. In the theater, if the play succeeds, the audience responds together, beginning to end, and if the audience does not do its part, the play fails. The same audience might sit in the very same seats at a concert, but on that occasion they know to sit still and keep quiet. There is no confusion in the concert hall about who the orchestra is, or when or where, as they perform—and they all wear the same costumes the whole show long. But in the theater, the audience has to learn the time and place of the story, and who is who, as the show begins, and the show will die if the audience does not accept the premise of the story and respond along the way. The audience is part of the show, written in. In this way, plays are not even like movies and television stories, where the audience has no effect on the production at all. In the theater, the audience brings the show to life and carries it to the end.

This general principle applies to every show in every theater, but it is especially important in beginning theater when the actors are sometimes unsure and are focused on themselves. Children on stage have to learn that theater is not personal but public and social. After they memorize their lines and movements, they have to understand that their purpose is to affect the audience. Beginning actors, whatever their ages, usually care less about the audience's feelings than about their own, and what they want from the audience is support for themselves. But at some late point, when

45

they become true actors, true to the play, they know that it is the audience at stake. The promise of children's theater, as of every theater, is to engage and affect the audience for the better.

To understand how this works (when it does), we need to see how an audience not only enjoys children's theater but also credits and values it. If this idea seems sophisticated for children's theater, too deep for Little Red Riding Hood, watch out for the Wolf! Even in a good production he probably gets more laughs than gasps, but laughter is part of the fears we carry as children and as adults. If the audience is willing and the production succeeds, even a comical Wolf in a children's theater production leaves questions. When you walk through the woods, who is behind the tree? Is your Wolf my Wolf? What costume does he wear? Can we laugh the Wolf away?

This chapter will focus on what the audience brings to children's theater and where it leaves them. Examples from around the world show the personal—and even political and religious—power that children's theater can have.

e

Oyster River Players is a sample of American middle-class children, with happiness on one side of the studio and a variety of personal problems on the other, visible at times of stress. In larger, professionally oriented companies, there is usually more distance among the members and sometimes a code that keeps personal problems aside. But in a company of our size, there are always personal "issues," and as a matter of policy no child's issue is ignored. Hard as it can be for the company and for classes, here issues are allowed to upset the schedule and interfere with the day's lessons—or they become part of the day's lessons, as part of the larger drama of life.

Points of view and time and setting are always built in, and so even the most imaginary or remote story affords us a chance to learn about life. How can New Hampshire children know enough about Austria and World War II to perform *The Sound of Music*? That will take work—difficult but valuable work—for them and for the audience. *Our Town* is an easier case for us: a New Hampshire play, with voices and manners we recognize as local, even though the story is dated. This might mean that in this play the actors and the audience can take on harder questions. Do we know our neighbors? What is our place in history? What is the meaning of birth and death in Grover's Corners? These are big, important issues, and a children's production of this play can be an effective way to represent and understand them.

To turn this point around, a small hometown children's theater can confront serious issues as issues, even if only indirectly. This is a challenge of theater—any theater—and the personal rewards for the actors and the audience can be great, even if they all are children.

Serious issues tie in with voice projection and blocking, and in that sense the skills children learn in the theater can affect their personal and social development. When children work hard and achieve expertise in theater they gain confidence and authority, and this naturally strengthens their roles in their families and among friends and others. In the past, company parents actually took small parts in our spring productions. Most of their performances were what you would call "okay," but there was some real benefit to our families when children became examples for their parents to follow. "That's not how Mother Abbess *feels*, Mommy. You love Maria, and you're only partly sad when you send her away from the convent. You should seem happy *and* sad." This child has learned something to say on a difficult, important subject, even at home, and now can carry this wisdom out into the world.

In the theater, on the stage, children naturally learn about social relationships, sharing authority and responsibility and, as we have tried to show throughout this book, building trust. New Hampshire is a relatively affluent and stable place, where social conflicts and personal crises are not easily acknowledged. But all children have the capacity to take in new worlds and not only imagine but enact them. We see them put on parts and devise their own scripts at home before they can read. Then when they enter the wonderful world of Oz or the chamber of Dracula, their personal stories expand, and they can learn the differences between good and bad witches—a lesson that we all keep learning over again. Pure fantasy can be made compelling on the stage, and it can have lasting effects on the moral imaginations of those who perform, as well as on their audience. From this standpoint, "the theatre arts are necessities, not luxuries to be enjoyed by the privileged few but things to which everyone is entitled."[2]

Parents who are involved in children's theater productions are aware that they can have an important ethical dimension.

> The beauty of ORP for me as a parent is seeing the director explain to the actors how the action in the play they are laboring to master connects to the real world they are growing into. I spend a lot of time building stage sets for ORP, when my schedule allows, and whenever I am doing so I always keep an ear out for the director's rehearsal "ethical" messages to the kids. It's all very easy for the actors to just think that whatever they are doing is "just a play," more fantasy than not, a way to spend free time or whatever, quite another to understand that playwrights for the most part write these pieces to illuminate or illustrate something profoundly human. There is always something to be learned and taught. For instance, during *West Side Story*, the message communicated to the troupe was essentially that the action was about racism at its vilest, that if the differences we have as a people can't be resolved peacefully and responsibly, we have failed as human beings. The character Maria's bedroom purposely included sacred images and she wore a cross around her neck not to enforce any Christian polemic, but rather to communicate that Maria and her Latino family were not "bad" persons, just culturally "other," like we all are. The point is to find reconciliation, understanding, and respect in our own lives with those who are different than we are way before we get selfishly and ignorantly violent. The final scene in *West Side Story*, where the two crowds finally intersperse with one another over a shared tragedy, the death of Maria's lover, Tony, is the visual enactment of this message.

These are very powerful scenes in children's theater, for you have to believe that it stays with them for a lifetime, especially when previously understood as the key to all their hard work. (Richard Belshaw, ORP parent)

Powerful scenes are never simple in the lessons they convey. An earlier generation of ORP students received a grant to carry a production of *West Side Story* to two public middle schools in the area. The initiative came from the children of the company themselves, partly because they wanted to keep the show going after its three-day run was over and partly because preparing this play took a lot of discussion about street gangs and social prejudice. They thought they had learned something important to share. Again, this is small-town New Hampshire, where conflicts among young groups are usually played out on sports fields. What could these students learn and convey about West Side New York in 1961?

After the show, members of the company were joined by a police officer for a discussion with the students in the audience. The idea was that the students could apply this story to their own lives, even here, where most children still think of themselves as innocent. The officer testified that fights like these do happen, not only in cities but in communities like ours, and that young people can be seriously hurt when fights get out of hand. So what went wrong with the characters in this story? What lessons could the audience learn? Everyone agreed that this aspect of the story could be especially valuable for young people, even in New Hampshire.

The discussion went well, and then at one point somebody asked not about the story but about the show. It is full of fighting, and people get killed. So why is there so much singing and dancing? Why is it sometimes very funny? How do such different feelings go together in the audience? These were harder questions. They talked about how good stories can confuse the audience's feelings. When did you laugh? Did you care about all of the characters? Did you enjoy the big musical numbers, even though the characters were angry and destructive and you knew where the story was going? Finally the students and the company decided that the happiness of this show actually makes the tragic ending harder and more powerful—and that this, too, is a lesson about life. The Sharks and the Jets are exciting in their anger, and then suddenly all of the singing and dancing comes to an end. The scene that turns the story around comes right after the montage "Tonight" is sung and danced by everyone in different places on the stage: the Sharks, the Jets, Tony and Riff, Maria, Anita, all with separate parts and opposite tones but on the same beat and harmony, singing the word "tonight" over and over, as earlier in the lovers' duet. Then suddenly the passion is destroyed. We learn that people with different names and accents must get along. Life in the city can be dangerous. Love can be dangerous. But the musical comedy continues. What is the lesson there?

In the passage cited at the beginning of this chapter, Walter Benjamin extols children's theater as the best means for children to learn social values and responsibility. He is talking about theater not as a paradigm or example, but as theater, with children on stage performing: "The education of the child requires that his total life be affected. . . . Only on the stage does all life in its unlimited fullness appear framed and as a circumscribed area. . . . The most powerful force of the future [is] summoned up in children by the theater."[3] Benjamin is speaking to adults about reconstructing society by "guaranteeing" children "the fulfillment of their childhood" through theater.

This process is not as simple as drawing a moral from a story. In a good play performed well, fantasy affects the moral imagination, but precepts and lessons can be very difficult to spell out along the way or at the end. Every character represents a different point of view, and every point of view can be compelling. With enough distance from the show, the audience might be able to detach itself from the story, and some simple lessons might seem clear. But good playwrights and good productions rope you in. Your feelings become complex, especially where the characters are concerned.

Children show that they understand the complexity of stories when they are able to represent characters and what they represent well on stage. The Witch in Sondheim's *Into the Woods* is a bad witch, and nothing redeems

her. But she catches the audience in moments of sympathy, even loyalty, through the songs she sings.

The evil Captain Hook is a contrary character, a comical villain with big musical numbers.

There might not seem to be much complexity in Hook's story, for the actor or the audience. But *Peter Pan* is a fairy-tale comedy built on the sadness

of lost children, especially those at home. What is Captain Hook's role in that story? Musicals sometimes give us characters like *Carousel's* Billy Bigelow or *Sweeney Todd's* Mrs. Lovett, who can make an audience feel contrary ways at the same time, even during songs and dances.

These characters probably best suit older children actors and audiences, but the youngest children can be drawn to funny stories about fears and

the ugliness of life, and adults seem not to worry about printing these stories or putting them on stage. Think of the vicious comedy of Punch and
Judy, or the horrors in stories from the Brothers Grimm or Hans Christian
Andersen, or Maurice Sendak's illustrated nightmares. In Roald Dahl's
version of *Little Red Riding Hood*, the title character whips out a pistol and
shoots the Wolf dead. David Wood, who has been called England's greatest
children's dramatist, explains that Dahl was an extremely moral children's
writer: "[H]is child heroes and heroines always defeat the representatives
of evil or unfairness. But the audience, in order to experience the cathartic
joy of triumph over villainy, needs to be shown the nasty things that need
punishing!"[4] If these lessons are simple, they are also important. They can
be appreciated and understood.

Whatever the story, producing theater can help children learn broad lessons about community. To return to a theme of this book, trust is a formal
function in theater: Performers, stagehands, the orchestra, the lighting crew
all depend on one another, and the whole show will fall if somebody trips
and is not caught by everyone else. Actors might compete for attention on
stage, but they learn that they cannot succeed alone. The trust that theater
requires offers a deep, built-in lesson about human relationships. What
more important lesson is there for a child to learn than to trust? What aspect of the arts has greater social value?

℘

Children's theater has the power to affect the deep attitudes and beliefs in
an audience.[5] Religious communities sometimes use children's theater to
celebrate their stories and doctrines, sharing them outside the congregation
while focusing within. Curtain Call in Phoenix, Arizona, is the "educational
arm" of the Arizona Jewish Theatre Company, though it is nonsectarian, extending its teaching "to children of all backgrounds." The Jewish Children's
Theater in Los Angeles, California, targets children from observant Jewish
families, holding weekend classes on Sundays, though the outlook is broad,
including a commercial workshop for students professionally oriented to
theater in the outside world. Jewish Youth Theater, the only student theater
club in Vinnitsa, Ukraine, uses theatrical performances on Jewish holidays
to convey lessons as they celebrate life.

Riding Lights Theatre Company in York, England, "engages children in
theater in an atmosphere where Christian faith and art can be explored side
by side, but membership is open to all, irrespective of religious beliefs."[6]
The Christian Youth Theater identifies itself as the largest youth theater program in the United States, with twelve locations reaching from Vancouver,
Washington, to Anderson, South Carolina, as well as touring groups. Its
mission statement is not partisan to the faith, though its orientation is clear

in its title. In all of these cases, children's theater helps an audience appreciate serious religious doctrine, with no apology to theater critics.

NANA Theater in East Jerusalem is expressly interfaith and has political importance: It draws together Muslim, Christian, and Jewish youth and "puts them together on one stage. There, their cultural differences are expressed and dealt with, only to bring actors and audiences alike in touch with their common humanity and feel how similar they really are."[7] From the perspective of all of these programs, an important purpose of children's theater is to strengthen the bonds of a religious community by orienting children to religious stories and rituals.

Children's drama has a social mission when actors are taught that transforming themselves can transform the audience. Interactive Drama for Education and Awareness in Schools (IDEAS), a company based in Brooklyn, New York, operates through in-school residencies, using role-playing techniques and improvisation to educate disabled and disadvantaged children.

> IDEAS aims to provide an avenue for interaction in a congenial atmosphere, where students can exercise their creativity, self-expression, and risk-taking skills in a safe space while learning about themselves and others, . . . creating a theatrical ensemble, where all the players work together.[8]

In this company, drama provides positive therapy for students with learning disabilities, developmental delays, deafness, blindness, and emotional and behavioral problems. Their work as an ensemble can affect them personally, and at the same time the ensemble can affect the audience.

"Involvement" and "confrontation" make the medium of the theater, even children's theater, a natural vehicle for politics, religion, and other strong points of view. Children are not too innocent to engage an audience in critical issues and affect their sympathies and judgments. Children's theater can be powerfully persuasive, and this power can be exploited to the point that there is no theater at all, but only placards and slogans, illustrations, sermons, and speeches, with no characters, no scenes, and no story. But without being narrowly polemical, children's theater can engage and inform an audience's understanding of the world. If this claim seems exorbitant, consider the following examples.

Children's Performing Arts Workshop (CHIPAWO) is a broad-scale, complex program of support for children in Zimbabwe that involves a variety of arts and cultural activities.[9] Children's theater is at the center of the program. Charitable organizations like the United Nations help to support Zimbabwe through CHIPAWO, focusing on children's health and hunger, but they recognize the importance of cultural activities for children. There can be no more effective means than the theater to engage children in their history and their hopes. Children have to overcome a disposition in the dominant native society against children being seen and heard at all, and so this project has not been easy. But for the same reason, it has had great effect.

CHIPAWO is affiliated with the Zimbabwe Association of Theatre for Children & Young People (ZATCYP), a chapter of the International Association of Theater for Children and Young People that puts children in the audience. From that standpoint, too, theater is recognized as a unifying cultural voice for children in the country. But the emphasis in CHIPAWO is on the participation of students—the word "chipawo" is a Shona word meaning "give also." Its success has been remarkable: There are now thirty-one centers throughout the country, where students are selected to participate in the national Harare Youth Theatre and Junior Theatre.

In this case, specific social skills are part of a curriculum that centers on the arts: decision making and empowerment; schoolwork; health and sex education; and financial, educational, and health problems. This is an example of how theater that is oriented to the welfare of children can transform their lives.

Another example is the People's Recovery, Empowerment, Development Assistance Foundation (PREDA) in the Philippines. There the focus is on abused and exploited children, who are rescued from their circumstances and located in foster homes or trained in the arts throughout the country. Children's theater is at the center: "We train youth in arts and advocacy theatre and they are ambassadors of advocacy and through powerful theatre performances they enlighten and encourage Filipino youth to get involved in helping others and once a year they travel abroad inspiring people to action."[10] These children enact the stories of their lives to an audience that understands what they suffer. In this way, they make their suffering an important issue. Advocacy theater puts these stories even into musicals. The Philippine Educational Theater Association (PETA) offers these students training, which includes scriptwriting, directing, choreography, and the visual arts. There is a focus on the process of improvisation, where children are taught to make independent decisions about how to affect the audience.[11]

The AKBAY Advocacy Theater Group, part of PREDA, has carried its productions into European countries, enlisting other societies than their own to recognize and respond to exploitation and abuse. Their program shows how effective theater can be as it objectifies children's emotions and engages an audience in social issues that can affect all children.

The Bangladesh chapter of Action against Trafficking and Sexual Exploitation of Children (ATSEC) likewise uses children's theater in response to the abuse of children.[12] Street drama is used to expose street trafficking, and the performance is followed by discussions between the performers and the audience. The target is the audience, but the benefit is also enormous for the children who present stories of their own suffering.

Another program in Bangladesh that uses theater to transform the lives of children has been sponsored by the Swedish International Development Cooperation Agency (SIDA). The broad objective of the program is to enable children to "enjoy basic rights, including the right to theatre, and the effects have been positive for all the children participating in the program: better self-confidence, better creative thinking, and a better capacity to discuss and express their opinions." But for children in the harshest circumstances, theater has been a redeeming gift. The question was what could be done for "a sex-worker's children, children living at the streets, vagrants, blind children, other physically handicapped children as well as with mentally handicapped children." Ali Lucky, long identified with children's theater across Bangladesh, has rediscovered through the SIDA project the deep effect that theater can have on children who suffer from poverty and other kinds of personal hardship:

> Children in our hierarchic society often are oppressed. They have to obey without asking why. We shall use our theatre training to help the children not only to express themselves in theatre, where we already have a deep knowledge. But we shall now also train them in asking "why," we shall train them not to be afraid of asking, to start dialogues, to dare to speak with their teachers and their parents. We shall train them to express their opinions. This is a new task for us, and it is a challenge.[13]

The best-known example of political advocacy in children's theater is probably La Colmenita ("The Little Beehive") from Cuba. Founded in 1990, it has expanded through regional programs to include ten thousand Cuban children. It has a particular focus on children with disabilities, but it also has a distinct social mission, explained in the Global Exchange Web site. On the front page of this site, children in the program are called "ambassadors for change,"[14] touring all over the world. This Web site publicizes a frankly political tour to California: "Global Exchange's Cuba Program works to educate government, mainstream media, US institutions and the public to raise awareness about the need to end the US embargo of Cuba and its impact on the Cuban people."

If politics is a facet of La Colmenita, it is not its only reason for being: The social impact of art does not preempt its art, and politics is not simply propaganda. An example of the heart of La Colmenita is its response to a Cuban community devastated by a hurricane. What you see is generosity, pride in the performance, and the kind of political assertion that is a public blessing. "Solidarity" with the audience is beyond politics: "[W]ithout changing their costumes our children mingled with the public, shared their experiences, and exchanged addresses and telephone numbers. More than art, we're interested in creating a participatory environment, full of solidarity."[15]

An organization called DramAidE originated in the drama department of the University of Zululand in South Africa. Because there is no better means than the drama to address the subject of human relationships—in particular serious personal issues that have a social context—the faculty took on the subject of HIV/AIDS. Plays were performed at first by trained counselors and then by young participants themselves, locally at the university and over time throughout the country. Young people learned to create their own plays and to perform them, with dialogue, songs, dances, poems, and posters. This is what DramAidE calls "action media": "communication for development and the applied arts for social change."[16]

Storytelling and theater are proud traditions in South Africa, and "where young people present their own creations to their parents and other community members, they are very well received." Beyond the lessons taught and learned is the capacity to understand themselves: "[T]he complexity, range and subtlety of this approach allows young people to genuinely explore their own attitudes, values and beliefs."[17]

Theater can also be redeeming to children caught in political conflict. An example is the Al-Rowwad Children's Theater established in the Aida Refugee Camp in Palestine. Whatever our views of that conflict, we can respect the objective "to help children to overcome and manage the recent stress and violence imposed on them and encourage self-expression through peaceful means (Drama and Art) in a secure and healthy environment." The motive behind this children's theater reflects a particular time and place, but in broader terms it speaks for any child in any place. Its purpose is to "initiate the children to the art of theatre and drama, and train them on acting and prepare plays which reflect their situation and their rights and other subjects of interest for their age, so that they benefit of this as a means of self-expression and creation to widen their horizons."[18]

In this chapter we have explored the vitality and the determination of children's theater worldwide. Even as children train in theater and learn the forms and effects of dramatic literature, they develop values and skills to carry through life.

NOTES

1. Walter Benjamin, "Program for a Proletarian Children's Theater" (1928), in *The Weimar Republic Sourcebook*, ed. Anton Laes, Martin Jay, and Edward Dimendberg (Berkeley and Los Angeles: University of California Press, 1994), 233.

2. Gary Meredith, *The Future* (2006), Gwent Young People's Theatre, Abergavenny, Wales, 50th Anniversary brochure, 4.

3. Benjamin, "Proletarian Children's Theater," 232–33.

4. "All about David Wood," http://www.davidwood.org.uk/an_interview.htm.

5. We identify theater companies in this section of this chapter by name only, and not Web address. See app. B and C for more information about individual companies.

6. Riding Lights, http://www.ridinglights.org/sub_sites/sts09/welcome.html.

7. Additional Jewish and Christian children's theater companies listed in our appendices include Berkshire Institute for Music and Arts Summer Program in Waltham, Massachusetts; Winnipeg Jewish Theater in Winnipeg, Manitoba, Canada; A Three Fold Cord in Washington, Missouri; Mishpachah, Inc. in Mason, Ohio; Ragamuffin Children's Theatre in Charlevoix, Michigan; and Spiritual Twist Productions in Fuquay-Varina, North Carolina.

8. Interactive Drama for Education and Awareness in Schools, http://www.ideasdrama.org. In its various programs, IDEAS is affiliated with the New York City Department of Education and the Brooklyn Public Library.

9. See "Children's Performing Arts Workshop (CHIPAWO)," Early Childhood Development, http://www.comminit.com/en/node/135060/303.

10. Preda Foundation, Inc., "Introduction," http://www.preda.org/intro.htm.

11. Preda Foundation, Inc., "Preda-AKBAY Theater Group," http://www.preda.org/work/akbay/theater.htm.

12. See Action against Trafficking and Sexual Exploitation of Children, Bangladesh Chapter, *ATSEC Newsletter*, 2nd Issue, http://atsec.tripod.com/atsecbangladeshchapter/id9.html.

13. SIDA, *The Regional Children's Theatre Project in South Asia* (2007), http://www.sida.se/sida/jsp/sida.jsp?d=118&a=32971&language=en_US.

14. Global Exchange, *La Colmenita: Children, The Most Powerful Ambassadors for Change*, http://www.globalexchange.org/countries/americas/cuba/LaColmenita.pdf.

15. "La Colmenita Cuban's Children Theater Company Performs for Hurricane Victims," Cubaheadlines Digital Edition, http://www.cubaheadlines.com/2008/09/24/13575/la_colmenita_cubans_children_theater_company_performs_hurricane_victims.html.

16. DramAidE, "About DramAidE," http://www.dramaide.co.za/contentpage.aspx?pageid=2208.

17. University of KwaZulu, "About DramAidE," http://www.ukzn.ac.za/dramaide/about.asp.

18. Al-Rowwad, "Goal," http://alrowwad.virtualactivism.net/mission.htm.

Conclusion

The Oyster River Players has grown in size and evolved from cardboard sets to a barn full of backdrops, stage furniture, and costumes, but it has not changed its mission. It is a teaching theater for young people, most of them beginners who want more learning in the arts than they are offered in school. Students have never been recruited for the company. They come in through family and friends, and they stay, enjoying the experience however far they carry it.

In principle, but also for practical reasons, company members are encouraged to audition for any parts that interest them in any plays the company puts on, and roles are double and triple cast—whatever it takes to assign roles all around. Like any other performers, ours are motivated by competition. But the spirit even of auditions can be open and encouraging, if the children who are putting themselves to the test are given the right assurances. To recruit or reject company members through auditions would damage the spirit of the company. Instead, our focus will always be on expanding opportunities. Performers are "ready" for roles, or they are not yet; roles "fit," or they do not quite.

The students complain about too much Shakespeare ("Not that we don't like it . . ."), and they want more contemporary plays if we can afford them. We have talked about expanding experiments in musical theater, like the time when a rock band made up of company members composed and performed background music for *As You Like It*. We have dreamed about constructing our own theater (maybe another barn renovation at Kelly's father's farm). More importantly and realistically, over the years we have expected senior members of the company to assume more and more responsibility for classes and productions. Now our graduates come back to help out, even sometimes to take a part or run the lights. Their solidarity is a function of their trust, reinforced in theater.

Just where smaller companies like this go depends on the interests and energies of the students, but all of the companies described in this book go in more directions than one at a time. The mission is always the same— good theater and the welfare of children—and so the questions are always the same. How can we make these shows more enjoyable and important to families and communities? What can these children learn, not only about theater but about their lives? Most private theater companies in this country, like ours, do not have any formal relationship with the towns and cities in which they are located. Instead, their focus is on the skills that children gain and the satisfaction of their audience, mostly parents and friends. Their talents and dedication fan out as the children go out into the world, in most cases leaving the stage.

A small company like ours, in a small town in the woods, will never directly be a part of the international enterprise we have described. The discussions among parents at the back of the Exeter Town Hall before the show have mainly to do with children and families. We celebrate holidays, graduations, and reunions together, as a group of friends, and we enjoy remembering productions and the roles that the children played. Remarkably many ORP graduates have stayed with theater in one way and another—you can find a small colony of them in New York City—and faithfully they come up here to be part of the audience and applaud their younger counterparts.

Looking not too far forward, we can see this company coming to its end. Those children of ours grew up and graduated from ORP, hard as that is to believe, and teachers graduate too. But students teach in turn, and in that way we can expect the spirit of this company to carry on.

Appendix A: Children's Theater Agencies and Organizations

The following is a list of Web sites for agencies and organizations that promote children's theater. Although this list is not comprehensive, it's a good start. These lists will be posted online at http://www.childrenstheaterinfo. com, and revised as further Web sites and information becomes available. If you wish to suggest additional sites, please send your recommendations to us at ctsurvey2@aol.com.

GENERAL

Alliance for the Arts	http://www.allianceforarts.org
American Alliance for Theatre and Education (AATE)	http://www.aate.com
American Society for Theatre Research (ASTR)	http://www.astr.org
Americans for the Arts (AFTA)	http://www.artsusa.org
Arts Education Partnership (AEP)	http://aep-arts.org
ARTSEDGE: The National Arts and Education Network	http://artsedge.kennedy-center.org
ArtsEdNet—The Getty Education Institute for the Arts	http://www.getty.edu/artsednet
Association for Theatre in Higher Education (ATHE)	http://www.athe.org
Association of Performing Arts Presenters	http://www.artspresenters.org

Association International du   http://www.assitej.org
  Theatre pour L'Enfance et la
  Jeunesse (ASSITEJ)
Children's Theatre Foundation of   http://www.childrenstheatre
  America (CTFA)   foundation.org
Educational Theatre Association   http://www.edta.org
  (EdTA)
International Thespian Society.
  See EdTA
Lincoln Center Institute for the   http://www.lcinstitute.org
  Arts in Education
National Endowment for the   http://www.nea.gov
  Arts (NEA)
National Foundation for   www.artsawards.org
  Advancement in the Arts (NFAA)
National Youth Theatre (NYT)   http://www.nationalyouththeatre
                                        .com
Performing the World   http://www.performingtheworld.org

AFRICA

Eastern Africa Theatre Institute (EATI)   *see* http://basata-tz.org/eatheatre.php

ASIA

India

International Festival of Performing   http://www.ryanicfpa.com/home
  Arts, Ryan International School   .html
Rangshala   http://www.rangshala.com

Singapore

Singapore Drama Educators   http://www.sdea.org.sg
  Association (SDEA)

AUSTRALIA AND NEW ZEALAND

ArtsEdge   http://www.artsedge.dca.wa.gov.au
Australian Capital Territory Drama   http://www.pa.ash.org.au/actda
  Educators' Association

Drama Australia: The National Association for Drama in Education, Inc.	http://www.dramaaustralia.org.au
Drama New South Wales	http://dramansw.org.au
Drama New Zealand (NZADIE)	http://www.drama.org.nz
Drama Queensland—Queensland Association for Drama in Education (QADIE)	http://www.dramaqueensland.org.au
Drama Tas—Tasmanian Association for Drama in Education	http://www.dramatas.com.au/index.htm
Drama Victoria—Drama in Education Association of Victoria	http://www.dramavictoria.vic.edu.au
DramaWest: The Professional Association of Drama Educators in Western Australia	http://www.dramawest.com
International Drama/Theatre Education Association (IDEA)	http://www.idea-org.net/en/
Regional Arts Australia Online	http://www.regionalarts.com.au/raa1/default.asp
South Australian Association for Drama in Education (SAADIE)	http://www.ceasa.asn.au/cgi-bin/assoc.pl?assn=SAADIE

EUROPE

General

International Drama in Education Research Institute (IDIERI)	http://www.idieri2009.org
International Museum Theatre Alliance (IMTAL)	http://www.imtal-europe.net
International Schools Theatre Association (ISTA)	http://www.ista.co.uk
International Society for Education through Art (InSEA)	http://www.insea.org
World Festival of Children's Theatre	http://www.weltkindertheaterfest.de

Countries

Belgium

Asociación Internacional del Teatro de Arte/International Amateur Theatre Association (AITA/IATA)	http://www.aitaiata.org

Cyprus

Theatre Education Association   http://www.humanrights-edu-cy
    Cyprus (TEA)   .org/tea.htm

Finland

Finnish Drama and Theatre   http://www.fideahomepage.org/
    Education Association (FIDEA)   eng/fideahome.htm
Murros: Nuorten teatteritapahtuma   http://www.tnl.fi

Germany

"Fantastic—Fantastisch":   http://www.theater-spiel-laden.de/
    Internationales Kinder- und   fileadmin/dateien/festivalzeitung
    Jugendtheaterfest   _web-1.pdf

Hungary

The Hungarian Drama and Theatre   http://www.drama.hu
    in Education Association (HUDEA)

Italy

Hollawind: International   http://www.tpz-brixen.org/holla
    Children's Theatre Festival   wind_international_encounter_
                                          of_kids_theatre.htm

Romania

Educational Drama Association   http://www.drama.ro/hornby.html
    in Romania (EDAR)

Sweden

Riksorganisationen Auktoriserade   http://dramapedagogen.se
    Dramapedagoger (RAD)

NORTH AMERICA

United States

Regional

New England
New England Drama Council   http://spiddington.com/nedrama/

Southeast

The Southeast Center for Education
    in the Arts (SCEA) http://www.utc.edu/SCEA/

Southeastern Theatre Conference,
    Inc. (SETC) http://www.setc.org

Southwest

Southwest Theatre and Film
    Association (SWTFA) http://swtfa.com

States

California

California County Superintendents
    Educational Services Association
    Arts Initiative http://www.ccsesaarts.org

Connecticut

Connecticut Drama Association
    (CDA) http://www.connecticutdrama
    association.org

Florida

Florida Association for Theatre
    Education (FATE) http://www.fatefirst.org

Hawaii

Alliance for Drama Education http://www.rehearseforlife.com

Illinois

Youth Theater Coalition of
    Chicago (YTCC) http://www.CCAP.us/ytcc

Iowa

Iowa Alliance for Arts Education
    (IAEE) http://www.iowaalliance4artsed.org

Massachusetts

The Massachusetts High School
    Drama Guild, Inc. http://www.mhsdg.com

Michigan

Theatre Alliance of Michigan (TAM) http://www.theatreallianceof
    michigan.org

Mississippi

Mississippi Theatre Association http://www.mta-online.org

New York

The New York State Theatre
    Education Association (NYSTEA) http://www.nystea.org

North Carolina
North Carolina Theatre Arts   http://www.nctae.org
    Educators (NCTAE)

Ohio
Ohio Alliance for Arts Education   http://www.oaae.net
    (OAAE)
Ohio Arts Council (OAC)   http://www.oac.state.oh.us
Ohio Educational Theatre Association   http://www.ohioedta.org

South Carolina
South Carolina Theatre Association   http://www.southcarolinatheatre.com

Tennessee
The Tennessee Theatre Association: http://www.tn-theatre.com/tta-
    Children's Theatre (TTA)   divisions-childrens.html

Texas
Texas Educational Theatre   http://www.tetatx.com
    Association (TETA)

Utah
Utah Theatre Association   http://www.utahtheatreassociation
                                           .org

Virginia
Virginia Theatre Association   http://www.vtasite.org
Wolf Trap Foundation: Institute for   http://www.wolftrap.org/Education/
    Early Learning in the Arts   Institute_for_Early_Learning_
                                           through_the_Arts.aspx

Canada

Canadian Children's Theatre Co.   http://www.childrenstheatre.ca

SOUTH AMERICA

Brazil

Proscenio: Teatro Brasileiro, Escolas   http://www.pagebuilder.com.br/
                                            proscenio/bibliote.htm

UNITED KINGDOM AND IRELAND

England

Action for Children's Arts (ACA)   http://www.childrensarts.org.uk
Arts Council England   http://www.artscouncil.org.uk

Arts4Schools: National Grid for Learning — http://www.arts4schools.com

Centre for Applied Theatre Research — http://www.arts.manchester.ac.uk/catr/

Drama Teachers Association North (DTA North) — http://www.nationaldrama.co.uk/index.php?content=nd_links&linkgroupnr=6

English National Youth Arts Network (ENYAN) — http://www.enyan.co.uk

National Association for the Teaching of Drama (NATD) — http://www.natd.50megs.com

National Association of Youth Theatres (NAYT) — http://www.nayt.org.uk

National Campaign for the Arts — http://www.artscampaign.org.uk

National Drama — http://www.nationaldrama.co.uk

National Operatic and Dramatic Association (NODA) — http://www.noda.org.uk

National Resource Centre for Youth Theatre. *See* NAYT

National Youth Music Theatre (NYMT) — http://www.nymt.org.uk

The Society of Teachers of Speech and Drama — http://www.stsd.org.uk

Ireland

Association for Drama in Education in Ireland (ADEI) — http://www.ict.mic.ul.ie/adei

National Association for Youth Drama (NAYD)—Ireland — http://www.youthdrama.ie

Northern Ireland

Ulster Association of Youth Drama (UAYD) — http://www.uayd.co.uk

Scotland

Promote YT — http://www.promoteyt.co.uk

Appendix B: Programs and Companies: United States and Canada

This list contains several hundred programs and companies throughout the United States and Canada, along with some basic details for each. Further information may be obtained by visiting the Web sites provided. This list will be revised and amended as needed, so please visit http://www.child renstheater.com for periodic updates. If you wish to suggest additional sites, please send your recommendations to us at ctsurvey2@aol.com.

UNITED STATES

General/Various

Christian Youth Theater [CYT]
http://www.cyt.org
The largest youth theater program in the United States, committed to developing performing arts skills and helping youth develop character and self-confidence. Three times a year—in the fall, winter, and spring—CYT offers theater arts classes for six- to eighteen-year-old children as an after-school activity. Each local branch conducts three ten-week sessions throughout the school year, teaching drama, voice, dance, and a broad spectrum of specialty theatrical workshops in weekly two-hour classes. Students have the opportunity to work behind the scenes or to audition and perform on stage in a Broadway-style musical performed for the community. Additional performance opportunities are available in CYT Tour Groups, which perform musical reviews for community and civic functions. Internships, director training, teacher aiding, and shadow aiding provide older students

with the opportunity to gain additional training and experience. Programs are located in Anderson, South Carolina; Atlanta, Georgia; Chicago, Illinois; Denver, Colorado; Kansas City, Kansas; Phoenix, Arizona; Richmond, Virginia; San Diego, California (founding program); Spokane, Washington; Tucson, Arizona; Vancouver, British Columbia; Washington, D.C.

Alabama

Alabama Shakespeare Festival Acting Academy (Montgomery)
http://www.asfeducation.com/academy/index.html
Encourages high achievement; builds creative problem solving, analytical, and collaborative skills; refines judgment; and stimulates thinking "outside the box." Students exposed to theater arts are often more confident, creative, and self-assured, developing a lifelong appreciation of language.

Birmingham Children's Theatre (Birmingham)
http://www.bct123.org
Provides educational activities in connection with theater productions and auditions children for roles.

Fantasy Playhouse Children's Theater (Huntsville)
http://www.letthemagicbegin.org
A volunteer organization offering personalized instruction to preschool and school-aged children.

Madison Children's Theatre's School of Cultural & Performing Arts (Madison)
http://madisontheatre.com
Designed to provide an innovative and high-quality performing arts education, the school strives to create an environment where students are encouraged to express themselves to the best of their ability in a fun and enjoyable way. Offers classes during the school year and a summer camp.

Tuscaloosa Children's Theatre (Tuscaloosa)
http://www.tuscaloosachildrenstheatre.com
Organized in 1986 to educate and expose the children of Tuscaloosa County to all aspects of stage performing and production. Offers summer courses as well as productions year-round.

Alaska

Alaska Theatre of Youth (Anchorage)
http://www.alaskatheatreofyouth.org

Aimed at developing the human potential in young people through performing arts training and performance, and exposing the community to the finest in theater for young people. As a long-standing member of Alaska's vigorous arts community, the Alaska Theatre of Youth teaches everything from Japanese culture (as part of staging *Otogibanashi*) to sword fighting. It collaborates with native organizations and the schools to reach children in many different situations. Its original mission focused on using the performing arts to help youth trapped in destructive life patterns. Now, in addition to a mainstage season, its activities include a summer conservatory, a Touring Young Shakespeare Company, and an education program.

Arizona

Actor's Youth Theatre (Mesa)
http://www.actorsyouththeatre.org
A performing arts organization with the mission of educating, entertaining, and enriching the lives of young people and their families through the art of theater. Provides opportunities for youth to develop their acting abilities and musical talents through comprehensive performing arts workshops, community outreach, performance opportunities, and the presentation of theater productions for school and family audiences.

Ahwatukee Youth Theater (Phoenix)
http://www.azact.org
Provides local children and adults education in, appreciation for, and opportunities to participate in all aspects of the performing arts, as well as offering family-friendly entertainment to the community at large.

ArtsWork (Phoenix)
http://artswork.asu.edu
A broad arts program for children that includes "Summer on Stage," a five-week intensive workshop that teaches students basic acting techniques, movement for the theater, character development, and more. Students end the course with fully mounted productions.

Childsplay, Inc. (Tempe)
http://childsplayaz.org
Encourages self-esteem building and creative expression through pantomime, role-playing, dancing, and production of short plays. Summer campers explore a variety of theater genres and the world of script development, creating backdrops, props and scenery, auditioning for roles, and producing, directing, and taping productions in order to create a special performance at the end of the camp session.

Cookie Company [Phoenix Theatre] (Phoenix)
http://www.phoenixtheatre.com/homeCC.aspx
Offers classes, camps, and workshops for developing talent and a chance
for accomplished actors to audition into youth performance troupes. The
PT Players perform original works at schools, libraries, and special events.
The company also offers a broad variety of summer classes in progressive
stages for different ages.

Creative Youth Theatre (Phoenix)
http://www.cryt.org
Produces a season of four mainstage plays (for students age ten and over)
and a three-week summer session (a one-act play with mini-workshops
including comedy, improvisation, voice, and diction). Students learn
about the audition process, backstage, and directing.

Curtain Call (Phoenix)
http://www.azjewishtheatre.org/youth.html
The educational arm of the Arizona Jewish Theatre Company, a not-for-
profit, nonsectarian professional theater company. Open to children of all
backgrounds.

East Valley Children's Theatre (Mesa)
http://www.evct.org
A place where children can grow and develop into confident young adults,
gain self-esteem, and develop creativity. Its mission is to offer youth ages
eight through eighteen opportunities to experience the process and product
of live theatrical performances, by children and for children. No previous
experience is required for children to audition and no advance preparation
is needed.

Fountain Hills Community Youth Theater (Fountain Hills)
http://www.fountainhillstheater.com
A community theater with an extensive program of youth education for
children and teenagers ages seven to eighteen. Youth education programs
are offered year-round: Fall Workshops, Spring Workshops, Summer Mini-
Camps, and a Teen Summer Camp.

Gilbert Youth Theater (Gilbert)
http://www.gfaa.com/youththeater.html
Offers classes to children at different levels of age and experience, culminating in public shows. Young actors with experience are given opportunities
to write their own commercials and to learn improvisation, pantomime,
and stage techniques, while learning basic theater directions and skills.

Greasepaint Youtheatre (Scottsdale)

http://www.phxtheatre.org/HomeGP.aspx

Programming is designed to develop the life skills and aesthetic knowledge that youth will carry with them as both artists and audiences of tomorrow. Its mission is to nurture intellectual, artistic, and personal development through a range of professionally managed and directed theatrical experiences, drama education, and the power of live theater performances.

Herrera School for the Fine Arts and Dual Language (Phoenix)

http://www.phxelem.k12.az.us/school_sites/Herrera/index.htm

Teaches students to express their emotions and perspectives through drama. Student actors and actresses perform regularly for other classes, demonstrating their understanding of newly learned concepts and skills. A yearly production provides older students with a professional drama experience and allows them to share their accomplishments with the community in a professional setting.

Music Theater Conservatory (Phoenix)

http://www.musictheaterconservatory.com/project.asp

A two-week summer workshop designed for singing actors in grades 7 through 12 who are serious about developing and refining their auditioning and performance skills.

Summer Centerstage (Phoenix)

http://www.cstage.com/summer/

Founded in 1969 as a college preparatory program for high school–aged performers, through the years Centerstage has grown to be respected throughout North America as a training ground for career- and college-bound talent. Its unique system of training has inspired dozens of newspaper and television features.

Vagabond Youth Theatre (Avondale)

see http://www.wwar.com/categories/Theater/Youth_Related/

A nonprofit organization devoted to introducing theater to children through education and performance. Offers apprenticeships and workshops in both performance and technical areas of a professional theater for kids, by kids.

Valley Youth Theatre (Phoenix)

http://www.vyt.com

Provides positive exposure for children, adolescents, and teens to skills through community theater activities. Casts are always primarily people from seven to eighteen years of age. Offers classes, workshops, and camps.

Young Actors Theatre [Edna Vihel Center for the Arts] (Tempe)
see http://www.tempe.gov/arts/art/yasyat.htm
Teaches the basic skills of acting and improvisation through theater games
and exercises. Students aged seven through twelve work on a script and
learn about set, costume, makeup, and other technical elements of theater,
while getting ready for the final production at each session's end.

Arkansas

Arkansas Arts Center Children's Theatre (Little Rock)
http://www.arkarts.com/childrens_theatre/
An art museum with a children's theater and a studio school.

Camden Fairview High School Thespian Troupe 5780 (Camden)
http://www.freewebs.com/cfhsthespian/index.htm
A privately sponsored theater group and a member of the International
Thespian Society. In addition to performances, the troupe attends a statewide drama festival each year.

The Foundation of Arts Youth Repertory Theatre Company (Jonesboro)
http://www.deltaboogie.com/features/youthrep/
The Foundation of Arts Youth Repertory Theatre Company is made up of
students in grades 2–12, from the after-school drama program.

Sonshine Academy, Inc. (Conway)
http://sonshineacademy.com
Offers boys and girls gymnastics, dance, cheerleading, swimming, and
children's theater. Students receive instruction in storytelling, dramatic acting, characterization, improvisation, role-play, and much more. Students
also participate in short sketches, plays, and learn the art of making props
and backdrops.

California

Academy of Creative Education (North Hollywood)
http://www.academyofcreativeeducation.com
Students focus on a particular aspect of theater as they work collectively to
produce a final piece, presented at the end of the five-week program.

Actors' Conservatory Theatre San Diego (San Diego)
http://www.actsandiego.com/index.htm
Provides educational and artistic opportunities to young actors to perform,
act, and learn the art of stagecraft in a fun, satisfying, yet highly professional

environment. This is accomplished by teaching, practicing, and performing live theater with youth who are interested in learning and becoming more involved in stage acting.

Actors Workout Studio (Los Angeles)
http://www.actorsworkout.com
Offers professional acting training and coaching for adults, teens, and children.

Adda Clevenger Junior Preparatory and Theater School for Children (San Francisco)
http://addaclevenger.org
A coeducational school for students in grades K–8.

American Conservatory Theater—Young Conservatory (San Francisco)
http://www.act-sf.org/site/PageServer?pagename=conservatory_yc
The large and well-established students' component of the American Conservatory Theater. The standard curriculum offers between twenty and thirty different classes and intensive programs designed for beginning, intermediate, and advanced-level study, all set according to age. Courses include Improvisation, Acting, Voice and Speech, Dialects, Audition, Professionalism, Creating Physical Character, Musical Theater, Dance, Shakespeare, Alexander Technique, Directing, On-Camera Acting Techniques, Active Play Reading (in various styles of theater and dramatic writing), Technical Theater Lab and Design for the Theater, Senior Seminar (to aid graduating students in the transition to college, university, or conservatory), and various master classes. The Young Conservatory Company, the production and public performance arm of the school, offers a season of four plays, many of which are commissioned and original creations. Additional emphases include new plays written, performed, and published; and international programs in cooperation with distinguished companies and schools abroad. Financial assistance is based on need for each session, and funds for these scholarships are raised through annual events and private donations. Additionally, the Young Conservatory has a long history of working with special-needs groups in the San Francisco Tenderloin neighborhood (Glide Memorial Church, the Vietnamese Youth Development Organization, the Columbia Park Boys and Girls Club, and more).

ARIEL Theatrical, Inc. (Salinas)
http://www.arieltheatrical.org
A nonprofit theater arts program for children throughout Monterey County. ARIEL provides a comprehensive theater experience that imparts the joys of learning and performing while teaching positive values and enhancing self-esteem.

Bakersfield Music Theater (Bakersfield)
http://www.bmtshowtiks.com
Offers children's theater and workshops.

BB's Kids (Los Angeles)
http://www.bbskids.com
An acting school for kids and teens interested in commercials, TV, film, or music videos. The school produces three showcases per year for agents and managers.

Biola Youth Theatre (La Mirada)
http://youth.biola.edu/theatre/
Offers a summer program of basic, intermediate, and advanced classes in acting, voice, and dance, held at the Biola University Campus in La Mirada. Students range from age ten through eighteen.

Blue Room Theatre (Chico)
http://www.blueroomtheatre.com/young_company.html
A nonprofit educational organization dedicated to providing children and teens with the opportunity to experience the performing arts. The Blue Room Young Company offers year-round productions, classes, and workshops for students ages three through eighteen.

Boxtales Theatre Company (Santa Barbara)
http://www.boxtales.org
Storytelling, music, masks, and movement present world myths and folktales to audiences of all ages, and this company offers professional theater training for students ages fourteen and up.

Broadway Bound and Temecula Performing Arts Co. (Temecula)
http://www.broadwayboundonline.com
Offers children's classes and performances at the home theater and throughout Southern California at hospitals, retirement homes, county fairs, and more.

Broadway on Tour (Yorba Linda)
http://www.broadwayontour.org/default.htm
With the motto "Children Bringing Theatre to Children," provides theater for children both on stage and in the audience. Children who are cast are typically aged from eight to eighteen, with auditions open to the public. Parents of company members help with the staging of productions.

Broadway Starz (Temecula)
http://www.broadwaystarz.com
Serves the community as an educational resource dedicated to the promotion, development, and celebration of all creative and performing arts. This is accomplished through an innovative and comprehensive theatre arts program in which children, youths, and adults can develop their creative potential while experiencing the enjoyment of self-expression.

Buena Park Youth Theatre (Buena Park)
http://www.buenaparkfinearts.com/youth.php
BPYT has produced fully staged Broadway musicals since 1981. Over the years more than twenty-five hundred young people between the ages of eight and eighteen have participated. Full-length shows are presented with professional lighting and sound, full costumes, and complete sets. All productions are presented with highest quality production values possible and have consistently received outstanding critical acclaim.

Cal Shakes Summer Theater [California Shakespeare Theater] (Oakland)
http://www.calshakes.org/v4/educ/summertheaterprograms.html
Provides invaluable training for young people ages eight to eighteen who are interested in the pursuit of acting, as well as for those who want to create through other means of expression, with the goal of nourishing imaginations in preparation for the work of life.

California Young Actors Conservatory (San Diego)
see http://www.sandiego.org/listing/Visitors/12788
Offers classes and workshops taught by well-respected professional actors and teachers. Produces youth theatre productions staff led by professional actor/directors, producers, musical directors, and choreographers.

Chico Children's Theatre Workshop (Chico)
http://www.chicotheatercompany.com
Since 1998, has offered nearly two hundred children ages four to seventeen twelve productions and workshops. A school for performing arts includes courses for teenage students.

Children's Civic Light Opera (Culver City)
http://www.cclo.org
Presents musical theater productions that tell stories through a combination of song, dance, and dialogue. Classes and workshops open doors for creative expression and performance through an intermediary program between educational theater and the professional stage.

Children's Musical Theater San Jose (San Jose)
http://www.cmtsj.org
The nation's largest youth theater company, producing seven or eight shows a year, with performers ranging in age from six to twenty. Also offers a Conservatory Program and online theater as a digital activity program, where young people can work with theater professionals to create new work for the stage.

Children's Musical Theaterworks (Fresno)
https://www.cmtworks.com
A nonprofit theater company dedicated to the training of young performers in the area of musical theater and the arts. Since 1997 it has produced more than thirty mainstage and touring productions, seen by more than forty-five thousand audience members. All who audition are cast.

Children's Playtime Productions (Palm Desert)
http://www.childrensplaytimeproductions.com
A nonprofit education-based theater company for children and adults. Founded in 1995, it has grown to reach more than nineteen thousand children and adults each year.

Children's Theatre Workshop (Mission Viejo)
http://www.childrenstheatreworkshop.org
A nonprofit community-oriented organization providing interactive theater opportunities for young people ages five through sixteen since 1981. Its fundamental mission is to let children experience dramatics that enhance their self-esteem and reward them for their creativity.

Christian Arts & Theatre [CAT] (Corona)
http://www.catcorona.org/aboutus.asp
An after-school theater and visual arts educational program for students ages six through eighteen. CAT is committed to building up kids through excellence in the arts as well as modeling for them the highest morals through traditional biblical values.

Classic Youth Theatre (Carlsbad)
http://classicyouththeatre.org
Offers workshops, auditions, and performances, recruiting children with no limits on age. Motives include declining school budgets and the uncertainties of children in contemporary society.

Creative Acting Theater School (Simi Valley)
http://www.youththeater.com/
Stages productions for young audiences and also offers a summer children's camp and courses throughout the year for children.

Developing Stages (San Francisco)
http://home.comcast.net/~scottnbecky
Teaches Shakespeare's plays through performance and educational theater programs, including workshops for children ages nine through eighteen. Encourages creativity and provides opportunities for participants to grow mentally and spiritually in an atmosphere that is as edifying as it is exciting and fun.

Dublin Theatre Company (Dublin)
see http://www.oakland.com/dublin-theatre-company-b2150521
A children's theater providing summer camp, after-school programs and classes, workshops, and shows.

Easily Distracted Theatre (San Jose)
http://www.easilydistracted.com
A collaboration of various student artists who self-produce animated, cinematic, and theatrical productions.

Education Unlimited Actors Workshop (Berkeley)
http://educationunlimited.com/actors/index.html
Offers middle school, high school, and intensive workshops dedicated to the craft of stage acting. Whether or not a student intends eventually to study film, television, or theater acting, the techniques taught here serve as essential building blocks for any actor. All programs combine a level of intensity appropriate for students who recognize that they must work hard to maximize their mastery of their art, along with the "playing" inherent in the job of acting. Working actors are guest visitors and speakers.

Encore Youth Theatre (Vista)
http://www.encoreyouththeatre.com
A not-for-profit educational association that specializes in theatrical training for young people. Young aspiring actors are prepared to pursue their dreams by producing shows and theatrical workshops. Education in theater arts includes encouraging teamwork and developing leadership skills in a supportive setting.

Fallbrook Players (Fallbrook)
http://www.fallbrooktheater.com
An arts education program founded in 1980, specializing in training in the arts (singing, drama, dance, comedy, and technical theater) to give young people a wholesome, fun, and safe place to learn.

Fullerton Children's Repertory Theater (Fullerton)
http://boneplate.com/takeda/fcrt/
A nonprofit company composed entirely of youths ages ten to thirteen performing Broadway musicals. In repertory spirit, they play together until they graduate from the company. In each production, all students are assigned lines and parts, and major roles are double cast in order to give more members the opportunity to perform. In addition to presenting two Broadway musicals per year, the group also entertains for local community organizations. It also travels frequently to international festivals and musicales.

Gypsies in a Trunk Touring Troupe (Simi Valley)
http://www.youththeater.com/
Stages productions for young audiences and also offers a summer children's camp and courses throughout the year for children.

JCompany Children's Theater Group (La Jolla)
http://www.lfjcc.org/youth/arts.aspx
Offers many classes and workshops and summer camps in theater and related kinds of performance.

Jewish Children's Theater (Los Angeles)
see http://www.jewishjournal.com/community_briefs/article/young_jews_can_act_out_on_sundays_20050902_11830/
A serious acting program targeting children from observant Jewish families, offering classes on Sundays. While sessions usually end with a low-key performance for parents, the focus is on acting techniques, improvisation, theater games, and even a commercial workshop.

Kids 4 Broadway [The Way Off-Broadway Theatre Workshop] (Kelseyville)
http://www.pacificsites.com/~kidsplay/about.htm
A theater company for students ages seven to seventeen. The program motivates young people to appreciate the value of learning and discovery, while helping to build their confidence and self-worth. The company also offers worldwide a series of original one-act plays written for elementary and middle school children to perform in schools and learning centers.

Kids on Broadway (Santa Cruz)
http://www.kidsonbroadway.org
Offers young people (ages eight through eighteen) the opportunity to learn about and participate in quality professional theater in a supportive environment where they can acquire communication, performance, and

technical skills; develop character and self-esteem; and experience the pride of accomplishment and the joy of working as a team.

Kids Take the Stage, Inc. (San Leandro)
http://www.kidstakethestage.com/index.html
A not-for-profit organization established in 1998 to provide the highest quality in youth theater in both an artistic and technical arena. All productions employ top-of-the-line lighting, costume, scenic, and sound design in addition to an award-winning staff of directors, choreographers, and musical directors. The company strives to give each participant the most authentic off-Broadway experience possible and to prepare them for careers in professional live theater.

The Laguna Playhouse Youth Conservatory (Laguna Beach)
http://www.lagunaplayhouse.com/education/conservatory/
Unique in the region for its approach to theater education for young people, this company offers talented youngsters a small-enrollment, high-level program of instruction in theater skills taught by theater professionals. The curriculum encompasses acting, theater production, and dramatic literature. Admission is highly selective and by annual audition.

Magic Circle Theatre (Roseville)
http://www.mcircle.org/children's_theatre/childrens_theatre.html
Offers performance-oriented Little Ones Workshops for children ages four through six and Youth Workshops for ages seven through seventeen. Students use original scripts as well as some popular music to learn their chosen craft. Productions never double or triple cast, and everyone sings, dances, and acts, regardless of experience.

The Marsh Youth Theater (San Francisco)
http://www.themarsh.org
Provides youth ages four through fifteen with a high-quality theater arts experience integrating music, dance, drama, stagecraft, and performance into one holistic program. Open to all young performers without audition and regardless of financial limitations, the Marsh exposes children to the vast world of multicultural arts by working with a diverse group of professional performing faculty.

Metropolitan Educational Theatre [MET2] (San Diego)
http://www.met2.org
A nonprofit educational organization that provides young people with an opportunity to be participants in the dramatic process as actors, singers, dancers, and good members of an audience. MET2 has performed

in high school, college, and community theaters; dinner theater settings; large outdoor tents; and professional theaters in the United States, Europe, Australia, and New Zealand. Multiple locations in San Diego–Metro, San Diego–North County, San Fernando Valley, East San Gabriel Valley, and Torrance/South Bay, California.

Music West, Inc. (Westchester)
http://www.musicwest.org
Provides young people an opportunity to perform and experience large-scale musical theater. Actors also have the opportunity to go behind the scenes of a full-scale production and assist in set building, crew, choreography, and other aspects vital to producing musical theater.

Musical Theatre Works (San Francisco)
http://www.musicaltheatreworks.org
An after-school academy and performance company for children in grades 1–12 with classes in musical theater, voice, acting, and dance. The diverse school is made up of beginning students (with little or no experience in performing arts), as well as students who have had previous stage and performance experience.

Musical Youth Artists Repertory Theatre [MYART] (Long Beach)
http://www.myart.org
A nonprofit youth theater that provides instruction and performance experience in acting, singing, dancing, and stage movement to help students discover their own power as individuals. Students also learn how to create and work together as a cooperative group in a positive manner. Each year MYART presents three mainstage productions with casts of 160 to more than three hundred participants. Multiple leads and large ensemble casts allow all participants to shine.

No Limits Theater Program (Culver City)
http://www.nolimitsspeaksout.com/index.php?page_name=theater_program
Provides deaf children the opportunity to improve their speech and language skills as well as self-confidence in a professional theatrical environment.

Orange County Children's Theatre (Stanton)
http://www.occt.org
A community theater program for actors ages eight through nineteen, with an emphasis on education and family involvement, self-esteem, and confidence.

Palo Alto Children's Theatre (Palo Alto)
see http://www.cityofpaloalto.org/childrenstheatre
A seventy-five-year-old public-private partnership serving children and young adults aged eight to twenty-four years old. Over the years this program has expanded its scope to include radio, television, film and video, classes, camps, and special events, during both the summer and the school year.

Pam Donkin's Theater Workshops for Young Performers (Millbrae)
http://www.pamdonkin.com
A summer drama camp for children ages eleven to seventeen, with improvisation, clowning, and basic acting.

Peninsula Youth Theatre (Mountain View)
http://www.pytnet.org
A unique family atmosphere that successfully uses theater performances and classes to develop a strong sense of self-esteem and to nurture social and communication skills that are useful in all walks of life. This program is committed to providing an enriching theatrical experience in schools, thereby reinforcing the positive role the arts play in academic success.

Peter Pan Junior Theater (La Mesa)
http://www.ppjt.org
A program that has served the community since 1970, specializing in creating a family experience like no other after-school organization can. Volunteer teachers and past students play an integral role in each production as designers, choreographers, vocal directors, orchestra directors, and musicians.

Premiere for Kids (San Diego)
http://www.premiereforkids.com
Year-round youth theater presented by youth performers, including auditions, workshops, and special events.

Riverside Youth Theatre (Moreno Valley)
http://riversideyouththeatre.org
A program dedicated to providing training for children and youth in the theater arts. All musicals and plays are reviewed for content that is appropriate for young people. Program costs are kept as low as possible by efficient management and parent volunteers.

Roberta Jones Junior Theatre [formerly Santa Clara Junior Theatre]
(Santa Clara)
see http://santaclaraca.gov/park_recreation/pr-junior-theatre.html
Offers theatrical experience for youth aged eight to eighteen. Full participation is encouraged, whether on stage, as part of the technical production staff, or as a makeup artist. This program helps youngsters find their creative niche wherever they feel most comfortable.

Runaway Stage: Musical Theater (Elk Grove)
www.runawaystage.com/ymtw.html
Dance workshops, vocal workshops, acting workshops, and a parents' seminar. The acting workshops include instruction on acting, stage movement, theatrical terms and definitions, awareness games, theater games, blocking (stage movement), character analysis, voice projection, anatomy of a theater, respect for the art of performing, dialogue and diction, and having fun on stage.

Sacramento Theatre Company (Sacramento)
http://www.sactheatre.org/index.cfm?page=585072
Offers ensemble classes and summer camps with concentration on character development, improvisation, and the rehearsal process. STC-2 is the company's premier training program for young professionals, who are selected for their acting, dancing, and musical ability; high academic standing in their schools; a willingness to attend master classes; a willingness and availability to attend all rehearsals for assigned shows; and a high level of maturity and family support.

San Diego Junior Theatre (San Diego)
http://www.juniortheatre.com
The oldest continuing children's theater program in the United States. Offers hundreds of classes and camps and is committed to providing engaging, innovative, high-quality theater education and productions for children of all cultural heritages, ages, abilities, and levels of interest.

Shenanigans' Youth Theater (Victorville)
http://www.sytg.org
A nonprofit organization that provides opportunities for performers in singing, dancing, and acting, as well as stage management, lighting, and sound control.

Showstoppers Theatre Productions (Santa Barbara)
http://www.showstopperstheatreproductions.com
A musical theater training program that provides students the opportunity to learn by participating in quality musical theater productions. The pro-

gram focuses on teaching youth about all aspects of musical theater. Young performers of all skill levels are welcome, and no previous experience is required. Shows feature large casts, so all members enjoy the opportunity for featured parts, lines, solos, or small-group songs.

Siskiyou Performing Arts Center (SPAC): The Children's Summer Shakespeare Theater (Yreka)
http://www.siskiyouspac.org
A six-week summer workshop and final Shakespeare production for students ages seven to nine.

Solano Youth Theatre (Suisun City)
http://www.solanoyouththeatre.com
The award-winning youth division of Solano College's celebrated conservatory theater training program. Surrounded by dedicated educators and industry professionals, young people participate in quality productions, workshops, and classes. Programming is designed to strengthen communication skills, promote team building, supplement teachers' classroom efforts, and promote theater arts.

South Coast Repertory (Costa Mesa)
http://www.scr.org/education/
Offers fun and formative acting classes for young people, with ongoing training throughout the school year in fall, winter, and spring sessions. Available to kids in grades 3 through 12 and at every level of experience, from beginners to serious acting students, classes are taught by a faculty of theater professionals.

Southern California Youth Theater (Whittier)
http://www.southerncaliforniayouththeater.com/
Launched its first production in spring of 2000. K–12th grade productions have been offered in Whittier, Fullerton, South Bay, Hermosa Beach, Pasadena, Van Nuys, Tustin, Pasadena Christian School, and Chatsworth.

Spotlight on Youth Theatre Company (Glendale)
http://www.spotlightyouththeatre.org
A youth theater group that teaches all aspects of theater, including acting, directing, singing, and backstage activities. Young people can learn and grow within a safe and fun environment.

Star Struck Children's Theatre (San Jose)
http://www.starstrucktheatre.org
A nonprofit organization dedicated to providing excellent, accessible theater training for youth, with high-quality performances for families and

the entire community. A positive environment in which young people can learn teamwork and communication skills and build self-esteem.

Stepping Stone Players (Glendale)
http://www.steppingstoneplayers.com
A nonprofit children's theater company dedicated to bringing quality theater arts experiences to individuals from age eight to adult. School-aged children are encouraged to create original plays, set designs, and costumes.

Theatre 360 [formerly Pasadena Junior Theatre] (Pasadena)
http://www.pasadenajuniortheatre.org/home.shtml
A company committed to creating an environment in which children develop imagination, talent, and self-esteem by learning how to act in theater, film, TV, and commercials. Acting, dance, and voice training programs provide challenging, innovative, high-quality classes to students of all ages, cultures, and levels of interest. Seasonal classes teach students theater skills which help them grow as artists and as people.

TheatreWorks (Palo Alto)
http://www.theatreworks.org/educationcommunity/theworkshop.htm
Engages and exposes educational and community organizations to the art of theater using TheatreWorks productions and artists in programs that build theater professionals and audiences. Acting classes are available in the form of camps and conservatories that create a solid foundation of experience and theater appreciation.

Town Hall Kids (Lafayette)
http://www.thtc.org/education/
World-class shows designed for kids from preschool through high school. Classes expose children of all ages to theater arts while developing self-esteem, confidence, leadership, team-building skills, and advanced acting techniques. Each class culminates in a performance.

Truckee Tahoe Youth Theater (Truckee)
see http://www.sierragiving.org/Non-profits/non-profits.html
Dedicated to providing a full spectrum of education in the theater arts to the youth of Truckee and North Tahoe by holding workshops and staging productions in the region.

The Unusual Suspects Theatre Company (Los Angeles)
http://theunusualsuspects.org
A program that helps at-risk youth create original theater and to foster pride, self-confidence, and racial tolerance. Youth are empowered by giving

them an effective tool for communication—the theater. Professional actors, writers, and directors work with groups of at-risk teens, helping them create original plays.

Willow Glen Children's Theatre (San Jose)
http://www.freewebs.com/bramhall/
A theater program for children up to age eighteen, offering summer theater camps, Theatre Connection Workshop (culminating in the production of an original play), and fairy-tale and puppet theater programs. Every child is given the chance to succeed by being cast in every production.

Wordical Productions (San Diego)
http://www.wordical.com
A Christian youth group program that offers children ages fifteen through nineteen opportunities to display their performing talents in a professional and moral setting. Teens are involved in multicultural and urban-style performances for live theater and film, comprising acting, dancing, and singing. Although there is no cost to participants, they must maintain a satisfactory school record.

Yorba Linda Spotlight Theater Company (Yorba Linda)
http://www.ylspotlight.org
A nonprofit organization dedicated to education in the performing arts through summer youth productions and instructional workshops for children and teens eight to nineteen years old. In addition to focusing on a top-notch final production, the program is structured to provide a broad education in the theater arts.

Young Actors Camp (Hollywood)
http://www.youngactorscamp.com
Young actors and their parents are invited to examine the Hollywood film and television industry firsthand. This acting camp educates those preparing to enter into the acting business, introduces the young stage actor to the art of acting for the camera, and offers a dynamic camp experience for any young actor captivated by the movie screen. A three-day summer camp is also offered to parents interested in professional careers for their children.

The Young Actor's Studio (Los Angeles)
http://www.youngactorsstudio.com
Offers students introduction and training in various theatrical media: stage, screen, TV, or film. Acting is oriented to the Stanislavsky system, and students are exposed to dramatic literature. Classes include Teen Acting, Kids Acting, Orientation for the Younger Young Actors, Acting for the Camera in Los Angeles, and Summer Camps.

Young Actors' Theatre [YAT] (San Diego)
http://www.yatsandiego.org
Produces five musicals a year and offers an all-inclusive performing arts studio with a variety of classes in voice, drama, and dance. Classes at YAT teach technical skills, and productions give students the opportunity to apply what they learn in front of an audience.

The Young Artists Ensemble Youth Theatre Company (Thousand Oaks)
http://www.youngartistsensemble.com
Dedicated to providing the highest quality performing arts experiences for the youth of the Conejo Valley and beyond, instilling a seed of love for the arts that continues to grow and blossom throughout their lives. Hundreds of kids between the ages of ten and nineteen have the opportunity to perform in well-known musicals and plays.

Young People's Teen Musical Theatre Company (San Francisco)
http://www.yptmtc.org
A performing arts program for San Francisco teenagers thirteen to eighteen years of age. The company has been in existence since 1984, and its alumni have gone on to national tours, Broadway shows, national commercials, and conservatory BFA programs.

Young Performers Theatre (San Francisco)
http://www.ypt.org
A company that produces children's classics, adaptations, and new works, with children from all backgrounds working alongside professional actors.

Youth Academy of Dramatic Arts [YADA] (Los Angeles)
http://www.yada.org
Theater arts training programs for children eight to seventeen. Classes are delineated based on age and ability. Designers, directors, choreographers, musical directors, stage managers, and running crew are all on staff. Private coaching is available in voice, music, and dance, and YADA also offers stagecraft internships.

Youth for Asian Theater [YFAT] (San Francisco)
http://www.yfat.org
A youth-run acting group that writes, directs, and performs original plays focusing on Asian themes. YFAT aims to introduce youth to the many aspects of theater, teaching them the skills necessary to create a theater production and be strong leaders in their communities. Although many of YFAT's members are Asian, they come from a diverse mix of ethnic backgrounds. The goal of YFAT is not to exclude youth but to build ties between different cultures and promote an understanding of Asian heritage and culture.

Youth Theater Conservatory (El Cajon)

http://www.broadwaybythebay.org/ytc.html

A nonprofit summer theater conservatory designed to produce high-quality theater education for students thirteen to nineteen years of age. Students take master classes in costume design, voice, acting, stage management, technical theater, and stagecraft. The term ends with a production.

Youth Theatre Company (Walnut Creek)

http://www.youththeatrecompany.org

Engages children from kindergarten through high school age in musical theater performance and theater education. Classes and productions are offered in "stepping-stones" (four age groups). Performs student matinees for school groups.

Colorado

Castle Rock Theatre (Castle Rock)

http://www.crplayers.org

A nonprofit theater company dedicated to the promotion and presentation of the arts, with an emphasis on youth participation.

Denver Center Theatre Academy (Denver)

http://www.denvercenter.org/aboutdenvercenter/DenverCenterDepartments/
DenverCenterTheatreAcademy.aspx

Academy classes empower children and their imaginations through the discipline of theater. Creating theatrically rich opportunities to discover then shape and share creative expression is the goal in all of the children's classes. This is accomplished through storytelling, improvisation, group building, learning to accept and work with others' ideas, developing a theatrical vocabulary, and becoming comfortable with performing in front of others.

La De Da (Fort Collins)

http://www.ladeda.ws/

A performing arts studio specializing in musical theater training and original new musicals for young actors.

La Junta Children's Theatre (La Junta)

see http://www.visitlajunta.org/arts.html

A program dedicated to giving students a professional theater experience: a professional, personal, and creative perspective on the crafting of theater. Creates an environment where both the creative process and a professional performance experience are spotlighted.

Northglenn Youth Theater (Northglenn)
see http://www.northglenn.org/p364.html
A popular and highly honored children's theater group from the Denver area. The success of this program depends on a network of volunteers and committed young people.

Peanut Butter Players (Boulder)
www.peanutbutterplayers.com
A well-established and comprehensive program providing training in singing, dancing, and acting for the young, summer day camp, summer theater, and luncheon theater for the family. Classes and the summer program grow as children return, some with ten years or more of experience. Auditions for summer theater are open to all who are interested, and everyone gets a part. A distinctive program is the Children's Luncheon Theatre, "just like adult dinner theatre, only it's lunch on Saturdays." The actors, professional at only seven to seventeen years old, perform at least weekly for six months a year. The company members are paid for their work, just as adults. And they learn to sing, dance, and wait tables (when the audience arrives, they are greeted, seated, and served). Their productions are intended to have Broadway quality, and many Peanut Butter Players have continued in the professional theater world.

The Rising Curtain Theatre Academy (Denver)
http://www.curtainproductions.org
An arts education organization that seeks to develop confidence in students' own sense of creativity and understanding of the creation of live performance. Arts education ultimately cultivates lasting performance skills, self-discipline, interaction, creative thought, public speaking, and other essential life skills. The Rising Curtain was founded by Christians, but students of all faiths are welcome.

Rocky Mountain Theatre for Kids (Boulder)
http://www.theaterforkids.net/youth_rep_entry.php
Offers children's theater, creative arts classes, summer camp, mime, scene study, storytelling, directing, improvisation, and dramatic performance. The Youth Actors Conservatory offers pre-professional training year-round (mid-September through mid-April). Focus varies depending on the program but typically includes character work, scene study, musical theater, dance, voice, and performance training.

Walden Family Playhouse (Denver)
http://www2.waldenfamilyplayhouse.com/theworkshop/index.html
A cultural and educational venue for musical theater productions that focus on children and families. Classes are available in theater arts for children

ages five and up. The workshop offers various sections of technique classes and performance classes grouped by age. Each semester, performance classes culminate in a production presented to the public.

The Younger Generation Players (Englewood)
http://www.ygplayers.org
A children's musical theater company featuring classes in drama, dance, and voice, which have provided a catalyst for many young performers who have chosen a professional career in musical theater. In addition, the students develop strong self-esteem and lasting friendships.

Connecticut

Center for Creative Youth: Theater and Technical Theater (Hartford and Middletown)
http://www.crec.org/ccy
A summer pre-college program that offers talented high school students five weeks of intensive study in the arts at Wesleyan University, including theater, musical theater, technical theater, and dance.

Children's Associated Summer Theatre [C.A.S.T.] (Manchester)
http://casttheatre.org/index.html
C.A.S.T. has grown from a children's theater group doing summer musicals to a full-scale theater group offering year-round productions and classes for children. There is also a splinter group known as C.A.S.T. After Dark that offers theater productions for teens and adults.

Connecticut Children's Theatre (Essex)
http://discovercct.org/ws_workshops.html
Offers classes for children in Essex, New Haven, and Waterbury. Pre-K and kindergarten-age children build self-confidence, interactive communication, and teamwork through theater games and performance activities. The Young Stars (grades 1 through 3) memorize lines and become part of a scene while learning basic performing techniques. Broadway Bound students (grades 4 through 6) use their voices, bodies, and minds to pursue objectives, overcome obstacles, and create characters and scenes, all while working as an ensemble.

Edgerton Center for the Performing Arts (Fairfield)
http://edgertoncenter.org/summer_camps.php
Offers musical theater workshops for young performers ages eight through seventeen, culminating in a free live performance at the end of each two-week session. This program encourages the development of a young

performer's talent while also encouraging socialization among peers and, most importantly, fun.

FOOTELights Youth Theater Company (Oxford)
http://www.electronicvalley.org/oxford/footelights/
Offers area youth the opportunity to come together to produce and perform educational and responsible theatrical productions.

Hartford Children's Theatre [HCT] (Hartford)
http://www.hartfordchildrenstheatre.org
Offers year-round programming for children ages three to seventeen: the HCT Drama School, the Hartford Summer Youtheatre, the after-school outreach program, and mainstage programming. Through these activities, HCT brings together children of all ages, social, economic, and cultural backgrounds in a safe, supportive, and encouraging environment.

Oddfellows Playhouse Youth Theater (Middletown)
http://www.oddfellows.org
A nonprofit theater and performing arts program for children. The core program consists of performing arts classes and mainstage and mini-productions for participants ages six through twenty. The Neighborhood Troupes program offers free after-school weekly performing arts classes throughout the school year for at-risk youth.

Polka Dot Playhouse (Bridgeport)
http://www.polkadotplayhouse.net
Offers creative dramatics classes for children ages six through twelve and auditions for actors seventeen and older for a children's theater performance group.

Simsbury Summer Theatre for Youth [SSTFY] (Simsbury)
http://www.sstfy.com/index.html
Since 1966 SSTFY has provided quality onstage, backstage, and orchestra opportunities for young adults interested in musical theater. Professional staff members provide guidance and direction, and adult volunteers assist with the production of the show.

The Southeastern Connecticut Regional Youth Theater (Oakdale)
http://www.thesecryt.com
Provides children, youth, and young adults throughout Eastern and Southeastern Connecticut opportunities to learn and apply essential theater skills, not only performance but the administrative, operational, technical, and managerial disciplines of live theater. Offers preschool, home school, and after-school classes.

Warner Theatre Center for Arts Education (Torrington)
http://www.warnertheatre.org/aboutWTCAE.htm
Offers a dramatic arts curriculum that takes students on a hands-on journey through improvisation, character development, movement, and scene study. More advanced levels of acting classes explore the various master teachers of the craft, such as Meisner, Stanislavsky, Strasberg, Adler, and Suzuki. Branching out from its dramatic arts courses is a highly acclaimed dance program.

Wilton Children's Theater (Wilton)
http://www.wiltonchildrenstheater.org
A nonprofit volunteer organization with the goal of exposing as many children as possible, in grades 4 through 7, to high-quality theater through two musical productions per school year. In addition, Summerstage is geared toward children in grades 7 through 10.

Yale University's Children's Theatre Program (New Haven)
http://www.yale.edu/yct/
An organization with a broad mission and numerous programs, including original shows that feature children in local public schools.

Delaware

The Children's Theater of Delmarva (Delmar)
http://www.theaterofdelmarva.org
Founded in 1996 as a nonprofit community performing arts organization that has since produced more than forty-four programs. More than four hundred participants ranging in age from four to twenty-five have performed and participated in workshops and live productions. All programs and events are free; all labor is provided by volunteers, including the founder.

The Children's Theatre of Dover and Kent County (Dover)
http://www.thechildrenstheatre.org
A volunteer, nonprofit, tax-exempt community theater that offers five shows and a series of workshops and seminars. Includes a Traveling Troupe of children performing different shows.

Delaware Children's Theatre [DCT] (Wilmington)
http://www.dechildrenstheatre.org
Founded in 1973 as a theatrical repertory troupe touring to schools, churches, senior centers, and parks, now established in a historic theatre-house and performing in major theaters in the region. This company is

dedicated to community outreach and offers many free workshops to underprivileged children.

Doorway to Drama [Wilmington Drama League] (Wilmington)
http://wilmingtondramaleague.org/opportunities/classes
Kids ages seven to fifteen learn the fundamentals of acting, auditioning, singing, and dancing on the stage. A summer camp concludes in a performance.

District of Columbia

Kelsey E. Collie (Washington, D.C.)
http://www.kelseyecollie.com
A children's theater group offering summer workshops and courses. Includes a semiprofessional troupe of young performers selected to perform on tour.

OneStage Productions (Washington, D.C.)
http://www.onestageproductions.com
Teaches young actors the fundamentals of acting and how to stage a live theatrical production. Acting theory and techniques, character development, plot and script development, and principles of theater are covered as participants work to focus their energies, build self-confidence, and improve their communication skills. The session culminates in the performance of an original stage production—written by the participants—for friends, family, and the general public.

The Studio Theatre Young Actors Ensemble (Washington, D.C.)
http://www.studiotheatre.org/conservatory/youth_classes.php
A program of activities that introduces young actors ages twelve through seventeen to realistic acting. Through experiences such as theater games, pantomimes, improvisation, ensemble work, monologues, and/or scene study, students acquire and expand skills in concentration, observation, stimulus-response, and interplay. This curriculum provides disciplined, process-oriented training for young actors with or without prior experience or training.

Florida

All Children's Theatre (Gainesville)
http://www.afn.org/~act/Act.htm
A nonprofit theater company dedicated to the enrichment, entertainment, and education of all children ages four to eighteen. Children in the Not

Ready for Bedtime Players learn about the theater through games, songs, costumes, makeup, and laughter. They also rehearse and perform their own small production for friends and family.

American Stage (St. Petersburg)
http://www.americanstage.org/education1.php
Provides students access to the art of the theater through productions, camps, and internships. A summer children's class concludes in a showcase.

Center Stage Academy (Casselberry)
http://dancecsa.com
Dedicated to dance and performing arts instruction to children and adults of all ages. Offers cutting-edge dance instruction in ballet, jazz, hip-hop, musical theater, ballroom, Latin, and cheerleading, as well as acting and modeling classes for prospective entertainers.

Fort Lauderdale Children's Theatre (Ft. Lauderdale)
http://www.flct.org
A not-for-profit developmental center for the theater arts founded in 1952. Classes follow the form and purpose of "creative dramatics," using theater skills for personal development. Plays are produced with a cast and crew of students aged six to eighteen.

The Hippodrome State Theatre (Gainesville)
http://thehipp.org/education/classes/
A series of classes and fast-paced workshops designed to expose students to all aspects of theatrical production. Examples of acting classes include improvisation, acting for the camera, movement and dance, Shakespeare, and interactive performance. Workshops not only cover areas such as costuming, voice, prop making, and other aspects of technical theater, but also expose young people to different creative outlets, such as doll making, Capoeira, and bookbinding and art. Additionally, the Hippodrome Improvisational Teen Theatre helps teens explore their attitudes about critical issues they face daily.

Learning Theatre (Sarasota)
http://www.learntheatre.org/index.html
Sponsors the Encore! Summer Theatre Program where youth from around the world (ages fourteen to eighteen) study theater arts in Valbonne, France. The ensemble technique, which is at the heart of Learning Theatre's approach to educational theater and theater in education, celebrates creativity and exploration, involving all participants in the creative process.

Orlando Youth Theatre and Academy (Orlando)
http://www.orlandoyouththeatre.com
Dedicated to providing quality theatre opportunities for young people in central Florida. Offers training and performance opportunities for students ages four to eighteen. Classes, workshops, and seminars are offered throughout the year.

Patel Conservatory Youth Theater (Tampa)
http://www.patelconservatory.org/disciplines/youththeater.htm
As part of the broad Conservatory program, offers students the chance to put the experience they have gained into practice. The facility includes studios and classrooms for dance, media arts, theater, on-camera acting, and private lessons in all disciplines, plus a piano lab, a recording studio, a scene shop, a costume shop, a library, and a "black box" theater. In the performance lab, students have a chance to work in a demanding and nurturing rehearsal environment. The lab culminates in a final performance piece that incorporates acting, dancing, and singing.

Riverside Children's Theatre (Vero Beach)
http://www.riversidechildrenstheatre.org
A volunteer-run company offering drama instruction and performances for more than fifty years. Classes are held throughout the year. Class size is limited, and there is a two- or three-year waiting list for admittance. The company produces two musicals a year, in the fall and spring.

Georgia

Alliance Theater Company Acting Program (Atlanta)
http://www.alliancetheatre.org/education.aspx?id=50
Offers youth and summer camp classes and productions for all ages.

Atlanta Workshop Players (Atlanta)
http://www.atlantaworkshopplayers.com
A nonprofit, professional children's theater company with a theater school and performing arts camp. Instructors and guest artists are industry professionals with significant TV/film and Broadway credits. Original musicals, focusing on social issues, are made available internationally through publication. Offers a "Kids' Cabaret" at a comedy club.

Cobb Children's Theatre (Powder Springs)
http://www.cobbchildrenstheatre.org
A repertory stock company founded to provide for children of all ages, middle school, high school, and college students. Youth express themselves

and develop character through avocational theater. Over the years, CCT has produced many musicals, "Storytime" shows, and touring productions. The objective is not training children for the profession but helping them through the trauma of adolescence.

Fayette-Coweta Family Theatre, Inc. (Sharpsburg)
http://www.fcft.net
An educationally based organization that offers workshops, production camps, and weekly acting classes throughout the year. These workshops, camps, and classes are designed for participants five to eighteen years of age and foster creativity and a love of theater. All workshops, camps, and classes are taught by theater professionals, and all ages are cast in FCFT shows.

Holly Children's Theatre & Education (Dahlonega)
http://www.hollytheater.com/content/blogcategory/47/47/
Provides the youth in the community with theater education at an affordable tuition and presents public children's theater performances. Children are exposed to a variety of different classes and plays to bring the wonder and magic of theater into every child's heart, and to prepare each child to feel confident onstage or behind the scenes. Classes are available for all ages, and the children's program includes summer camps and six productions through the year.

PushPush Theater—SmallTall Theater Projects (Atlanta)
http://www.pushpushtheater.com/youth/index.html
A program designed to bring adults and youth together for shared and accessible productions. Offers workshops and camps for children.

Savannah Children's Theatre (Savannah)
http://www.savannahchildrenstheatre.org
During the school year, offers classes in creative dramatics, theater performance, and dance for musical theater. Summer camp produces a full-scale musical. Classes include diction, dance, vocal performance, theater etiquette, scene studies, improvisational skills, prop making, costuming, scenic painting, and other aspects of performance and technical theater.

Youth Ensemble of Atlanta [YEA] (Atlanta)
http://fhyea.org
Utilizing the power of the arts, YEA fosters the personal growth of hundreds of young people from childhood to adulthood. Along the way, these talented and dedicated performers develop crucial communication and life skills that result in heightened cultural awareness, a commitment to excellence and community service, and an appreciation for diversity. In addition

to renowned training and performance programs, YEA also serves the community through Intern, Youth Empowerment Summer (YES), Tippy Toes Arts, Tutoring, College Scholarship, and International programs.

Hawaii

Hawaii Children's Theatre (Lihue, Kauai)
http://www.hawaiichildrenstheatre.com
Offers two programs for students in grades 2 through 6 and 7 through 12, each culminating in a full-scale production. There are also after-school programs throughout the year. Serves more than three hundred young people each year, some through scholarship subsidy and work-study programs.

Idaho

Camp Crescendo (Twin Falls, Idaho, and Bethel Park, Oregon)
http://www.campcrescendo.com
A summer music camp for children, designed for children grades 2 through 7 who enjoy music and dance performance.

Illinois

About Face Youth Theatre (Chicago)
http://www.aboutfacetheatre.com/?pg=afyt_about
An innovative and rigorous arts-based series of programs that increase the safety, empowerment, and leadership capacity of lesbian, gay, bisexual, transgender, and questioning youth and their allies in order to catalyze youth-led civic dialogue and action within schools and communities. Produces ensemble-based plays in dynamic collaboration with a community of accomplished adult artists.

Actors Gymnasium (Evanston)
http://www.actorsgymnasium.com
Offers classes for child actors, including circus, physical comedy, dance, music, mime, and puppetry.

Adventure Stage (Chicago)
http://www.adventurestage.org
Offers performances for young children and also interactive workshops.

Awkward Alliance (Evanston)
http://www.repla.com/awkward
An independent teenage theater group that performs wacky skit comedy/performance shows at people's homes, instead of in traditional theaters.

Chicago Kids Company (Chicago)
http://www.chicagokidscompany.com
Offers classes in movement, acting, singing, dancing, and improvisation for children ages three to fourteen, all taught by Chicago theater professionals with years of experience. Classes are held once a week for eight weeks and each session ends with a final presentation, recital, or performance.

Children's Theatre of Elgin (Elgin)
http://www.cteelgin.com
Provides high-quality theatrical experiences for children and young adults, by children and young adults. Encourages family support and participation in theater, makes live theater affordable and accessible, and instills a standard of performance excellence.

Children's Theatre Project (Rockford)
http://www.ctpytp.org
Produces "plays with music" adapted from Broadway and television scripts. The company is split into two groups. Younger children (ages six through twelve) learn the arts of improvisation, pantomime, dramatic arts, singing, dancing, and even script writing; older children (ages thirteen through eighteen) expand their abilities, learning lighting, sound, set design, construction, costumes, makeup, technical assistance, stage management, choreography, and box office, while honing their acting skills. As they are educated in all aspects of musical production, they gain feelings of self-identity and purpose. There is a determination in casting to give speaking roles to all the children. No one gets a throwaway role; instead, each child is a real part of every production. The CTP After School program brings professional actors in for workshops. Families are involved in productions by volunteering their help, and the company strives to make itself better known and more affordable to families that need it.

Child's Play Touring Theatre (Chicago)
http://www.cptt.org
Staffed by theater arts educators who promote literacy and are dedicated exclusively to performing plays written from the stories and poetry of children. Summer workshops give children the opportunity to perform.

Emerald City Theatre School (Chicago)
http://www.emeraldcitytheatre.com/mainclass.shtml
Offers children's theater camps throughout the year. Parents are enlisted to help with teaching and productions. Touring classes are designed for the very young and children with special needs. The objective is to give students greater self-confidence and problem-solving skills.

Hands Together, Heart to Heart (Chicago)
http://www.thelightbeyond.com/forum/showthread.php?t=757
A program presented by Roosevelt University designed for children seven to fourteen years old who have experienced the death of one or both of their parents. Employing several different areas of the performing arts, the program encourages communication, fosters emotional growth, and provides the consolation of friendship and compassion.

Lookingglass Theatre Company (Chicago)
http://www.lookingglasstheatre.org/content/education/welcome
Offers a variety of studio classes (experiential, technique, and performance) and a Young Ensemble that performs a full season of family shows. Participation is by invitation, based on audition, and is free of charge.

Northbrook Theatre Children's Company (Northbrook)
http://www.northbrooktheatre.org/children's_company.htm
Providing "theatre by youth for youth" for more than twenty-three years. Actors in grades 6 through 9 perform age-appropriate plays and musicals suitable for family viewing.

Open Door Repertory Company (Oak Park)
http://www.opendoorrep.org/class_children.shtml
A variety of classes in theater skills for children ages four through fifteen.

The Piven Theatre Workshop (Evanston)
http://www.piventheatre.org
A leading and acclaimed training center for both children and adults, accommodating all levels of experience, from professional actors honing their skills to beginners who wish to explore their creativity through the theater arts. Classes include Story Theatre and Theatre Games, elements of the Stanislavsky system, mime, a basic focus on "the other person," and concentration on the task at hand. Offers a fall session, a spring session, and a six-week Summer Institute.

Prologue Theatre Productions (Chicago)
http://prologuetheatreco.org
Participants work with professionals to develop improvisational and acting skills. Offerings include children's theater productions (grades K–8) and Young Actors Performance Studio (ages ten to seventeen).

Raven Children's Theatre (Chicago)
http://www.raventheatre.com/children.shtml

Offers a fall workshop and summer Kids in the Spotlight program. Through dance, movement, theater games, and improvisation, young aspiring actors learn how to use both body and voice to create characters and build basic acting and performance skills.

School of Performing Arts (Naperville)
http://www.schoolofperformingarts.com
Offers instruction for beginning, intermediate, and professional-level students. The Theatre Department offers classes in various styles and focuses. Students can look forward to testing out their techniques in a fully staged spring musical production each year. Offers group instruction for all ages of children.

Special Gifts Theatre, Inc. (Northbrook)
http://www.specialgiftstheatre.com
A nonprofit group providing creative drama classes and theater programs for children with special physical, cognitive, social, emotional, and learning needs. Its aim is to provide children and teens with special needs a unique, creative drama experience enabling personal growth while breaking down stereotypes related to disabilities within the community at large. Mainstreaming is encouraged whenever students have developed the appropriate social and artistic skills necessary to succeed.

Storycatchers Theatre (Chicago)
http://www.storycatcherstheatre.org
Prepares young people to make positive life choices by training them to write, produce, and perform original musical theater inspired by personal stories.

Village Players Performing Arts Center (Oak Park)
http://www.village-players.org
Offers classes for adults and children and also has a junior ensemble for children ages thirteen to eighteen who have an earnest desire to make theater an important part of their lives.

Indiana

Asante Children's Theatre of Indianapolis (Indianapolis)
http://www.asantechildrenstheatre.org
A professional theater organization committed to preserving the tradition of African and African American performing arts. Instructors and mentors use the basic genres of performing arts (theater, music, dance, and storytelling) to develop the life skills of young people ages twelve to twenty-one.

Civic Youth Theatre (Lafayette)
http://www.lafayettecivic.com
Provides a noncompetitive atmosphere in which young people can develop their imagination, explore their creative potential, and feel positive growth in self-confidence and self-expression. Group-building and ensemble support create a no-failure environment. The classroom is a stage, scene shop, and lighting booth where students experience hands-on learning in a vital and creative arena.

Ole Olsen Memorial Theatre: Children's Theatre Workshop (Peru)
http://www.oleolsen.org/ctw/index.htm
A nonprofit organization promoting interest in the theater arts. Workshops are offered free to children in different age groups.

Iowa

Black Hawk Children's Theatre (Waterloo)
http://www.wcpbhct.org/bhct_classes.html
Offers classes for students in two age groups, and a summer camp.

Kate Goldman Children's Theatre at the Des Moines Playhouse (Des Moines)
http://www.dmplayhouse.com/kg_childrens.html
Offers winter and spring terms of classes for ages four to adult, with a special program for elementary school children during winter and spring breaks. Summer classes for kindergarten through adult boast more than fifty offerings, taught by area professional teachers, directors, choreographers, and actors.

Old Creamery Theatre (Garrison)
http://www.oldcreamery.com/workshops.php
Offers weeklong camps for students seven to twelve in the school year and seven to fifteen in the summer. The camps conclude in theatrical performances.

Stebens Children's Theatre (Mason City)
http://stebens.com
Offers seven tiers of classes, enrolling students ages seven through eighteen. The year's schedule includes five mainstage productions, a professional tour, a variety show, and a summer project. Additional programs have included school production workshops and a musical review that traveled around northern Iowa performing at nursing homes, libraries, and restaurants.

Kansas

Topeka Youth Players [Helen Hocker Center for the Performing Arts] (Topeka)

see http://www.topeka.org/parksrec/Hocker.shtml
A troupe of eleven- to thirteen-year-olds is selected through auditions for productions twice a year. Those not selected for a production are encouraged to take part in the volunteer theater crew. Various summer camps are offered, and the Bath House Players (ages fourteen to eighteen) perform two to three shows annually and tour.

Kentucky

Lexington Youth Theatre (Lexington)

http://www.lexingtonyouththeatre.com
A nonprofit touring theater company that also includes classes and workshops for young people ages four to eighteen.

Louisville Youth Theatre [LYT] (Louisville)

http://www.louisvilleyouththeatre.com
Provides youth with the opportunity to participate in theatrical performances for the purpose of developing talent, self-confidence, creativity, imagination, discipline, and teamwork. LYT is dedicated to theatrical excellence and providing wholesome, quality entertainment for the community.

Sunburst Youth Theatre (Bowling Green)

http://www.ptkbg.org
Theater professionals work with youth ages eight to eighteen in numerous programs such as youth-acted one-act plays, acting classes, and the famous Shakespeare Summer Day Camp.

Walden Theatre (Louisville)

http://www.waldentheatre.org
A theater conservatory and producing organization for young people. Its mission is to provide the opportunity for young people to grow and develop through the comprehensive study of theater. It offers a formal curriculum.

Louisiana

The Children's Theatre Company (Lake Charles)

http://0087bd7.netsolhost.com
Offers training in theater for children ages three and a half to eighteen, taught by a team of professional directors. Students learn to act, sing, and

dance while building self-confidence, discipline, self-awareness, and leader-ship skills. Classes include Storybook Drama (ages three and a half to four), Creative Dramatics (ages five through eight), and Stageworks (ages nine to eighteen).

Civic Student Theatre (Lake Charles)
http://www.actstheatre.com/cst.html
Children in the youth division of Artists Civic Theatre & Studio learn the theater, learn to follow directions, and learn voice control through classes in the spring. Students participating in classes are cast in a special production presented during Contraband Days.

Crescent City Lights Youth Theater (New Orleans)
http://www.summerstages.org
Professional theater experiences for young people ages seven to seventeen. The theater offers a forum for collaboration of artists, designers, and playwrights and enriches the entire community with its professional quality stage productions and classes. Crescent City Lights instills an early appreciation of literature, art, and the performing arts in tomorrow's artists and patrons.

Jefferson Performing Arts Society Youth Musical Theatre (Metairie)
http://www.jpas.org/education.php?ID=11
For more than ten years has offered more than four hundred youth from the greater New Orleans area the opportunity to participate in musical theater productions. Two camps are offered, for students third through seventh and eighth through twelfth grades. They work with professional directors, conductors, costumers, and an array of technical staff.

Peter Pan Players (Shreveport)
http://www.peterpanplayers.org
Founded in 1973, a city institution known widely for the training it gives its young thespians and the entertainment it gives to the audiences. The region's first children's theater company.

Maine

Bearnstow (Mount Vernon)
http://www.bearnstow.org
A nonprofit organization offering an arts day camp for children, including classes in theater.

Children's Museum and Theatre of Maine (Portland)
http://www.kitetails.org/theatre/theatre-info/

Founded in 1923, the oldest private children's theater company in the United States. Merged with the Children's Museum of Maine in 2008. Engages children and the community in the magic of live theater, enabling young people to gain confidence while discovering their unique power. A professional, nonprofit theater providing educational opportunities for children.

Hackmatack Playhouse (Berwick)
http://www.hackmatack.org
A summer theater that includes a summer drama camp and children's theater geared for children between the ages of seven and thirteen.

Lakewood Children's Theater and Young Performers Camp [YPC] (East Madison)
http://www.lakewoodtheater.org/ypc.html
Offers children the opportunity to grow creatively in professional theater setting. A nonresidential day camp at Lakewood Theater, the nation's oldest summer theater, YPC is open to youth from six to sixteen years old who want to learn theater craft from theater professionals. Every camper performs in costume and makeup before a set and an audience.

Maine Youth Summer Theatre Institute (Machias)
see http://www.stageeast.org/brocure_rj_2.pdf
Located on the campus of the University of Maine at Machias, a summer theater camp offering creative young people ages ten to eighteen a fifteen-day program. The focus is the art of Shakespeare.

The Theater Project (Brunswick)
http://www.theaterproject.com
Teaches theater to young people through two programs: the Young Company, a group of bright and energetic high school and college-age actors performing and directing their own works, new plays, and works from the theater repertory; and the Young People's Theater, a long-standing program for elementary through middle school actors, including classes and productions by young actors.

Maryland

Actors Anonymous [Maryland Ensemble Theatre] (Frederick)
http://www.marylandensemble.org/ensemble_school
Offers various theater classes for students seven to seventeen years old. Committed teens write and produce their own work as they grow as actors. Adult members of MET serve as mentors, and AA members act as apprentices, learning about the technical aspects of theater.

Adventure Theatre (Glen Echo)
http://www.adventuretheatre.org
Students are challenged artistically and encouraged to have fun while exploring a variety of theatrical roles. In addition to theatrical skills, students will learn how to enunciate, project, work as a team, and solve problems creatively.

The Black Box Theater: Stage Training Apprentice Mentoring Program (Indian Head)
http://www.indianheadblackbox.org
An innovative theater program designed to give support and guidance through a mentor-based theatrical apprentice program to at-risk youth between the ages of fourteen and seventeen.

Bound4Broadway (Rockville)
http://www.angelfire.com/musicals/b4bensembles/
A nonprofit, all-volunteer youth theater dedicated to providing high-quality programs for the young people of the community. All proceeds are used for productions, enabling children to expand their talents and develop the skills needed in the world of professional theater.

The Children's Playhouse of Maryland (Baltimore)
see http://www.ccbcmd.edu/performingarts/childrensplayhouse.html
Offers classes, summer camps, and theater opportunities for young performers under eighteen years of age, and produces five musicals a year.

Children's Theatre of Annapolis (Annapolis)
http://www.childrenstheatreofannapolis.org
A community-based nonprofit organization dedicated to nurturing the growth and development of children ages eight to eighteen through participation in all aspects of the theatrical experience.

Columbia Center for Theatrical Arts (Columbia)
http://www.cctarts.com
Educates through the arts by creating theatrical experiences that "inspire thought, action, creativity, and change." The Conservatory offers several performance arts classes, three summer theatrical arts camps, a summer teen professional theater program (featuring professional guest directors and staff), and the Young Columbians, a professional performance ensemble that has performed widely, including a special performance at the White House.

The Conservatory [Baltimore Actors' Theatre] (Baltimore)
http://www.baltimoreactorstheatre.org/conservatory.html

An accredited college preparatory school of the arts, for students in pre-K through grade 12. A strong academic program is provided in the morning hours, followed by professional training in three disciplines: music, drama, and dance.

Drama Kids International [DKI] (Ellicott City)
http://www.dramakids.com
Offers several different after-school and summer camp programs for children and high school students, ages five through seventeen. DKI students gain greater confidence and self-esteem while also improving verbal skills and acting abilities.

Imagination Stage [Bethesda Academy of Performing Arts] (Bethesda)
http://www.imaginationstage.org
This program has grown from a handful of children in a single classroom to a full-spectrum theater arts organization that includes nationally acclaimed programs for children who are deaf (Deaf Access) and children with physical or cognitive disabilities (AccessAbility Theatre). Includes short-term camps and courses, as well as acting and musical theater conservatories.

Performing Arts Factory (Frederick)
http://performingartsfactory.com/theatre/
A performing arts school that includes a theater program with a curriculum that covers focus techniques and exercises in bringing a character to theatrical life from read-through to performance. The methods used and experiences gained are not only applicable to performance situations, but also invaluable tools to enhance self-esteem and self-awareness, increasing participants' confidence to their entire approach to life.

Pumpkin Theatre (Baltimore)
http://www.pumpkintheatre.com
A children's theater founded in the Drama Department at the College of Notre Dame in Maryland. Includes children's programs pre-K to age eighteen and a Musical Theatre Conservatory for the more experienced performers, ages ten through eighteen.

Round House Theatre (Bethesda and Silver Spring)
http://www.round-house.org/education/forstudent.php
Offers a student matinee program, apprenticeships, internships, and the Sarah Play: the country's only theatrical production offered as part of a regional theater's regular programming that is directed, designed, stage managed, and performed entirely by high school students.

Three-Ring Theater (Baltimore)
http://www.threeringtheater.com
Offers a complete musical theater experience to children ages five and up.
Young people have fun while acting, singing, and learning staging, costuming, and set design. Many students begin theater at age five, moving up
through the age-grouped sessions, and students in high school or college
assist weekly with the younger groups.

Thurmont Thespians (Thurmont)
http://thurmontthespians.org
A summer music theater workshop focused on teaching all aspects of theater to children and teens. The workshop is open to teens and children at
no cost, everyone who auditions and attends rehearsals gets an onstage
role, and actors learn about a local charity, to which all of the profits from
the performances are donated.

Variety Children's Theater and Dance (Baltimore)
see   http://www.ci.baltimore.md.us/government/recnparks/downloads/
0309/Rec_Parks_Special_Events%20(3-1-09).pdf
An inclusive, instructional program in theater and dance, free and open to
the public, for children with and without disabilities. Recommended for
ages eight to eighteen.

Wildwood Summer Theatre (Bethesda)
http://www.wst.org
A fully independent youth-run summer theater. Initially created, and now
sustained, by theatrically minded students and young professionals, Wildwood produces at least one musical each year. Participants initially learn
about, and subsequently come to teach, the practical realities of mounting
a full-scale theatrical production. The most remarkable aspect of the theater
is that all company members are fourteen to twenty-five years of age, and
all are volunteers.

Young Artists Theatre (West Laurel)
http://www.yatheatre.com
Offers performing arts instruction for children and teens, paid opportunities in original productions, summer camp, and musical theater. Students
from this program have gone on to perform on television, in professional
theater, and with touring companies.

Massachusetts

Academy of the Company Theatre (Norwell)
http://www.companytheatre.com/academy.html

Strives to discover the creative spirit in each child in an enjoyable and challenging atmosphere and to build self-confidence through the experience of the arts. Includes the Teen Conservatory Program (ages thirteen through eighteen) and the Academy of the Company Theatre Program (ages seven through twelve).

Arlington Children's Theater (Arlington)
http://act.arlington.ma.us
A nonprofit organization dedicated to creating positive theatrical experiences for children aged four through eighteen.

Barre Players Theater (Barre)
http:/barreplayers.homestead.com
A nonprofit theater that offers youth programs in the summer.

Belvoir Terrace (Lenox)
http://www.belvoirterrace.com
An educational summer camp for girls in grades 3 to 11. Fourteen professional teacher/directors teach classes in acting techniques, musical theater, improvisation, directing, Shakespeare, and all aspects of technical theater.

Berkshire Institute for Music and Arts (Waltham)
http://www.brandeis.edu/bima/
A summer arts program for teenagers to develop their imaginative and artistic faculties and explore the relevance of Jewish tradition to their lives. Actors focus on character development, scene work, crafting and presenting monologues, voice, movement, and other core techniques.

Berkshire Theatre Festival (Stockbridge)
http://www.berkshiretheatre.org
A primarily summer theater with mainstage as well as children's and experimental productions.

Boston Children's Theatre (Boston)
http://www.bostonchildrenstheatre.org
A year-round program that offers a season of mainstage productions, summer creative arts programs and Teen Stagemobile Tour Company productions, theater classes for students in grades K through 12, community-wide special events projects, school collaborative projects, and other opportunities.

Brookline Smart Summers Theater Arts Program for Kids (Brookline)
see http://www.bostoncentral.com/activities/activities/p1339.php
A summer program offering classes for children in music, acting, dance, and art. Participants work together to create an original musical production.

Chapel School of Creative Arts (Lexington)
see http://www.bostoncentral.com/activities/activities/p191.php
Offers after-school theater classes for children in grades 2 through 12. In
the fall there is a fifteen-week theater workshop that focuses on teaching
children a specific set of drama skills. In the spring there is a fifteen-week
production class that introduces all aspects of show production, including
costuming, set design, and stage presence.

Children's Theatre of Nantucket (Nantucket Town)
http://www.nantucketchildrenstheatre.org
Takes over the six-hundred-seat auditorium of the Nantucket High School
for weekly productions in the summer. Students between eight and sixteen
develop general acting skills and may enroll in multiple sessions.

Concord Youth Theater (Concord)
www.concordyouththeatre.org
A nonprofit educational organization founded in 1976 as Act/Tunes;
committed to making high-quality live theater accessible, relevant, and
memorable for young people and their families. Brings the excitement of
live theater to hundreds of participants and audience members each season
through company productions, theater arts classes, summer workshops,
and guest artist performances.

Creative Arts (Reading)
http://www.creativeartsforkids.org/theatre_kids.php
Founded in 1978 by a group of local parents concerned about arts in the
community; its goal is to serve elementary schoolchildren with enrichment
programs. The theater program offers classes to children as young as three
years old. Classes range from stage to screen (television as well as film).

Fiddlehead Youth Theatre Company (Norwood)
http://www.fiddleheadtheatre.com/classes.htm
A summer program that provides students with the opportunity to participate in a drama or musical theater production. Students learn a variety of
theater arts skills, including acting, voice, dance, improvisation, technical
theater, and theater games. Students gain self-confidence and learn to grow
as performers. Students also get the chance to perform in a professional
theater setting before a live audience on their last day of class.

Harwich Junior Theatre (West Harwich)
http://www.hjtcapecod.org/home.html
Offers children the enjoyment of being in a theater audience as well as
in-house classes and workshops. The range of opportunities is wide, from

creative movement for preschool and kindergarten children to outreach programs in connection with the schools. The theater includes around six hundred students each year in classes and reaches many more through its acclaimed educational outreach programs.

Island Theatre Workshop (Vineyard Haven)
http://www.itwmv.org
Primarily a music theater camp, with four two-week sessions and an original musical presented at the end of each session. Everyone, regardless of age, is involved in each class, with the exception of the acting classes, which are broken up into age-appropriate groups. The Children's Theatre is a summer drama program in music, theater, voice and speech, and body movement, for young people from six to sixteen years old. The Apprentice Players is a winter drama program for young people ages seven to fifteen with classes and productions. The performances include everyone, as interaction among different ages enhances the learning experience and makes productions more enjoyable. A Mugwump program provides students with an opportunity to work as junior staff, together with theater and music theater majors from Carnegie Mellon University, who are training for professional careers in theater. Many graduates are currently working as professionals in the world of stage, television, and film. They return from time to time for performances, master classes, and summer staff.

JM Productions & Children's Corner (Quincy)
http://www.jmproductionspresents.com
Presents dinner theater and children's classes for theater, dance, and music in the South Shore.

Kids' Cabaret! (Hingham)
see http://gocitykids.parentsconnect.com/attraction/kids-cabaret-post-office-box-239-hingham-ma-02043-us
A nonprofit community youth theater program producing an annual summer musical involving children. Kids' Cabaret! is designed to give kids the opportunity to sing, dance, and act in a full-length feature musical production. It also gives young adults the opportunity to direct, produce, choreograph, paint, design, build, teach, conduct, and play for a musical production.

Kidstock (Winchester)
http://www.kidstocktheater.com
Offers dozens of theater workshop programs year-round for students in preschool through high school. A hands-on approach involves students working cooperatively with professional actors, musicians, and designers in

developing the characters and plot scenarios for their scripts; penning lyrics for songs, and creating steps for dances; designing scenery and costumes that later become projects they complete; and rehearsing a production as a team where every member is a vital piece of the puzzle.

Methuen Young People's Theatre (Methuen)
http://www.mmmh.org/VSM/templates/temp.asp?articleid=228&zoneid=47
Seeks to provide an excellent summertime educational and cultural experience in musical theater. Each summer, children of ages from those about to enter grade 4 through high school learn and rehearse a full-scale Gilbert & Sullivan operetta.

Musical Theater Experiences (Lincoln)
http://www.MusicalTheaterExperiences.com
Develops original scripts appropriate for children's theater, and then stages these plays with local children, performing for their families and the community. Some musicals are based on original Broadway plays but edited for age appropriateness.

Neverland Theatre (Hamilton)
http://neverlandtheatre.com
Offers summer workshops in which children participate in music, drama, and dance activities, as well as after-school drama classes.

Pocket Full of Tales Children's Theater (Natick)
http://www.pocketfulloftales.com
Provides children and young families with a warm, nurturing environment in which to explore their imaginations, their bodies, their voices, and their world through the arts.

Priscilla Beach Theatre (Whitehorse Beach)
http://www.priscillabeachtheater.org
Focused on developing professional communication and acting skills for children ages four to seventeen. Children are introduced to the techniques of voice, concentration, speech, creative movement, vocal expression, and poise. Their study culminates in public performances of their work.

Riverside Theatre Works (Boston)
http://www.riversidetheatreworks.org
A nonprofit performing arts center that works as a school for both children and adults. Mixed Emotions is the young adult company, and the Next Generation is the children's company. The repertoire includes Broadway classics.

Shakespeare and Company (Lenox)
http://www.shakespeare.org
Provides resident instruction and productions in four programs: the Fall Festival (mainstage productions for which high school students rehearse at their high schools), Shakespeare & Young Company (actor programs for youth aged sixteen to twenty), Riotous Youth (summer program for students aged seven to fifteen), and Shakespeare in the Courts (productions sponsored by the Berkshire Juvenile Court System).

Stageloft Repertory Theater Summer Theater Camp (Sturbridge)
http://www.stageloft.com/camps/youthcamps.htm
Two-week camp sessions teach kids skills associated with theater production and performance. Mornings are devoted to specific skills, and afternoons are used to transfer those skills to full-scale productions.

True Colors: Out Youth Theater (Cambridge)
http://www.thetheateroffensive.org/truecolors.html
A theater troupe for lesbian, gay, bisexual, transgender, and questioning youth and their allies, ages fourteen to twenty-two, dedicated to presenting an honest portrayal of the lives of LGBTQA youth. Twice a year, during the fall and spring school terms, True Colors recruits a culturally diverse theater troupe of ten to twelve participants. A team of artists and teachers guides troupe members in creating a new theater piece based on their lives and experiences. The troupe then tours this original play to schools and community groups.

The UnCommon Theatre [UTC] (Mansfield)
http://uncommontheatre.com
Provides aspiring young actors, singers, musicians, and technicians an opportunity to work under the guidance of theater professionals and to perform in a professional theater house. UTC seeks to develop children's confidence, self-esteem, teamwork, and effective life skills. Adults are welcome to join volunteer crews, which are an integral part of each production.

Vineyard Playhouse Youth Theater (Vineyard Haven)
http://www.vineyardplayhouse.org
Offers several theater programs meet the needs and encourage the ambitions of young players. Summer Stars Theater & Art Camp is a fun weekly program exploring the magic of theater and art for ages nine through fourteen. Fourth Grade Theater Project offers every fourth grader on Martha's Vineyard an introduction to all aspects of the theater; each original play is backed by production, artistic, and technical teams. Rising Stars is a small, friendly program incorporating theater, movement, and art for children ages nine through thirteen.

Walpole Children's Theatre (Walpole)
http://walpolechildrenstheatre1.homestead.com/wcthomepage.html
A specialized group with the sole aim of educating, enlightening, and entertaining youths in the local community through theater arts. The intent is to preserve the tradition of children's theater within the community, providing the children involved with more than just onstage experience but also the many behind-the-scenes aspects that go into a production.

Watertown Children's Theatre (Watertown)
http://www.watertownchildrenstheatre.org
Provides a cultural and educational resource for children of all ages. Offers classes, productions, workshops, and mini-musical opportunities for all children to appreciate and participate in the performing arts.

Weston Drama Workshop (Weston)
http://www.westondramaworkshop.org/program/index.html
A summer camp where students between ages ten and twenty-three participate in two to three shows, whether in the spotlight or behind the scenes.

Wheelock Family Theatre (Boston)
http://www2.wheelock.edu/wheelock/x1010.xml
Supports children's intellectual, emotional, creative, and social development through drama activities. Educational programs include fall and spring courses, summer acting classes, vacation week institutes, a summer matinee series for lower-income youth, and an after-school theater training program for deaf teenagers.

Winchester Cooperative Theatre for Children (Winchester)
http://www.winchestermass.org/coop.html
Musical theater for children ages six through fourteen. Throughout their experience, they are encouraged to reach a level of performance far beyond that which is typically expected of their age group. The staff consists of accomplished dramatic coaches, musicians, choreographers, and stage, costume, and lighting designers who support the children as they develop to their fullest potential. This program includes a summer camp.

Your Kids' Theatre [Your Theatre Inc] (New Bedford)
http://www.yourtheatre.org/ytkids.htm
A five-week workshop, meeting twice a week. Throughout the workshop, children build and enhance many skills essential for the stage and for life. They strengthen communication skills and articulation while learning to collaborate on a play together without competing.

Michigan

All-of-us Express Children's Theatre (East Lansing)
http://www.allofusexpress.org
Offers theater for and by children. Provides young people with an opportunity to produce plays of professional quality.

Downriver Youth Performing Arts Center (Trenton)
http://www.dypac.com
DYPAC involves young people ages five to nineteen in three major theatrical productions per year and also offers a Summer Fine Arts Camp. In addition, DYPAC performs for local service organizations, charitable causes, and community events. DYPAC's mission is to offer quality arts entertainment and develop a state-of-the-art performing arts center in southeast Michigan.

Flint Youth Theater (Flint)
http://www.thefim.org/fyt-homepage
Offers classes year-round for students age three through grade 12. Classes are taught by FYT's professional artists. With small classes and one-on-one coaching, the faculty takes great pride in nurturing creative spirits while teaching the practical skills of performing on stage.

Grand Rapids Civic Theater (Grand Rapids)
http://www.grct.org/school/grctschool.html
Offers a complete range of acting, dance, and technical theater classes for preschool children through adults. Each year more than eighteen hundred students attend classes, workshops, and seminars. In the summer term as many as thirty-five instructors teach regular classes, summer theater camps, summer stock, and special programs.

The Kalamazoo Civic Youth Theatre (Kalamazoo)
http://www.kazoocivic.com/shows/youth.shtml
Offers classes taught by area professionals with a wide range of expertise. Fun-filled educational opportunities are available for students at all levels of skill and experience.

Michigan Youth Theatre (Holly)
http://www.michiganyouththeater.org
A youth-centered performing arts organization, developing leadership, teamwork, and communications skills in youth ages twelve to nineteen through theater production experiences, while providing professional quality, classics-based live theater experiences and education for community schools and audiences of all ages.

Mosaic Youth Theatre (Detroit)
http://www.mosaicdetroit.org/home.htm
A program designed to empower young people to maximize their potential through professional performing arts training and creation of first-rate theatrical and musical art. Young artists come from more than fifty city and suburban schools, and a variety of social, economic, racial, cultural, and religious backgrounds. Through a professional performing arts program, these young artists blend their ideas and talents and achieve excellence in their theatrical and musical performances.

Motor City Youth Theatre (Detroit)
http://mcyt.org
Organized exclusively for educational purposes and to bring the excitement and magic of live theater to young people and their families as performers and audience participants. Motor City Youth Theatre educates, enriches, and enlightens the lives of children and adults in the community and surrounding areas by offering plays, musicals, and workshops that address literary and musical works, current issues, and multiculturalism. It trains a youth population ages five through eighteen, many of whose recreational needs are not often met through sports.

Ragamuffin Children's Theatre (Charlevoix)
http://www.ragamuffintheatre.com
A Christian nonprofit organization dedicated to instructing young people in all areas of the performing arts: dance, mime, acting, drama, and singing. The company includes many adult artists, actors, singers, and dancers.

Taylor Youth Theater (Taylor)
see http://www.cityoftaylor.com/node/18293>
A theater featuring children ages six to fourteen performing musicals and other plays.

Traverse City Children's Theatre (Traverse City)
http://www.tcctheatre.org
Provides an innovative blend of theater and education for young people from three to twenty-one years of age. Performance areas include a mainstage auditorium and a studio theater, while touring productions visit various schools to bring shows that teach or reinforce core lessons for students from first grade to high school.

Young People's Theater (Ann Arbor)
http://www.youngpeoplestheater.com

Students are encouraged to explore the beauty, diversity, complexity, and challenges of the world around them through the dramatic process. Classes are designed for students at different ages and with different interests. Faculty at the summer camp specialize in acting, music, and choreography.

Minnesota

Chanhassen First Act Theater Camp (Chanhassen)
http://www.chanhassentheatres.com/summer_camp/
A unique camp taught by the professionals seen on stage and behind the scenes at Chanhassen Dinner Theatres. More than seven hundred children aged eight to eighteen participate in weeklong half-day summer sessions. They are divided into groups and all experience levels are welcomed.

Stages Theatre Company (Hopkins)
http://www.stagestheatre.org
A theater company committed to the enrichment and education of children and youth in an environment that stimulates artistic excellence and personal growth. Theater education programs and classes are designed to inspire creativity in youth ages four to seventeen, focusing on the techniques of drama, music, and dance. Students are taught to explore and express their own individuality and build self-confidence.

SteppingStone Theatre (St. Paul)
http://www.steppingstonetheatre.org
An alternative theater for youth, specializing in new works for the stage, classes, and outreach. The focus is on the process of making theater: how the company gets to the final day is as important as the final presentation itself. Students learn about setting, character, plot, problem, and solution (the where, who, what, why, and how of drama), and apply that to creating a play from the ground up. Rather than being assigned a part in an already formed script, students work together to create the work they will perform on stage.

The Children's Theatre Company (Minneapolis)
http://www.childrenstheatre.org
The largest children's theater in North America, serving children and their families. The Theatre Arts Training Program offers classes to students ages eight through eighteen. Each year, "ctc4teens" selects motivated high school juniors and seniors to act as school liaisons and sales and marketing consultants to build teen audiences for new productions and education programs created specially for teens.

The Great River Educational Arts Theatre (St. Cloud)
http://www.greattheatre.org
Performs for students and offers a variety of summer programs instructing children in theater skills.

Upstage! Musical Theatre Workshop (Minneapolis–St. Paul)
http://www.upstagemtw.org
Provides a fun and challenging environment for talented young performers ages four to thirty. Offers twelve weeks of formal instruction in drama, voice, dance, and movement, culminating in a production of a children's operetta or musical. Also offers summer programs, camps, and community workshops.

Youth Performance Company [YPC] (Minneapolis)
http://www.youthperformanceco.com
Offers winter classes for students from kindergarten through high school. A Young Artists Council is a leadership group of teen peers dedicated to the advancement of young artists. They meet monthly to support the main stage season. They also organize their own summer show, which is directed, created, and produced entirely by artists twenty-one or younger.

Mississippi

Acting Up Theatre Company (Grayling)
http://www.actingup.biz/workshop/workshop.html
An adult performance group that offers theater workshops for children eleven to seventeen on college campuses.

Missouri

Coterie Theatre (Kansas City)
http://www.coterietheatre.org/classes.html
Offers a variety of classes for children focused on process rather than product, providing educational experiences that challenge the child as audience and artist. Instructors are theater professionals—actors, designers, and directors. Classes are kept small enough that all students are able to participate and learn. Students are trained in interpreting and auditioning, as well as acting. Teenage actors are invited to audition for adult plays.

Crestwood-Kirkwood Youth Theater (Kirkwood)
see http://www.ci.kirkwood.mo.us/parks/com-center/theaterprograms.htm
Produces two productions per year—one in April and one in December—cast with sixty to eighty youth and teens between the ages of eight and

eighteen. The Kirkwood Summer Theatre performs one musical per year in the month of July, cast with performers age eleven and older.

The Muny—Muny Kids and Muny Teens (St. Louis)
http://www.muny.org/content/view/63/43/
A performance and training ground for talented youngsters. The program spotlights children (ages seven to thirteen) and teenagers (ages fourteen to nineteen) with exceptional voice and dance talent, stage presence, and discipline that make them standouts among their peers. Auditions and training are rigorous.

A Three Fold Cord (Washington)
http://www.3foldcord.org
A Christian youth theater that presents faith-based productions. In addition to summer musicals, the company presents Christmas musicals, promotes various other local organizations, and provides members, past and present, with experience, with wonderful memories, and a new way to serve the Lord in the community.

Montana

Equinox Theatre Company—Teen Theatre (Bozeman)
http://www.equinoxtheatre.com
After-school and summer programs that provide professional rehearsal experience for the teenagers utilizing uncommonly challenging material. Camp Equinox offers an broad program, from musical comedy to Shakespeare, to film acting, to mask making, to playwriting, to improvisation. Classes are divided into five age groups.

Missoula Children's Theatre [MCT] (Missoula)
http://www.mctinc.org
A large-scale and diverse musical theater program serving students from Montana, as well as from all over the country and around the world. More than sixty-five hundred young people participate in a regional residency week, which sets up theater out of the Little Red Wagon in metropolitan and rural schools; in addition, MCT reaches twelve hundred communities in all fifty states, four Canadian provinces, and overseas. MCT's nationally acclaimed performing arts camps bring two hundred of the finest young performers in the country to Montana for a two-week summer residency program. A new extended residency program is being negotiated with the Missoula public schools. Within each program, girls and boys are regarded as equal, and there is care and regard for the disabled and shy, as well as for the gifted. Productions receive excellent reviews, and outstanding theatrical

talent is discovered. But the primary purpose of these programs is to help children develop life skills through participation in the performing arts.

Nebraska

The Haymarket Theatre (Lincoln)
http://www.haymarkettheatre.org
Provides theater classes for children during the school year. A friendly, fun-filled, and fast-paced environment in which kids can explore their natural performing skills.

Omaha Theater Company for Young People (Omaha)
http://www.rosetheater.org/classes-about.asp
Offers year-round classes in acting, drama, and musical theater for children ages four to eighteen. All classes are professionally instructed and focus on the individual development of each child. Many offer performance opportunities. A program called Teens 'N' Theater offers young people opportunities to act, direct, write, design, and stage manage.

Nevada

The Rainbow Company Youth Theatre (Las Vegas)
http://www.rainbowcompany.info/index.html
A thirty-year-old youth theater program sponsored by the city of Las Vegas. At the core of the company is its Ensemble, a group of forty dedicated children, ages ten to eighteen, selected by open audition. A variety of classes in all aspects of theater is offered to students from age four through high school.

Sign Design Theatre Company (Las Vegas)
http://www.signdesigntheatre.org
A nonprofit youth development organization that provides an innovative program combining American Sign Language (ASL), dance, and the performing arts. Children ages five to eighteen learn and perform ASL through music. While bringing a creative and inspirational form of entertainment to their audiences, Sign Design members gain self-confidence, a sense of responsibility, and an understanding of the value of community service and disability acceptance.

New Hampshire

Andy's Summer Playhouse (Wilton)
http://www.andyssummerplayhouse.org

Produces creative collaborations between children and professional artists who work in a variety of media: performance art, theater, dance, music, puppetry, video, set and lighting design, and playwriting. In its more than thirty-five years, Andy's has grown from a summer play produced by two schoolteachers to its current state as a fully equipped summer theater, with a staff of more than thirty professional artists, involving more than 250 children and more than three thousand audience members each year.

Bedford Youth Performing Company [BYPC] (Bedford)
http://www.bypc.org/theatre.html
Offers courses in acting and musical performance for students as young as five. BYPC students and the general public audition for professional-quality productions of Broadway musicals with live accompaniment or full orchestration and complex choreography. All candidates who audition are cast.

Children's Stage Adventures (Sullivan)
http://www.childrensstageadventures.org
A nonprofit organization created for the sole purpose of enriching children's lives through participation in a live theater experience. Residency weeks and workshops are offered for school and community groups.

Kids Coop Theatre (Derry)
http://www.kids-coop-theatre.org
In addition to opportunities to perform in quality productions, provides children and teens with instruction, encouragement, and development in the performing arts. Also emphasizes (and requires) the active participation of parents and other adult volunteers as part of production teams.

Leddy Center School (Epping)
http://www.leddycenter.org/Leddy_School.html
Offers classes throughout the day in a wide variety of disciplines. The student body ranges in age from five to fifty-something years. Always strives to provide classes that will both interest and educate.

My Act (Merrimack)
see http://www.merrimack.lib.nh.us/contacts/m.shtml#MYACT
A nonprofit theater organization established in 1992 to promote the theatrical experience to all children in the Merrimack area from age three through high school. Encourages all interested to participate in all areas of theater, not just performing on the stage, but also including costuming, lights, sound, props, and related backstage activities.

North Country Teen Theatre Group (Lebanon)
http://northcountryteentheatre.fws1.com
Produces a teen musical show annually, with children from area schools routinely participating in all aspects of the production, from set design to acting.

Community Players of Concord: Children's Theater Project [CTP] (Concord)
http://www.communityplayersofconcord.org/4CTP/CTP.html
Founded in 1995 with a mission to "encourage, foster and promote the theatrical arts" to the younger generation, CTP produces one major show each fall and offers a children's theater camp during spring break week. All roles are open and available for young actors ages eight to fourteen.

Peacock Players (Nashua)
http://www.peacockplayers.org/programs/yc.html
Offers summer camps and the Peacock Players' Young Company, made up of performers between fourteen and eighteen years of age. Each year a group of twenty students is selected, through an intensive audition/interview process, to become the Peacock Players' summer work force, filling all the important positions in the theater—actor (performing in at least two fully produced shows), director, stage manager, producer, and backstage crew.

New Jersey

All Children's Theatre (Parsippany)
http://www.allchildrenstheatre.org
Provides children from age four to seventeen with experiences in comedy, creative dramatics, and musical theater. Offers additional summer day camps in Clinton, Jackson, Metuchen, Montville, Roxbury, Sparta, Tenafly, and Watchung.

BG Theatre Club (Pequannock)
http://www.wbgc.org/pqbgc/cultural.asp?ProgID=92
An organization dedicated to creating quality theater productions in two summer musicals: a Junior Company production with participants ages eight through twelve and a full-length Senior Company musical with participants ages twelve through eighteen.

Broadway Bound Theatrical and Dance Center (Lyndhurst)
http://www.broadwayboundnj.com

A stepping-stone for students who want to be on Broadway one day or a fun place for students who want to learn to sing, dance, or act. The Young People's Musical Comedy Workshop Program is for students between the ages of twelve and eighteen.

Essex Youth Theater (Essex)
see http://www.merchantcircle.com/business/Essex.Youth.Theater.Incorpo rated.973-746-3303
Offers musical theater for children age four to thirteen. Some shows are adaptations, and others are original. Each part has approximately the same amount of time on stage and at least one solo.

The Growing Stage (Netcong)
http://www.growingstage.com
Provides education programs created with the intent to provide young people the opportunity to experience and actively participate in the arts. Classes and camp are open to students with prior experience in the theater arts as well as those who would like to try something new.

The Kelsey Theatre at Mercer: Tomato Patch Workshops (West Windsor)
http://www.kelseyatmccc.org/tomato_patch.shtml
A community theater whose mission includes workshops for junior and senior high school students. They spend several weeks of the summer exploring the visual arts, dance, theater, and vocal music under the guidance of a highly qualified staff of teaching professional artists. Theater is viewed in a broad context, and classes are offered in stage combat, children's theater, computer art, "Who's line is it anyhow?," painting, drawing, jazz, musical theater, tap dance, cartooning and anime, hip hop, vocal ensemble, comedy, and video production.

Mainstage Center for the Arts (Sewell)
http://mainstage.org
Offers a broad range of classes and workshops in acting, voice, dance, and fitness. Various acting workshops and theater productions, school-year and "Summer Stage," are offered to children from fourth grade through high school.

Playwrights Theatre Creative Arts Academy (Madison)
http://www.ptnj.org/PubCL/ClassesMainPage.htm
Acting classes are offered in age-groups from kindergarten through age eighteen. At the older ages, theater skills are matched with the ability to write plays in a Creative Arts Academy.

Pushcart Players (Verona)
http://www.pushcartplayers.org
Offers a "Junior Broadway" program that gives students in grades 4 through 8 the chance to learn theater by doing it. Productions are cast, rehearsed, designed, costumed, and presented with the help of parents, teachers, and Pushcart staff. Dazzling performances are scheduled at the end of the twelve- to sixteen-week program.

Taubenslag Productions (New Brunswick)
http://www.taubenslagproductions.com/index.html
Offers two theater programs for young performers. Theater Week visits schools and produces theater with the resident students; half- and full-day theater camps are offered in the summer.

The Theatre School at Paper Mill Playhouse (Milburn)
http://www.papermill.org/outreach/theatreschool.php
Offers small classes taught by professional theater artists for groups aged four through twelve and thirteen through seventeen. Classes include acting, improvisation, musical theater, and production.

Tri-State Actors Theater: The Intern Company (Hardyston)
http://www.tristateactorstheater.org/interns.htm
A company of children ages thirteen through eighteen, auditioned to perform and produce plays on the highest professional level. Additional acting classes are offered to children as young as six. Originally children's theater only, Tri-State Actors Theater now includes an adult professional theater company.

New Mexico

Albuquerque Little Theatre (Albuquerque)
http://www.albuquerquelittletheatre.org/Edu.htm
Offers after-school and summer programs at different grade levels. A theater lab program offers productions, and children may audition for family and mainstage productions.

New Mexico Young Actors (Albuquerque)
http://www.nmyoungactors.org
A drama school that produces children's plays and musicals for and by students ages nine to nineteen.

Southwest Children's Theatre Productions (Santa Fe)
http://www.southwestchildrenstheatre.com

Offers after-school theater arts classes for kids in grades 1 through 9. The Young Actors' Class for grades 3 through 9 cast each child in a starring role in the semester's mainstage production. The Budding Actors' Class for grades 1 and 2 features a student showcase at the end of the semester. The Summer Theatre Session begins in June and continues through the end of July.

The Growing Stage: Children's Theatre in Albuquerque (Albuquerque)
http://www.thegrowingstage.com
Provides theatrical experiences to inspire, empower, and enrich children and communities. Offers a variety of classes for kids ages four through seventeen as well as very popular summer intensive workshops. Students are prepared not only to succeed in their personal endeavors but also to audition for mainstage shows.

New York

Adirondack Children's Troupe (Glen Falls)
http://www.adirondackchildrenstroupe.org
Provides a live theater experience for students in grades 4 through 12. ACT believes in a nonaudition program, and students are registered on a first-come, first-served basis, giving children of all abilities an opportunity to participate in live theater. Parents serve as support staff for the theater production in which their child is registered.

All-Stars Talent Shows Network (New York)
http://www.allstars.org/programs
Involves inner-city youth, ages five to twenty-five, in creating developmental culture through producing and performing in weekend talent shows, including theater, in their neighborhood school auditoriums. There are two major programs for young actors. The All Stars Talent Show Network is an after-school, performance-based enrichment program for inner-city youth. In the summer, Youth Onstage! offers an intensive theatre institute that meets four days a week. Admission is by audition.

Arts Connection (New York)
http://www.artsconnection.org
A comprehensive, not-for-profit, arts-in-education organization that provides programming in the performing, visual, literary, and media arts to the New York City public schools. The Young Talent Program reaches students in grades 3 to 6 with instruction in theater.

Attic Salt Theatre Company (Astoria, Queens)
http://www.atticsalt.org/arts_education.htm

Includes a program that takes a script created by students through the process that leads to performance: script analysis, character development, storytelling, stage presence, theater terminology, and the rehearsal process. Students analyze every aspect of the performance process as they bring a show from inception to curtain call.

Broadway Training Center of Westchester (Hastings-on-Hudson)
http://www.broadwaytraining.com
Broadway-oriented performing arts training with classes that include acting, dance, and voice. The most popular program, "Ensemble," is an intensive musical theater experience leading to a full-scale production. The atmosphere is noncompetitive, nonjudgmental, and safe.

Camp Broadway (New York)
http://www.campbroadway.com
A summer program offering classes and workshops taught by Broadway professionals in all aspects of musical theater, including a behind-the-scenes look at the business. Offers students from six to eighteen three programs plus workshops in dance, voice, acting, combat, improvisation, technical theater, and audition.

Children's Shakespeare Theatre and the Rogue Players (Nyack)
http://childrensshakespeare.org
An independent organization of children ranging in age from eight to fifteen. The group's chief goal is to give young actors an opportunity to experience Shakespeare's words and deep understanding of the human experience and to help them—through instruction in voice, movement, and acting techniques—to translate their experience to a broad audience of children and adults. Students are a company of players working together "in the best Shakespearean tradition," supporting each other and teaching each other. They mount six productions each year, in original language with period costumes, sometimes set in different time periods. They perform at Renaissance Fairs and have toured as far away as Texas; they offer in-school workshops and a CST Studio for beginning students. Parents are involved in productions, serving on the board, providing dinner for tech weeks, and even acting in fund-raising presentations.

The Children's Theatre Company (New York)
http://www.childrenstheatrecompany.org
Commissions and presents new and adapted pieces of professional theater that explore relevant and challenging social issues. Current events are interpreted from a historical and multidisciplinary perspective, utilizing drama, dance, music, and art. Students learn that they are the voices of positive

change in society. Four productions include four age groups from five to eighteen.

City Lights Youth Theatre (New York)

http://www.clyouththeatre.org

Provides young people from diverse backgrounds the opportunity to participate in theater experiences in order to develop confidence, responsibility, teamwork, and a greater sense of self and community. Performing arts classes, full-scale productions, and in-school residencies engage children and teens, ages three to nineteen. There are workshops in acting, improvisation, and musical theater. Classes are offered for children; high school students are cast in productions.

Clarkstown Summer Theatre (Clarkstown)

http://www.summertheatrefestival.com

A program that exposes high school students to the art of theater production. The program is open to students going into grade 9 through graduating seniors who live in the Rockland County area.

Creative Arts Team (New York)

http://www1.cuny.edu/portal_ur/content/academic_affairs/cat/index.html

The Creative Arts Team Youth Theatre is divided into three companies: the Youth Theatre (for high school students), the Junior Youth Theatre (for junior high school students), and the Ensemble (a training and performing company of former Youth Theatre members aged eighteen to twenty-five). Students are admitted on a first-come, first-served basis, with a membership of around thirty-five members and a waiting list.

Developing Artists Theater Company (New York)

http://www.developingartists.org

A nonprofit organization dedicated to providing eight- to nineteen-year-olds from culturally diverse backgrounds the opportunity to immerse themselves in the performing arts. Outreach programs and original productions maintain a focus on collaboration. Small classes are offered in Basic Acting (ages ten to fourteen) and Theater Studio (ages fourteen to seventeen). In addition, enrolled students are offered weekly workshops with artists from around New York City.

The 52nd Street Project [The Slightly Off-Broadway Theatre] (New York)

http://www.52project.org

A not-for-profit organization dedicated to matching the inner-city children of Hell's Kitchen (ages nine to eighteen) with professional theater artists to create original theater. Children are offered a succession of playwriting and acting courses, collaboratively with adult professionals. A "senior year" directing project is sometimes performed abroad.

Geneva Theatre Guild Youth Theater (Geneva)
http://www.gtglive.org/youththeatre.php
A summer theater program for young people in grades 3 through 12, founded in 1986. Its goals are to provide local youth with an opportunity to be involved in any and all aspects of the production of theater, to provide the community with theater that is both artistically and educationally challenging, to help local youth develop a better understanding of the potential of theater for fostering human development while also helping them understand the technical aspects of theater, and to use theater as a means of developing a sense of community. All interested students are given a part in the production. Students also have the opportunity to work on scenery, lighting, makeup, and other production areas under the guidance of adult volunteers.

Harbor Conservatory for the Performing Arts (New York)
http://www.harborconservatory.org
Offers pre-professional and introductory training in music, dance, and drama. A challenging, caring, and encouraging environment fosters positive self-image, an appreciation of the arts, and an understanding of cultural diversity.

Helen Hayes Youth Theatre (New York)
http://www.helenhayesyouththeatre.com
Offers year-round theater classes and performance opportunities for young actors ages five to eighteen from all backgrounds and at all levels of experience. Provides rigorous training in the theater arts while also offering training in life skills such as public speaking, improved focus, social skills, self-confidence, and teamwork.

Long Lake Camp for the Arts (Lake George)
http://www.longlakecamp.com
For boys and girls age ten to sixteen who want to immerse themselves in a performing arts/acting camp and a fine arts/visual arts camp. Subjects include theater, acting, dance, music, fine arts, rock bands, circus, and friendship.

Longwood Youth Theater Experience (Queens)
http://www.lyte.us
Offers New York–area students foundations in theater education. Programs are offered in drama and musical theater performance, as well as orchestral accompaniment and improvisation. Students develop critical thinking,

analysis, problem solving, organization, and writing and communication skills.

Manhattan Children's Theatre [MCT] (New York)
http://www.manhattanchildrenstheatre.org
Acting classes are offered in sequence—Storytellers/Playmakers, Creative Drama, and Beginning Acting—to students preschool to fifth grade. The focus is on learning all the elements that go into putting on a show.

MCC Youth Theater Company (New York)
http://www.mcctheater.org/youthcompany/index.html
A free after-school program for New York City youth, ages fourteen to twenty, interested in writing and acting for the theater. Students come from throughout the city to participate in weekly workshops led by theater professionals. The Youth Theater Company is designed to inspire young people to find and express their voices through the creation and performance of original theater pieces, while providing them with a safe artistic environment where they may grow and learn.

New Victory Theater (New York)
http://www.newvictory.org/educationNewVicStudio.m
Offers apprentice programs to students sixteen and older, in cooperation with schools. Workshops are available to children in music and storytelling, juggling and physical comedy, character creation, Shakespeare, circus, tap and choreography, mask, and puppetry.

Olean Theatre Workshop [The Washington Street Theatre] (Olean)
http://www.oleanworkshop.org/kids1.htm
A community theater school and performing company offering classes for children beginning at first grade; senior high school students perform a major musical.

The Open Eye Theater Youth Theater Workshop (Arkville)
http://www.theopeneye.org/workshop.html
A community theater that offers workshops in improvisation, theater games, and scene study. Summer youth theater workshops include auditions, rehearsals, and performances of a finished production.

The Pied Piper Children's Theatre (New York)
http://www.piedpipertheatre.org
Seven full-scale productions each season teach students performance skills, including acting, singing, and dance, as well as fine arts skills, through set building and the technical aspects of theatre-craft. Roles are assigned by

ability. In addition, a Pied Piper Society is a group of skilled and dedicated adolescents who participate in workshops and classes with invited guest artists. In addition to performing, they help direct and manage productions. They publish a quarterly newsletter and are involved in fundraising and maintaining the theater. For this, they receive scholarships.

The Play Group Theatre (Westchester)
http://www.playgroup.org
Produces original plays and musicals for children eighteen and younger. A not-for-profit theater company dedicated entirely to providing actor training and diverse performance opportunities for children and teenagers. Students learn through studio classes, an actor training program, an outreach program, and the PGT Summer Theatre.

Rochester Children's Theatre (Rochester)
http://www.rochesterchildrenstheatre.org/workshops.htm
Offers challenging, innovative, high-quality arts education opportunities for children ages eight through twelve, while teaching theater skills that will empower children—both as artists and as people. The workshops offer instruction in acting, music, and movement, and encourage exploration of all aspects of production, from set design to costumes and props.

Roundabout Theatre Company (New York)
http://www.roundabouttheatre.org/e07_students.htm
Offers a series of workshops and performances for young people through two student-driven theater companies. VOICES focuses on preparing students for post–high school life, including college and careers, through disciplined theater training. The Student Production Workshop is designed for students who are most at risk for dropping out of school, with a focus on reengaging students in their current education through student-driven theater creation.

SaBooge Theatre Company (Brooklyn, New York, and Montreal, Quebec)
http://www.sabooge.com/teaching/teaching.shtml
Dedicated to providing theater training and experience to students of all ages through workshops, summer arts camps, in-school programming, university residencies, and community initiatives. With instructors and artists from around the globe, SaBooge's education program draws on their experience with circus arts, mask, music, puppetry, and movement to create in-depth programming at all levels of experience.

School of Cinema & Performing Arts (New York)
https://www.socapa.org

A creative arts school offering visual and performing arts programs, includ ing youth summer camps and teen summer camps ranging in length from two to six weeks on campuses in New York, London, California, and Mas- sachusetts.

Stage Left Children's Theatre (Orangeburg)
http://stageleftchildrenstheater.com
Offers cultural inspiration and development for children through the me- dium of theater. Mainstage shows are supplemented by an extensive variety of classes in acting, scene study, rhythm and movement, dance, and song. They range from the Jelly Bean Society, ages four to five, to thirteen and up. The emphasis is on musical theater, and SLCT has received royalties for condensing classic Broadway shows into easy-to-learn mini-musicals for children to perform.

Stagedoor Manor (Loch Sheldrake)
http://www.stagedoormanor.com
A theatrical training camp for kids ages eight to seventeen that offers total theater immersion plus all of the fun of a great summer camp. Offers ac- cess not only to theater but to television and movies; students meet casting agents and talk to directors and producers. Performers of all levels—begin- ner and advanced—find expression and fulfillment on stage and in the classroom.

Summer Theatre Institute—New York City (New York)
http://www.youththeatreinstitutes.org/OpeningPage.html
A residential, intensive, theater-training program for teens, ages fourteen to nineteen (high school freshman and up). This program is to open to actors, musical theater actors, dancer-actors, playwrights, and directors. Admission is by audition.

TADA! Children's Theater (New York)
http://www.tadatheater.com
A multifaceted and multicultural organization that emphasizes diversity in all areas of its operations. TADA! offers a subsidized ticket program for mainstage shows, arts education in a wide variety of schools in low-income communities in all five boroughs, a free training/youth development pro- gram for New York City kids ages eight to eighteen, and the opportunity to critique, perform in, and be audience members for a playwriting contest and reading series. Children develop their imagination, talent, self-esteem, concentration, discipline, teamwork, public speaking ability, and vocabu- lary in a fun, safe, and stimulating environment.

Theatre Arts Centre (New York, New York, and Doylestown, Pennsylvania)
http://theatreartscenter.com
Offers classes and workshops in acting, musical theater, voice and music skills, dance (jazz, tap, lyrical, hip-hop, and ballet), on-camera technique, karate for kids, mime, and other theater arts throughout the year in Doylestown. Both locations offer professionally based summer workshops for children, teens, and young adults.

Theatre Arts School [New York State Theatre Institute] (Troy)
http://www.nysti.org/tas.htm
Offers workshops for young people by age groups: creative dramatics, theater fundamentals, theater skills, performance skills, and production workshop. WinterStage and SummerStage are training grounds for young performers, and Summer Theatre Institute is a selective program for high school and college students.

Usdan Center for the Creative and Performing Arts (Wheatley Heights)
http://www.usdan.com/theater.htm
Offers a variety of classes in acting, movement, voice, and dance skills for students in grades 5 to 12. Theater Adventure is for grades 2 to 4, and classes in musical theater, drama, and chorus are for older children. The Repertory Companies are for grades 9 through 12 by audition.

Woodstock Youth Theater (Bearsville)
see http://www.wavelinks.net/wyt.htm
Dedicated to helping young people discover a sense of self and others through the performing arts. The Youth Theater offers training and performance experience to students aged five through eighteen, and is committed to the highest quality of performance for the community through national and international touring. The company also provides Arts and Education programming in the schools.

The Youth Theatre Experience [TYTE] (New City)
see http://rockland.org/business.cfm?page=828&city=New%20City
A nonprofit youth organization for middle and high school students. Children have the option of being in the cast, playing in the pit, or helping to build the sets as part of the crew. They also have the option of learning the business side of theater ranging from working on the playbill to being assistant director.

Youth Theatre Interactions (Yonkers)
http://www.youth-theatre.org
A complete performing arts school for the youth of the Yonkers community, offering classes for students ages eight to nineteen. Operates two se-

mesters per year: the School Year Semester and the Summer Semester; also offers outreach residencies and additional theater classes.

North Carolina

Afro-American Children's Theatre (Charlotte)
see http://www.soulofamerica.com/charlotte-cultural-sites.phtml
Founded in 1981, mounts six to eight fully staged productions each year with local cast members. Children have the opportunity to develop a variety of skills: artistic, social, cultural, personal, and academic, with an emphasis on African, African American, and Afro-Caribbean cultural contributions.

Children's Theatre of Charlotte (Charlotte)
http://www.ctcharlotte.org
Offers a broad array of programs, from summer camp to classes organized by grades, pre-kindergarten through high school. Training classes are geared toward students who are dedicated to studying the skills and techniques of theater. An audition is required to place children in classes appropriate for their age and experience level. Provision is made for children with special needs.

The Children's Theatre Playhouse [Children's Theatre of Winston-Salem] (Winston-Salem)
http://www.childrenstheatrews.org/playhouse-classes.html
Three seasons of classes for children of different ages, prekindergarten through eighth grade. Classes include performances for families on the last day. A variety of birthday parties (including improvisation and performances) can be arranged.

KidShine [The Leavening Agency] (Asheville)
http://www.leaveningagency.org/index.cfm?i=1144&mid=3
Founded to provide creative, Christ-centered programs for kids in the church and community. Offers drama camps and productions. Teams travel throughout the United States.

Matthews Playhouse of the Performing Arts (Matthews)
http://www.matthewsplayhouse.com/
Classes are offered by the term or full-year for students from kindergarten through high school, "from page to stage" (adapting stories for performance) to the senior musical theater company.

Spiritual Twist Productions (Fuquay-Varina)
http://www.spiritualtwist.com

Allows children and youth the opportunity to experience the performing musical theater in a Christian context. Classes, offered September through May for ages eight and up, include skits, sketches, improvisations, role-play, and various other activities. There are Christmas skits for all classes, and four major musicals are performed each year.

Tanglewood Youth Theatre [Asheville Community Theatre] (Asheville)
http://www.ashevilletheatre.org/Classes/Classes.html
Offers daytime and after-school classes, Spring Break Camp, and Summer Camp. The addition of new courses and instructors, as well as the popular favorites that have been offered for years, makes this a wonderful program for all children interested in exploring the exciting world of theater. This program challenges the mind and strengthens theater skills, helping children to realize and build upon their natural talents and abilities.

YouTheatre [Flatrock Playhouse] (Flatrock)
http://flatrockplayhouse.org/education/youtheatre.php
Offers classes for students as young as five years old weekend day camps in the summer, and a summer drama boarding camp. This program produces two mainstage productions during the main season, as well as playwriting contests, informal cabarets, and informal community performances. Its mission is to foster the educational and artistic growth of the community's children.

North Dakota

Mouse River Players' "Mini Mousers" (Minot)
see http://www.minotdailynews.com/page/content.detail/id/525955.html?nav=5001>
Designed specifically for young students between the ages of six and fourteen. Program classes, taught by experienced and trained local artists, lead to auditions for the Mouse River Players' annual family production. In this production, the majority of support, on and off the stage, comes from the participants in the Mini Mousers program.

Shade Tree Players (Bismarck)
http://shadetreeplayers.com
Provides opportunities for children ages six to sixteen to develop and show off their talents on the stage, from summer theater productions to acting workshops and lessons.

Summer Performing Arts [SPA] (Grand Forks)
http://www.spacompany.org

Offers an eight-week summer arts program for students in the elementary, middle, and high schools. These programs are instructed by staff from the Grand Forks region (including the Grand Forks Public Schools and the University of North Dakota) as well as special guests from around the country. Students learn and grow through a variety of experiences in the arts.

Trollwood (Fargo)
http://www.trollwood.org
A major summer theater training "camp" for young actors. Each season, over four hundred students participate in the variety of summer programs. They enjoy a relaxed, outdoor atmosphere, learning alongside other students of their age and skill level, under the direction of professional artists and teachers. High school elective credit is available for participation.

Youth Education on Stage [YES] (Williston)
see http://www.kfyrtv.com/News_Stories.asp?news=32264
Produces three shows each summer—mostly musical theater and large cast productions—with children in grades 1 through 12.

Ohio

The Beck Center for the Arts Youth Theatre (Lakewood)
http://beckcenter.org/theater/youth.htm
Provides high-quality education in the arts to all people regardless of age or ability. The theater program offers a broad program for children and teens. Teens and adults share classes in sketch comedy and original theater; several full-scale dramas and musicals are scheduled over the year on the main stage and the studio theater. Here, theater is a part of a broad and integrated program in the arts.

The Children's Theatre of Cincinnati (Cincinnati)
http://www.thechildrenstheatre.com
Provides an opportunity for children to be exposed to the variety of art forms that come together to create the magic of theater. Two S.T.A.R. Programs are directed toward children ages nine to eleven and twelve to eighteen. A summer program for nine- to eighteen-year-olds offers professional classes and enrichment in musical theater. Led by professional teaching artists, students participate in workshops and training in acting, dance, and voice.

The Children's Theatre of Mason [CTM] (Mason)
http://www.childrenstheatreofmason.com

Exposes children to all aspects of theatrical production and helps them develop an appreciation for the performing arts. CTM produces two large-scale productions each season and offers children the opportunity to take part on stage as performers and off stage as crew members, set builders, makeup assistants, and in many other behind-the-scenes roles.

The Children's Theatre Workshop (Toledo)
http://www.childrenstheaterworkshop.org
Includes a Main Company (ages five to eleven) and Teen Company (ages twelve to eighteen), with full-fledged productions by both groups and technical training for the older students. The program teaches theatrical techniques through an informal, classroom-based structure, and promotes self-expression and teamwork. Classes are structured based on the age of the child rather than experience level or ability. Children are given a taste of live theater (as much as they want) so they can decide for themselves if and to what extent they might want to pursue the theater either as a career or as a hobby.

Cincinnati Playhouse in the Park (Cincinnati)
http://www.cincyplay.com/Education/Camp/
A professional regional theater committed to producing and presenting for diverse audiences the broadest range of theater in an inviting theatrical environment. A Summer Theatre Day Camp offers programs from creative dramatics to acting to musical theater for children ages five and up.

Columbus Children's Theatre (Columbus)
http://www.colschildrenstheatre.org
A children's theater company committed to the belief that the best way for young people to understand and appreciate the theater arts is through direct participation. Professionally directed, interactive, hands-on programs celebrate young people's spirit, creativity, and fresh perspective. Offers academy classes and workshops year-round for grades pre-K to 12 that teach acting technique, dance, voice, as well as many other specialized areas.

Geauga Lyric Theater Guild—Youth Theater Workshop and Teen Theater Workshop (Chardon)
http://www.geaugatheater.org/Art_education.htm
A nonprofit organization formed in 1954 to present live entertainment and give people an opportunity to participate in community theater. Art and theater education classes are offered throughout the year, and the young and old refine their talents.

Heights Youth Theatre (University Heights)
http://www.heightsyouththeatre.com

A nonprofit organization committed to providing quality children's theater on the East Side of Cleveland. Young people from kindergarten through grade 12 enjoy a safe, nurturing environment and a cooperative learning experience as they work together to mount a production. The extraordinary artistic quality of productions and the sense of connection to a larger community make children and adults choose to become involved in theater.

Mishpachah (Mason)
http://www.mish-inc.com
An auditioned Christian drama group made up of high school students. Offers performances about teen issues.

The Muse Machine (Dayton)
http://www.musemachinedayton.org
An art education organization that offers students opportunities to explore a variety of art forms—from ballet, instrumental music, and theater to contemporary dance and the visual arts. The secondary program is exposure based and is offered and administered through an extracurricular school club. The elementary program is co-curricular and takes place in the classroom setting. Teachers and professional artists combine their talents to provide integrated programming for students.

Near West Theatre (Cleveland)
http://www.nearwesttheatre.org
Since 1978 has engaged youth on the near west side of Cleveland. Its programs are now intergenerational, and KLAMOR (Kids Loud and Musical Organic Review) trains children to put on a mini-musical.

Ohio Lyric Theatre of Springfield (Springfield)
http://www.ohiolyric.org
Produces musical theater, adult and children choruses, and KidStage Children's Theater. Under the direction of a diverse variety of guest artists and instructors, KidStage members participate in regularly scheduled theater workshops, developing experience in the arts while gaining confidence and self-esteem.

Playhouse Youth Theatre (Youngstown)
http://theyoungstownplayhouse.com
Offers professionally taught classes offering the opportunity to nurture that imagination, develop creativity, and experience the theatrical process through active participation. From regular theater classes for all ages to four mainstage youth productions every year, attention and care for area youth is paramount.

Stagecrafters Youth Theater (Pepper Pike)
http://www.orangerec.com/stagecrafters/programs.html
Offers after-school, weekend, and evening classes, performance troupes, and private coaching.

Theatre Kidz (Toledo)
see http://www.myspace.com/theatrekidz
An educational theatre program for kids ages four to eighteen offering classes, shows, summer camps, touring troupes, technical programs, and much more.

Toledo Repertoire Theatre (Toledo)
http://www.toledorep.org/reped.htm
Offers acting, singing, dancing, art, and technical theater classes, as well as children's productions. In Young Playgoers, adults perform for young audiences, and in Armchair Theatre, adults and children perform together.

Town Hall Theatre (Centerville)
http://www.townhalltheatre.org/html/class_descriptions.html
Includes three production programs. The Landmark Children's Theatre Company features mixed casts of adults and children in "landmark productions of the world's finest children's stories." The All Children's Theatre presents "theater about children, with children and for children," featuring actors ranging from seven to eighteen years of age. The All Children's Touring Teens mount three to four productions each season that visit local elementary and middle schools in the community following their mainstage performances in the theater.

Yellow Springs Kids Playhouse (Yellow Springs)
http://www.yskp.org
A not-for-profit arts organization that enhances art awareness through the creation of original multimedia theater for youth. Each year approximately one hundred youth ages ten to eighteen participate in a six-week Summer Theatre Arts Immersion, from auditions through rehearsals and the final presentation of two summer productions, including a full-length musical. Other programs include Tween Youth Workshops, for students ages five to ten; a youth leadership program, DaBigs; and outreach programs to neighboring communities.

Oklahoma

Oklahoma Children's Acting Guild (Tuttle)
http://www.oklahomachildrensactingguild.com/

A professional acting school that provides opportunities for children to develop their creative potential through participation in theatrical productions and interactive educational experiences. Produces a collection of musical shows each year. Both group and individual lessons are available in theater and music.

Oklahoma Children's Theatre (Oklahoma City)
www.oklahomachildrenstheatre.org
Productions and educational programs for young students (five to thirteen years old), including preschool, homeschool, and school break programs, and the Young Company (eight and older) is selected by audition. Affiliated with Oklahoma City University.

Oregon

Ashland Children's Theatre [Oregon Stage Works] (Ashland)
http://www.oregonstageworks.net/kids.htm
Features a summer camp and productions. Offers classes for students aged four through seventeen, including musical theater.

Camp Crescendo (Twin Falls, Idaho, and Bethel Park, Oregon)
http://www.campcrescendo.com/
A summer music camp for children, designed for children grades 2 through 7 who enjoy music and dance performance.

Children's Educational Theatre (Salem)
http://cetsalem.org
A dramatic arts program for children that includes classroom instruction, performance, and technical training for students in grades 5 through 9.

Children's Musical Theatre of Oregon (Ashland)
http://www.cmtoregon.org
An emphasis on encouraging and training participating children, with the support of families and volunteers. The show constitutes an eight-week course for children and families. Set and costume designers are professionals, but parents who do not contribute to the production forfeit a deposit. No child who auditions is turned away, and scholarships are available based on need. A new Teen Musical Theatre of Oregon is focused on students twelve to nineteen.

Corbett Children's Theatre (Corbett)
http://www.corbettchildrenstheater.com

Provides high-quality training in the performing arts. Membership is open to all school-age children (ages eight to fourteen). Instructional classes are offered in acting, voice, and dance. Three full-length plays are performed for the general public each year.

Krayon Kids Musical Theatre Co. (Oregon City)
http://www.krayonkids.org
A self-sufficient children's musical theater offering interested children an opportunity to participate in original musical productions that feature a wide variety of performance disciplines. The company also provides a quality program for children to view and be introduced to musical theater.

Northwest Children's Theatre and School (Portland)
http://www.nwcts.org
Produces five mainstage shows a year and operates a year-round theater school. Offers skills classes and playlabs for ages four and a half to eighteen, an internship program, and summer employment/volunteer opportunities for teens. Off-site classes and production support are available to local schools, including programs that serve at-risk youth.

Northwest Youth Theatre (Troutdale)
http://www.nwyouththeatre.org
A not-for-profit children's theater company featuring classes in music, drama, dance, and voice. After-school and summer day-camp programs are available to children from preschool through high school. Children are not required to audition, and no child is denied access because of inability to pay.

On Broadway Theatre (Coos Bay)
http://www.onbroadwaytheater.com
Offers drama and comedy, musicals and children's theater, "enriching the lives of patrons and players of all ages, through the magic of live theatre."

Oregon Children's Theatre (Portland)
http://www.octc.org
Offers classes that allow young people aged four to seventeen to connect with professional actors who are skilled at teaching the art and craft of acting. Year-round classes and workshops encourage confidence by building theater skills in a fun, engaging environment.

Rose Children's Theatre (Eugene)
http://www.therct.com

A nonprofit, tax-exempt community organization providing a variety of theater opportunities to both youth and adults. Full and partial scholarships are available. Programs include Acting Academy, Summer Camp, and Musical in a Month. Interns aged twelve to eighteen are recruited, and parents are expected to volunteer.

Ross Ragland's Summer Youth Theater Day Camp (Klamath Falls)
http://www.rrtheater.org/learn/summer
A four-week, full-day Youth Theater Day Camp open to students K–12 and accommodating up to one hundred students.

Pennsylvania

Arden Theatre Company (Philadelphia)
http://ardentheatre.org/classes/
Offers a summer camp and theater classes for children and adults: preschool (Mommy and Me), the Ardens Kids' Crew (grades K–5), and Arden Teen Company (grades 6–12), as well as a professional apprenticeship program including children. Classes are interactive, and teachers are professional theater artists.

Camp Ballibay (Camptown)
http://www.ballibay.com
A summer camp for boys and girls ages six through sixteen, offering a wide range of noncompetitive fine and performing arts activities, including acting and technical theater.

Center for Theater Arts (Pittsburgh)
http://centerfortheaterarts.org
A nonprofit performing arts school for students four to eighteen years old offering classes in voice, acting, musical theater, ballet, pointe, jazz, tap, and musical theater for students with special needs.

DreamWrights Youth and Family Theatre (York)
http://www.dreamwrights.org
Founded in 1997 by a group of families who believed that a theater arts program would have a profound and valuable impact on their children. Classes, camps, and workshops are offered year-round, and they are made affordable and available to everyone, including home-schooled children. (A special program is offered to Brownies.)

Family Playhouse Academy of Drama: Littlest Players (Emmaus)
http://www.familyplayhouse.com/LPlayers.htm
A program for players between the ages of three and twelve years, performing abridged adaptations of classic stories. The acting roles are formidable
in their literacy and depth but simplified enough to capture the innocence
and delight that young children always bring to performance. These mini-
shows allow the children to double cast several roles and thus enhance and
refine their characterization and memorization skills.

Freedom Theatre (Philadelphia)
http://www.freedomtheatre.org
Pennsylvania's oldest African American theater, dedicated to serious training in the arts. Freedom Theatre's teaching staff believes that effective teaching includes the introduction of life skills that raise dignity, self-worth,
and pride through both cultural education and group theater art activities.
Students study traditional or modern performance skills, theory, various
techniques of a discipline, writing, and aspects of technical production.
Three age levels of theater classes are offered.

Gemini Children's Theater (Pittsburgh)
http://www.geminitheater.org
Produces original musical theater performances that focus on artistic,
cultural, and educational themes. Numerous acting classes and summer
camps are available to students aged four to seventeen. Learning techniques
include complex theater games, exercises and improvisation work, and self-
written monologues.

Hedgerow Theatre (Rose Valley)
http://www.hedgerowtheatre.org
Operates as both a professional theater and an educational center for the
training, development, and education of theater artists and enthusiasts, including classes for teens and youth and a children's summer camp.

Little Lake Theatre (Canonsburg)
http://www.littlelaketheatre.org
Instruction by adult professionals in a performance and production camp
for ages eleven to fifteen and an apprentice program for ages fourteen to
nineteen. Students receive training in the rehearsal process, vocal projection, movement, and other skills that build stage presence. In technical
theater, campers participate in the design, construction, and acquisition of
properties, scenery, costumes, and production playbills. At the end of the
program, campers select a specific area of performance or production for a
showcase.

Pennsylvania Youth Theater (Bethlehem)
http://www.123pyt.org
A nonprofit performing arts organization with the mission of educating, entertaining, and enriching the lives of young people and their families through the art of theater. Offers a broad variety of classes to students from preschool through high school. Includes a musical theater day camp, an acting intensive program for teens, and weeklong introductory classes.

Philadelphia Children's Theater (Philadelphia)
http://www.pctheatre.org
Offers classes for children in acting, puppetry, mask making, monologue and audition preparation, script writing, commedia dell'arte, and dance, all taught by professional teaching artists.

Popcorn Hat Players (Harrisburg)
http://www.gamutplays.org/education/camp.php
Offers a theater camp for students aged six to twelve. The goal is to enhance communication skills and develop self-confidence, imagination, and creativity, as well as to educate children on a general knowledge of the theater.

Prime Stage, Theatre for Youth and Families (Pittsburgh)
http://www.primestage.com/mentor.htm
Offers a Technical Theatre Mentoring Program to students who have a desire to learn about sound, lights, costumes, set design, props, back stage crew, and even box office management. The mentee becomes a working member of a production run crew under the guidance of a stage manager. The mentee learns the operation of the equipment, the work ethics of the position, and the responsibilities of a job.

The Rehoboth Summer Children's Theatre (Oreland)
http://www.rehobothchildrenstheatre.org
Offers a variety of opportunities for young actors to join the theater fun, including morning theater workshops for the youngest performers and a series of exciting weeklong summer theater camps for actors aged nine to fourteen.

Saltworks Theatre Company (Pittsburgh)
http://www.saltworks.org
A nonprofit, professional arts company that addresses the physical, emotional, and spiritual needs of children, youth, and families through the creation and performance of contemporary dramatic works.

Theatre & Kids (Lansdale)
http://theatreandkids.com
Offers a broad range of student-centered programs. Summer Show Camp offers young people in grades 3 through 9 the opportunity put on a full-scale Broadway show in two weeks of daytime rehearsals and camp activities. The Theatre for Young Performers Productions stages six to eight shows each year, alternately featuring performers in grades 3 through 9, 7 through 12, and 9 through college. Elaborate musicals, dramas, comedies, fantasies, and theater classics are performed at area theaters and centers with casts chosen through open auditions.

Theatre Arts Centre (New York, New York, and Doylestown, Pennsylvania)
http://theatreartscenter.com
Offers classes and workshops in acting, musical theater, voice and music skills, dance (jazz, tap, lyrical, hip-hop, and ballet), on-camera technique, karate for kids, mime, and other theater arts throughout the year in Doylestown. Both locations offer professionally based summer workshops for children, teens, and young adults.

Totem Pole Playhouse (Fayetteville)
http://www.totempoleplayhouse.org
A summer theater day camp for children between the ages of eight and fifteen. Their education culminates in a production. Enrollment is restricted, and a limited number of scholarships is available.

Upper Darby Performing Arts Center Summer Stage (Drexel Hill)
http://www.udpac.org/summerstage/
Offers three summer programs: Children's Theater (ages fourteen through seventeen), Apprentices (ages eleven and twelve) and Rising Stars, a three-week program for graduate Apprentices, culminating in the performance of a children's musical. Young people are encouraged to develop the magic of their talents and to share that magic.

Valley Forge Children's Theatre (Valley Forge)
http://wwwww.valleyforge.org/static/index.cfm?contentID=467
Offers Kids: The Heart of the Arts Summer Program, serving children between the ages of five and fourteen in various arts classes, and Student Music Theatre Workshop, two mainstage children's musicals directed, acted, and designed by children under the supervision of theater professionals.

Wolf Performing Arts Center (Wynnewood)
http://www.wolfperformingartscenter.org

Dedicated to enriching the lives of young people through learning, experiencing, and creating theater. Theater is the perfect venue for developing both a child's self-esteem and a sensitivity to the human condition. Students grow through theater, developing confidence and creativity, while deepening the community's appreciation of theater.

Young People's Theatre Workshop (Wallingford)
http://www.yptw.org
Offers classes and camps where children learn to use their imaginations, to celebrate differences, to reach out to an audience and to one another, and to gain self-confidence through taking risks. This program includes daytime and overnight camps, various courses, and shows throughout the year.

Rhode Island

All Children's Theatre [ACT] (East Providence)
http://www.actinri.org
A twenty-year staple of the Rhode Island theater community, this nonprofit theater company is dedicated to the education and enrichment of children ages four to eighteen. ACT enables children to use their imaginations and creativity to explore all aspects of theater production. Offers performances, outreach, classes, and summer camps.

Young Actors Studio [Trinity Repertory Company] (Providence)
http://www.trinityrep.com/education/student_programs/young_actors_studio.php
Offers students the opportunity to learn with company actors and education staff, culminating in performances that they have written, designed, and performed. Trimester sessions are offered for beginners, with year-round sessions for advanced students.

South Carolina

Clemson Area Youth Theatre (Pendelton)
http://www.clemsonlittletheatre.com
Produces two shows each year performed by middle and high school students. In the summer, students from kindergarten through grade 12 take over the theater with sessions that include makeup, costumes, acting, set construction, lighting, music, dance, and auditioning.

Columbia Children's Theatre (Columbia)
http://www.columbiachildrenstheatre.com
Provides a training ground in theater arts through the KidStage series, an intensive, production-oriented "boot camp" designed to give young

performers the opportunity to rehearse and perform in productions for live audiences. Instruction includes training in acting, singing, musical theater, dance, and movement by highly qualified master teachers and culminates in a live performance.

South Carolina Children's Theatre [SCCT] (Greenville)
http://www.scchildrenstheatre.org
A year-round program for students ages three through eighteen. The format includes intensive training, production classes, and workshops. Each format offers unique games, activities, and challenges for the theater student.

South Dakota

Children's Theatre Company of South Dakota [Black Hills Playhouse] (Vermillion)
http://www.blackhillsplayhouse.com/ctc
Provides a rare and unique theater experience for young people across the Midwest, allowing them the opportunity to perform with professional theater artists in a full-scale musical production. One-week residencies culminate in a musical production using up to fifty local children, with suitable parts designed for every age, skill, and experience level.

Tennessee

All Children's Theatre at Germantown Community Theatre (Germantown)
http://www.germantowncommunitytheatre.org/ACT.htm
A program of Fun in Theatre, including Saturday classes, home-school classes, summer camps, and special workshops. All Children's Theatre is a summer performance series that stages an outdoor musical and an outdoor play. Children learn the skills of technical theater and performance.

Dixie Youth Theatre (Huntingdon)
http://dixiepac.net/dixie_youth_theater.htm
Part of the civic center constructed with the cooperation of local businesses to serve as a venue for the performing, literary, visual, and media arts. Classes are offered in creative drama for the very young and acting for children through high school. Performances are scheduled through the year.

Nashville Children's Theatre (Nashville)
http://www.nashvillechildrenstheatre.org/orange/index.htm
Offers camps and classes year-round that are designed with a progressive curriculum to meet the developmental needs of children of different ages and abilities, providing an instructional ladder that allows children to build

on their previous experiences. Training classes are offered for older students who are interested in pursuing careers in the performing arts.

Nashville Shakespeare Festival (Nashville)

http://www.nashvilleshakes.org/students.htm

An Apprentice Company of twelve to fourteen theater artists ages thirteen and up, performing in the Nashville Shakespeare in the Park production and participating in a two-week training program. Also offers children's workshops on Shakespeare's language and the dynamics of theater (with children directing professional actors).

Texas

A. D. Players Theater Arts Academy (Houston)

http://www.adplayers.org/taa.html

Offers training for artists of all ages, including specific programming for inner-city youth and at-risk children.

Arts View Children's Theatre (Longview)

http://www.artsviewchildrenstheatre.com/education.php

Offers workshops (training in single theater skills), an academy (short-term, intensive classes and performances), and the production company (auditions, rehearsals, and full-scale performances).

Casa Mañana Performing Arts Conservatory (Fort Worth)

http://www.casamanana.org/cpac/

A theater school that trains both youth and adults in the performing arts. Offers a high school musical theater camp.

Centre Stage Theatrical School and Production Company (Kingwood)

http://www.centrestagekw.org/school.shtml

Offers vocal training along with musical theater movement: choreography, scene blocking, and body angles. Performance skills are also a part of the curriculum, including theatrical terminology and vocabulary, facial expression, acting, and vocal projection.

Children on Stage [Garland Civic Theatre] (Garland)

http://www.garlandcivictheatre.org/cos/about.php

Offers an open call for actors and crew, ages eight to eighteen. Children are afforded a wide variety of multi-age roles.

Class Act Productions (The Woodlands)

http://www.classactproductions.org

Offers classes and productions to students with different levels of experience and ability year-round: two full-scale Broadway musicals, two Broadway Jr. summer workshops, Premiere Performing Ensembles, and two semester sessions in theater dynamics. Stresses teamwork and responsibility, as well as the technical and artistic aspects of musical theater.

Creative Arts Theatre & School [CATS] (Arlington)
http://www.creativearts.org
Founded in 1977, one of the oldest operating youth theaters in the nation and the only youth theater in the Dallas–Fort Worth metroplex, where youth perform for peers and run the lights, sound, and crew. CATS is a theater by youth for youth, offering classes year-round for children ages four to seventeen and adults in all aspects of theater education.

DCT Academy and Teen Conservatory [Dallas Children's Theatre] (Dallas)
http://www.dct.org/index.php/academy
Offers a variety of theater and video classes taught by professional theater artists. Highly participatory, hands-on programs. Classes are divided by age level, and most classes include a performance at the end of the program.

Denton Community Theatre (Denton)
http://www.dentoncommunitytheatre.com
A theater school with performance classes and camps year-round. Seven to ten productions through the year include traveling and competition shows and showcases.

Express Children's Theatre Education Program [ETEP] (Houston)
http://www.expresstheatre.com/etep.html
Includes after-school theater arts programs and summer camps that focus on all aspects of rehearsing and performing a play. Students learn both the history of theater and theatrical skills as they participate in the rehearsal process and the excitement of performing on stage. ETEP also assists schools in implementing an art-based curriculum that contributes to the growth and development of students: raising self-esteem, fostering communication and collaboration, nurturing deductive reasoning, and enhancing problem-solving skills.

Hill Country Children's Theater (Fredericksburg)
http://www.hillcountrytheater.org
A theater program sponsored by the Salvation Army that stresses the community of children who participate. Productions are family-friendly and have strong moral and ethical themes. Main roles are filled by children, but parents often join on stage.

HITS Theatre (Houston)
http://www.hitstheatre.org
A nonprofit arts and education organization that provides theater training for children ages four to twenty. HITS is dedicated to providing school-age students the highest quality performing arts education with a focus on training in the musical theater disciplines of voice, dance, and acting. In addition, several community outreach programs provide arts education opportunities for underserved populations.

Humphreys School of Musical Theatre [Theatre Under the Stars] (Houston)
http://www.tuts.com/Education/HumphreysSchool/tabid/80/Default.aspx
Programs for students at different levels of interest and ability. The Studio offers early morning and evening classes, Saturday workshops, and summer and winter camps. The academy is for the career-track student auditioned for placement in acting, improvisation, scene study, voice and theory, musical theater, and directing.

Junior Players (Dallas)
http://www.juniorplayers.org
The oldest nonprofit children's theater organization in Dallas. Serves the youth of Dallas by providing free programming in local recreation and cultural centers, housing, elementary and middle schools, and through social service agencies serving youth at risk. Discover Theater summer camps and Discover Ourselves after-school workshops focus on children ages six to fourteen in underserved areas of the community. Junior Players' Discover Shakespeare! program combines the best of Dallas high school acting talent with the professional skills of the staff.

kidsActing (Austin)
http://www.kidsactingstudio.com
Provides a supportive environment where young people can be creative, expressive, and improve their communication skills—traits that improve performance in school and enhance one's life. Offers classes in screen acting, theater design, musical production; a full-year advanced play production class; and a winter holiday camp.

Kids-N-Co. [El Paso Playhouse] (El Paso)
http://www.kidsnco.org
A year-round children's theater company and school, dedicated to training youngsters ages five to eighteen in the craft of theater. Dedicated to providing a quality theater experience and hands-on theatrical training to the children of the El Paso area, regardless of their economic, ethnic, or

educational background. Children are in front of and behind the curtain, producing and performing in plays.

Kids on Stage [Main Street Theater] (Houston)
http://www.mainstreettheater.com/kos/
Classes and camps running by seasons through the year. Skills classes include the fundamentals of imagination, character development, and story, as well as the creation of basic sets, props, and costumes. Rehearsal and performance classes are offered in open lab and audition sections. In addition, there are summer and winter camps and workshops and audition coaching.

Kids Who Care (Fort Worth)
http://kidswhocare.org
Five main stage events per year and a program of education that includes camps, classes, and a resident company touring regionally and internationally. The participation of students is supported with endowed scholarship funds and the summer jobs of other company members. The company has a mission to serve special populations, like the hearing impaired and the mentally and physically challenged.

Lago Vista Players Youth Drama Workshop (Lago Vista)
http://www.lvplayers.org/Youth%20Drama%20Workshop.htm
Summer Youth Drama Workshops for youths ages eight to eighteen, free to children of company members. The terms are weekly, four days of rehearsals and a performance.

The Magik Theatre Acting and Creativity Academy (San Antonio)
http://www.magiktheatre.org/education/academy.html
Offers classes divided by age and focused on various theater styles. Some work on scenes, some on complete plays (including Shakespeare), and some on cinema, making short films in class.

Plano Children's Theatre (Plano)
http://www.planochildrenstheatre.com
Production classes and skills classes in acting and auditioning, as well as voice. Most twelve-week sessions conclude in performances. In major productions, all-youth casts experience auditions, casting, line memorization, blocking, choreography, props, set building, lighting, costumes, and make-up.

Playhouse 1960 (Houston)
http://www.ph1960.com
Gives kids of all ages a chance to be seen on stage, whether it is their first time or they are experienced actors. No prior experience is needed, and auditions are held at regular intervals throughout the year.

Repertory Company Theatre School of Musical Theatre and Dance (Richardson)
http://rcttheatre.com/Our_School.html
Offers year-round training in theater arts for all ages. Classes and workshops have a strong performance emphasis. Students are trained in theater arts by professionals in the fields. Private studies are available for children ages ten and older.

Second Youth Family Theater (Austin)
http://www.secondyouth.com
Gives each student the knowledge to gain confidence as a performer and to enhance collaborative and social skills. Works as an ensemble to develop a fully staged production from scratch, writing a script and using improvisational techniques.

Trinity Valley Community College Summer Drama Workshop (Athens)
see http://www.campchannel.com/summer-camps/Trinity-Valley-Community-College-Summer-Drama-Workshop-2862.html
An intensive theater camp that affords high school students from all over the state an opportunity to strengthen skills relating either to acting or to technical theater.

Unicorn School of Acting and USA Theatre (La Marque)
http://www.unicornschoolofacting.org
Offers affordable training in stage, film, and television with professional stage and screen personnel. Age groups are eight to eleven and twelve to fifteen. The company also provides educational outreach.

Young Actors Studio & Performing Arts Center (Farmers Branch)
http://www.youngactors.org
A program oriented toward professional training. Fall and spring dramatic performing arts classes cover comedy (scripts and improv), drama (scripts and improv), monologues (comedy and drama), voiceover technique, commercials and characters, cold reading and auditioning technique, character and role development, and green screen technique.

Utah

Children's Theatre and School of the Arts (Salt Lake City)
http://www.tctheatre.org/classesandcamps.html
Teaches drama and movement to children ages six to sixteen in twice-weekly after-school sessions during the traditional school year and summer theater camp sessions. The school's Youth Stage program offers students opportunities to work with professional directors, set designers, costumers,

lighting designers, and stage managers, while receiving more advanced performance training.

Youth Theatre at the U [University of Utah] (Salt Lake City)
http://www.youththeatre.utah.edu
Founded in the 1950s at the University of Utah, one of the first programs to offer theater for children and later by children. Now classes include students ages five through eighteen. Two or three performances each year include student members of the company, members of the community, and University of Utah theater students.

Vermont

Lost Nation Theater (Montpelier)
http://www.lostnationtheater.org/html/get_tickets.htm
A professional theater committed to community that offers a variety of training programs and residencies, including a high school conservatory, a Head Start arts program, Shakespeare workshops ("Will on Wheels"), and master classes.

New England Youth Theatre (Brattleboro)
http://www.sover.net/~stearns/neyt.html
A youth theater founded on the belief that young people can run their own theater with the guidance and assistance of professional adults. Students are exposed to a wide variety of dramatic mediums and exposed to every aspect of theater production, from acting to advertising, choreography to lighting, and direction to design.

Northern Stage Theater Arts Education Program (White River Junction)
http://www.northernstage.org/classes
Offers a theater arts education program that offers challenging classes for young artists from six to eighteen years old to develop their talents in an imaginative and stimulating environment.

Virginia

Appalachian Children's Theater [ACT] (Wise)
http://www.actshine.org
Promotes performing arts opportunities for children and their families of the Appalachian Region of Virginia, Kentucky, and Tennessee. Attempts to reach those groups who are not regularly exposed to live theatrical performances or have opportunities to develop their talent. ACT provides a pro-

fessional theater experience as well as art education for both the audience and the theater participants.

Camp Curtain Call (Dugspur)
http://www.campcurtaincall.com
A coeducational theater camp for children ages seven to eighteen that combines traditional summer camp activities with specialized performing and visual arts programming.

Classika Theatre Family Series (Arlington)
http://www.classika.org
Offers a conservatory-style studio in dramatic and visual arts for children ages four and up. Since its inauguration, more than seven hundred children have enjoyed creative classes in the visual and dramatic arts taught by professional artists.

Encore Stage and Studio (Arlington)
http://www.encorestage.org
Introduces young people to all aspects of theater arts through performances that are for children and by children and educational programs that are held year-round.

The Growing Stage (Purcellville)
http://growingstage.org
Teaches children from ages six to twenty the joys of acting on stage. Summer and fall workshops carry students from initial auditions to opening night.

Hurrah Players (Norfolk)
http://www.hurrahplayers.com
Dedicated to the idea of learning by doing, provides a joyous learning experience for children of all ages. Classes, offered for all age groups and experience levels, include acting, dancing, singing, musical theater, and stagecraft, all of which serve to build artistic and creative skills. This instruction is then translated into a hands-on educational experience through the mounting of four mainstage productions per season. Students have the opportunity to join in these productions.

Mount Vernon Community Children's Theatre [MVCCT] (Alexandria)
http://www.mvcct.org
A nonprofit organization committed to providing opportunities of creative expression to children of all ages through drama education and live theatrical production. MVCCT produces fall, winter, and spring performances and offers a comprehensive summer and spring break drama camp program.

Pied Piper Theatre (Manassas)
http://www.center-for-the-arts.org/piedpiper/
Offers regular-season and summer programs, specializing in musical theater, for children between the ages of eight and eighteen from all socioeconomic backgrounds.

Stage Door Productions (Fredericksburg)
http://www.stagedoorproductions.org
Offers a variety of workshops, classes, and camps throughout the year for children between the ages of four and eighteen. Weeklong summer camps culminate in performance at the end of each week. A scholarship has been established for a participating teenager.

Theatre IV Stage Explorers Camp [The Children's Theatre of Virginia] (Richmond)
http://www.theatreivrichmond.org/stage_exp.html
Offers a summer camp in which children participate. Campers are divided according to grade level and explore acting, singing, design, and other theater-related activities.

Theatrix Productions (Virginia Beach)
http://www.kidspaw.com/KidsteenPAWsummercamp.html
Offers two- to four-week tuition-based summer performing arts camps for children ages six to nineteen that rehearse and prepare full musical productions for public performance. Participants are exposed to and have their hands in virtually every aspect of the production, from helping with costumes and sets to singing, dancing, and acting on stage.

Young Peoples Theatre (Arlington)
http://www.yptnva.com
Gives home-educated students with an interest in acting and theater a chance to polish their skills and showcase their talents. Includes summer camps and an occasional small show.

Washington

Academy of Children's Theatre [ACT] (Richland)
http://www.academyofchildrenstheatre.org
Offers numerous classes for students from three to adult. Troupe is a small touring group formed from high school students; Studio 68 is a weekly

actors' studio for students grades 6 through 8; Repertory is a company in which students learn performing on stage and producing backstage.

Bainbridge Performing Arts Theatre School (Bainbridge Island)
http://www.bainbridgeperformingarts.org/Education/TheatreSchool.html
Numerous year-round classes offered to students of various ages and with different preparation. Outreach matinees are held in public and private schools, and an acting and improvisation workshop is offered for teens. Partial funding and scholarships are offered.

Bellevue Youth Theatre (Bellevue)
see http://www.ci.bellevue.wa.us/bellevue_youth_theatre.htm
Provides young children with the chance to explore the exciting world of theater, performing in a short play designed for their age group. Children learn the basics of theater character and presentation in a relaxed and fun environment. Also offers basic and advanced technical theater camps.

Broadway Bound Children's Theatre (Seattle)
http://www.broadwaybound.org
A transforming experience for children ages five to eighteen. Serves children of all experience levels and from all backgrounds. Challenges children to develop their mental, physical, emotional, social, and creative potentials.

Central Stage Theatre of County Kitsap (Silverdale)
http://www.cstock.org
Offers productions and workshops to students of various ages with different interests and abilities. Younger children are linked to a Director in Training program for older students, who learn essential theater management and theater production skills, including staging and blocking, choreography, music direction, set and costume design, and stage managing. In addition, a youth committee helps to sustain the various theater activities and liaisons with the adult company.

Columbia Gorge School of Theatre (White Salmon)
http://www.cgst.com/index.htm
A summer theater camp for children ages eight to eighteen. Students from around the world study acting, music, singing, dance, voice, TV/film acting, body awareness, theater potpourri, and the business of theater; perform in shows; and enjoy outdoor activities on the 142-acre Blue Moon Ranch with professionals from all over the country.

Creative Theatre Experience [CTE] (Olympia)
http://www.creativetheatre.org

A nonprofit children's theater that offers workshops in theater and the other arts, culminating in great stage productions. CTE promotes creativity, builds important life skills, and provides leadership opportunities for children and youth ages five to twenty-one.

KIDS AT PLAY [Capital Playhouse] (Olympia)
http://www.capitalplayhouse.com
A comprehensive musical theater and performance program using a summer stock model, with an enrollment of 350 students between the ages of eight and eighteen who are interested in expanding their performance skills and involving themselves in classes for dance, drama, voice, and technical theater.

KIDSTAGE [Village Theatre] (Issaquah)
http://www.villagetheatre.org/kidstage.shtml
A professional musical theater company with a year-round education program for ages three through twenty. Production programs include Company Originals, in which students collaborate in a workshop process with professional writers, composers, and lyricists to create original material. Students seeking behind-the-scenes experience are involved in a special program of orchestral performance, direction, design, or management. A Summer Independent program offers every aspect of training as an entry point to professional theater.

Lakewood Youth Theater (Lakewood)
http://www.lakewoodplayhouse.org/youth.html
Offers performance-based programs designed to immerse students ages seven to eighteen in a total theater experience. During the classes and workshops, young actors explore all facets of theater through the rehearsal and public performance of each story. All productions offer exciting opportunities for both actors and actresses, and provide a chance for both beginning and experienced students of theater.

Queer Teen Ensemble Theatre [Washington Ensemble Theatre] (Seattle)
http://www.washingtonensemble.org/qtet/
An educational outreach program giving voice and artistry to LGBT youth in the Seattle community. Teens work with Washington Ensemble Theatre members to explore their perspectives onstage in the creation of a new play.

Rainier Valley Youth Theatre (Seattle)
http://www.seedseattle.org/seedarts/rvyt.html
Offers arts and theater training for children at all levels of experience, led by professional artist educators and featuring a unique multi-cultural ap-

proach. The SummerARTS program features camps for elementary and middle school students and an acclaimed SummerSTAGE production for students age fourteen to twenty-one.

Seattle Children's Theatre (Seattle)
http://www.sct.org/classes/
Strives to enhance mainstage experience and provide theater education and theater arts training. Taught by professional artists through anticipatory experiences for young people. Through diverse programming, children have the opportunity to experience all aspects of the theater arts.

Seattle Playhouse for Young Performing Artists (Seattle)
http://www.seattleplayhouse.org
Provides an artistically sound and emotionally safe environment for students to learn the varied crafts of musical theater and experience performance opportunities.

Studio East (Kirkland)
http://www.studio-east.org
In addition to musical fairy tales performed by adults for young children, a program for children in theater, music, and dance. Courses are offered during the academic year and summer to enrolled and homeschooled students. Camps are smorgasbords of classes, such as musical theater, dance, stage combat, clowning, and audition technique.

Whidbey Children's Theater (Langley)
http://www.whidbey.com/wct/index.html
A children's theater program that gives children the opportunity to feel the excitement of live stage performances. Classes are offered for young players and for teens and youth. Special programs include Theater for Young Audiences and mentorship for children and teens.

Youth Theatre Northwest (Mercer Island)
http://www.youththeatre.org
A program that nurtures the intellectual, artistic, and personal development of children and youth through drama education, performing opportunities, and live theatre experiences. A wide range of classes and programs provides theatrical learning experiences for children age three to eighteen.

West Virginia

The Children's Theatre of Charleston (Charleston)
http://www.ctoc.org

Has educated children about the theater since 1932. Children are given an opportunity to learn and thrive by participating in plays, performing on stage or in important backstage roles.

Ice House Youth Theater (Berkeley Springs)
http://www.macicehouse.org/iht.html
During the school year, courses and workshops including creative dramatics and playwriting. During the summer, theater camp with a full production for a‍ s five to seventeen.

Morgantown Theatre Company (Morgantown)
http://www.morgantowntheatrecompany.org
A community theater company that provides children from six to eighteen years of age with the opportunity to participate in theater through classes, workshops, and full-scale productions. Students are involved in acting, directing, singing, dancing, lighting, sound effects, set and prop design and construction, fund-raising, publicity, makeup, stage crew, and stage management. Offers weekly classes for very young children as well as a summer camp.

Wisconsin

African American Children's Theatre (Milwaukee)
http://www.aact.us
Founded in 1989 to showcase African American writers, culture, and history in response to incidents of racial violence. Children explore the connections and similarities of a variety of cultures and traditions. Training is offered in basic acting skills, movement skills, singing, and music. A Youth Leadership Development Program is offered to students eight to eighteen. An Academy for Theatre Training, a four-week intensive theater experience, is required of students prior to auditioning for productions.

Central Wisconsin Children's Theatre (Wausau)
http://www.madstage.com/Companies/CWCT.html
A child/youth organization dedicated to education through dramatic arts, including the acting, theatrical, and managerial aspects of dramatic production.

Eau Claire Children's Theatre (Eau Claire)
http://www.ecct.org
A nonprofit, volunteer-driven community theater providing quality theatrical and educational experiences for western Wisconsin residents of all ages. ECCT provides opportunities for community members to participate in various phases of children's theater work, fosters an interest in the arts in

children through the viewing of and participation in theatrical productions, and promotes related activities such as storytelling, puppetry, and dance through workshops and performances.

First Stage Children's Theater (Milwaukee)
http://www.firststage.org
Offers a professional theater experience for young people and their families, including the Theater Academy, which teaches "life skills through stage skills" and has become a theater training school. More than two thousand students between the ages of two and eighteen participate in the program each year. The most advanced students—the Young Company—perform three shows each year.

Harand Camp (Kenosha)
http://www.harandcamp.com
A summer camp program that provides children ages eight to seventeen with a specialized musical theater program.

Madison Creative Arts Program (Madison)
http://www.madcap.org
In addition to theater for young audiences, includes performance ensembles and musical theater productions. Students take private weekly voice lessons, and during the school year, professional teaching artists work as a team to guide an ensemble of students in producing, rehearsing, and performing in plays, musicals, and concerts. Ensembles are open enrollment so that young people may find a place to develop their talents regardless of their experience.

Milwaukee Youth Theatre (Milwaukee)
http://www.milwaukeeyouththeatre.org
Involves children in all aspects of performances—not only acting but playwriting, sound, and stage management. Workshops and classes are tailored to specific age groups and often end with a performance.

Playtime Productions Children's Theatre (Mount Horeb)
http://www.playtimeproductions.org/cast.htm
A children's theater that includes twenty-five to thirty children from grade 3 through high school from many area communities and with varying interests and talents. For many, this is their first experience in theater. The unchanging objective is to give children a solid theater grounding. Not only do these young performers act, sing, and dance, they gain experience in all aspects of the production, from putting on their own makeup, caring for costumes and props, and loading in the sets.

SpotLight on Kids (Janesville)
http://www.spotlightonkids.org
Focuses on educating children and teens in the performing arts through classes, workshops, productions, and performances. School productions for local students are cast entirely with children so that young people are bringing live theater to other young people.

Young Shakespeare Players (Madison)
http://www.ysp.org
A children's theater program in which the children provide the theater. The program, in which young people perform full-length works of Shakespeare, is now over twenty-five years old, older than our actors who range in age from seven to eighteen years old. There are no auditions. Any child of the right age may take part simply by registering. Every young participant receives one or more speaking roles.

Zona Gale Youth Theater (Portage)
http://www.portagecenterforthearts.com/zgypt.html
Offers a Children's Theatre Workshop (theater games and scenes for young beginners), a Youth Theatre Workshop (classes tied to Shakespeare productions at the American Players Theatre), and Youth Theatre Productions (full-scale auditions, rehearsals, and performances, sometimes include adults). Productions are often centered on themes with social importance.

Wyoming

Casper Children's Theatre (Casper)
http://www.casperchildrenstheatre.com
A children's theater dedicated to providing training and diverse performance opportunities in the theatrical arts for youth ages four to seventeen in addition to producing quality live theatrical performances for family audiences.

CANADA

Alberta

Calgary Young People's Theatre (Calgary)
http://www.cypt.ca
A nonprofit charitable association dedicated to creativity and teamwork in young people. The caliber of instruction is professional, with classes ranging from introductory to advanced performance levels. Special programs with different goals include preschool classes and improvisation. Annual

Drumma classes create plays out of African drumming. Story Theatre visits Calgary public libraries. There is a strong emphasis on Shakespeare, including two-week summer classes that produce adaptations of the plays. Offerings include fall, winter, and spring classes as well as an extensive summer camp program, and are available to children of all walks of life and families with limited income.

Canadian Badlands Performing Arts Summer School (Drumheller)
http://www.cbsummerschool.com
A performing arts summer school that offers high school credit for choral work, dance, and the philosophy of performance. Students work with educators and professionals from colleges, theaters, and drama troupes, and they perform in the "Canadian Badlands Passion Play."

British Columbia

Carousel Theatre Company (Vancouver)
http://www.carouseltheatre.ca
A theater school program that includes more than eighty students each semester in various classes for ages three to seventeen. Each session includes a theater school showcase. Private instruction is available.

Drama Jockey Association: Enoch Drama Lab (Vancouver)
http://www.dramajockey.com
A Chinese-produced theater company for young people. Theater activity includes layout, script writing, dramatic interpretation, stage design, clothing style, and lighting effects.

Movimento! (Victoria)
http://www.earlydance.org
Offers dance and theater classes, including sixteenth- and seventeenth-century court dance and commedia dell'arte movement techniques, for children and adults.

Ontario

Canadian Children's Theatre Company (Aurora)
http://www.childrenstheatre.ca
Offers a wide array of children's theater programs from Pre-School Players (ages three and four) to Showtime for Teens (ages thirteen to eighteen). In addition, summer camps are available, including clowning, magic, movement, music, puppetry, mask, and basic acting instruction, as well as participation in theater games and production crafts. There are also year-round performance workshops.

Centauri Summer Arts Camp (Wellandport)
http://www.centauri.on.ca
A summer camp program for boys and girls ages nine to eighteen that offers a choice of more than thirty arts specialty programs, including theater, acting skills, Shakespeare performance, acting for the camera, television production, musical theater, comedy improv, ballet, and jazz.

Children's Arts Theatre School [CATS] (Toronto)
http://catsdrama.com/
Offers classes for students of different ages and abilities in improvisational training, trust-forming theater games, group improvisation, thinking processes, concentration, and self-confidence. Includes classes and summer camps.

The Children's Theater Project (Richmond Hill)
http://www.childrenstheatreproject.com
High-caliber theater training in a bright and clean environment, taught by dedicated and trained professionals. The focus is on the tools of the dramatic arts, offering different classes to students who wish to study drama at all different levels. Through the dramatic arts children can develop self-esteem, confidence, and self-discipline, which can prepare them for a successful future in any given profession.

Great Big Theatre Company (Dundas)
http://www.gbtc.com/index.shtml
A community-based children's theater company whose goal is to produce professional-quality performances of classic and contemporary children's theater productions. The objective is the enjoyment of family audiences as well as school groups and community organizations and also the advancement of drama education for children and teens by providing educational programs for young people of all ages.

Lorraine Kimsa Theatre for Young People (Toronto)
http://www.lktyp.ca/en/drama/index.cfm
Aims to stimulate the imagination, promote self-expression, and develop self-confidence. The drama school offers junior (grades JK to 6) and senior (grades 7 to 12) classes as well as the Ensemble, which performs mainstage.

Markham Youth Theatre (Markham)
http://markhamyouththeatre.wordpress.com
A nonprofit community group established to give young people the opportunity to focus their talents and aspirations in the fields of acting, pro-

duction, and musical and technical theater. The company is organized by youth in the area.

Original Kids Theatre Company (London)

http://www.oktc.ca

Includes Senior and Junior Theatre Kids Companies that perform and conduct discussion sessions for school groups. A Kidlets program, offered through year and in the summer, explores self-expression and creativity through music, movement, drama, and art.

Sudbury Theatre Centre (Sudbury)

http://www.sudburytheatre.on.ca/content/youth-drama

Classes include Discovery (ages eight to eleven) and Development (ages twelve to fifteen). Students from grades 4 to grade 11 may audition for Students on Stage, a special program where students learn all about producing a play while rehearsing a production.

Theatre Aquarius Classic Kids (Hamilton)

http://www.theatreaquarius.org/TheatreSchool/index.html

A training ground for young actors, singers, and dancers. The program is designed to develop theatrical communication skills and life skills as a means of fostering self-expression. Individuals explore their creative imagination and challenge their critical thinking process while achieving a higher level of self-confidence and self-discipline.

TheatreKids (Toronto)

see http://www.harbourfrontcentre.com/Camps/Summer_listing.cfm?id=64

A summer program created for campers who love being in the spotlight, explores the world of theater in a relaxed, hands-on environment. Working with their director, campers learn aspects of performance and theater production while rehearsing, preparing, and presenting their own show for friends and families. Special guests are brought in when available to showcase aspects of drama or stage production.

Manitoba

Manitoba Theatre for Young People (Winnipeg)

http://www.mtyp.ca

A large professional children's theater company, offering nine plays in the professional season; provincial, national, and international touring productions; and classes throughout the year, including eight weeks of intensive theater camps in the summer. Students learn fundamental theater performance techniques, as well as such related disciplines as moviemaking, animation, puppetry, musical theater, and acting for the camera. An integral part of the theater school is the Young Company, a pre-professional program for highly motivated teens. A distinctive feature of the program is a play development program for students, operated in cooperation with the Manitoba Association of Playwrights, in which playwrights work with a professional dramaturge, a professional director, and student actors. MTYP also offers a "drama residency" for elementary schools. In support of the Manitoba community, MTYP offers free acting, performing and film training classes to four hundred young people through the Aboriginal Arts Training and Mentorship Program.

Winnipeg Jewish Theater (Winnipeg)
http://www.wjt.ca/outreach/
Provides theater training to Winnipeg youth who may not have had the opportunity to become involved in professional theater. The goal of this program is to help local youth between the ages of sixteen and twenty-four secure some experience in the theater. Many of the students who apprentice with WJT go on to work at larger theater companies.

Quebec

SaBooge Theatre Company (Brooklyn, New York, and Montreal, Quebec)
http://www.sabooge.com/teaching/teaching.shtml
Dedicated to providing theater training and experience to students of all ages through workshops, summer arts camps, in-school programming, university residencies, and community initiatives. With instructors and artists from around the globe, SaBooge's education program draws on their experience with circus arts, mask, music, puppetry, and movement to create in-depth programming at all levels of experience.

Saskatchewan

The Improv Camp (Regina)
http://www.improv.ca/camp/
Uses improvisation as a learning tool to foster skills such as positivity, leadership, commitment, and teamwork. An exciting experience for any high school student who enjoys the art of improvisational theater and also a place for those recent graduates to expand their skills in the Leadership Program.

Appendix C: Programs and Companies: International

This list contains programs and companies throughout the world, along with some basic details for each. Further information may be obtained by visiting the Web sites provided. This list will be revised and amended as needed, so please visit http://www.childrenstheaterinfo.com for periodic updates. If you wish to suggest additional sites, please send your recommendations to us at ctsurvey2@aol.com.

ASIA

India

Association for Nascent Art and Natural Theatre [ANANT] (New Delhi)
http://www.anantindia.org
Creates in children's theater a space for wide and rich exposure, capacity enhancement, self-learning and realization, and a platform for self-expression. In 1999 the management and running of the group was taken over by a group of young people. From the beginning ANANT has been conscious of the need to include the disadvantaged—mentally, physically, economically, and socially—within this space.

Evam Youth Forum [The Company Theatre] (Bangalore)
http://www.thecompanytheatre.net/youthforumnew.htm
Conceived as an initiative toward creating a vibrant and thriving culture of theater among youth across India, seeks to bring together talented, commit-

ted, and hardworking young artists and provide them with opportunities and a platform to explore their art further and produce exciting new theater.

International Children's Festival of Performing Arts (New Delhi)
http://www.ryanicfpa.com
Participants prepare a twenty-five- to thirty-minute performance and a folk dance from their native country. They also wear native folk costumes at the opening and closing ceremonies.

International Children's Theatre Festival [National Institute of Performing Arts] (New Delhi)
http://www.nipaindia.com/event_delhi.html
An annual festival for children between the ages of eight and fourteen. Includes interactive sessions, cultural ceremonies, and folk and traditional dances.

Little Theatre in Chennai
see http://www.asiarooms.com/travel-guide/india/chennai/things-to-do-in-chennai/theatres-and-entertainment-centres-in-chennai/little-theatre-in-chennai.html
Focuses on the creative talent of the children by guiding them into theater. Workshops are conducted by professionals in dance, drama, arts and crafts, mime, music, poetry, puppetry, magic, and photography. Children between the ages of five and fourteen are enrolled, and scholarships are afforded to the underprivileged.

Mazhavillu [Lokadharmi Theatre] (Tripunithura)
http://lokadharmi.org
A group of about forty children ages ten to seventeen, assembling under "the tree of theater" for improvisation, games, play readings, and other theater activities.

Indonesia

Teater Tanah Air (Jakarta)
http://teatertanahair.org/en/home
Introduces about one hundred children to their multiple cultural backgrounds through modern dance, acting, and poetry. This company has extensive international experience.

Malaysia

The Academy [The Actors Studio] (Kuala Lumpur)
http://www.theactorsstudio.com.my/the-academy/

Focuses on training and nurturing of children as young as three. One objective is to encourage public participation in all aspects of performing arts regardless of race, class, or creed. The Academy works with children with special needs, shelter homes, schools, the disabled, and the deaf.

Philippines

Preda Akbay Advocacy Theater Group (Olongapo City)
http://www.preda.org/work/akbay/theatergroup.html
Advocates the rights of the children and youth empowerment, raising the consciousness of the general public regarding social issues confronting the children and youth, using theater as an effective tool. Young people enhance their talents as playwrights, stage directors, performers, visual artists, singers, musicians, dancers, choreographers, youth facilitators, community organizers, stage technicians, and production managers through a series of training and participatory artistic interactions. The company carries its mission worldwide.

Singapore

Act Three International (Singapore)
http://www.act3international.com.sg
An arts company that believes in an all-around learning environment. Projects are commissioned in private and public sectors that marry the arts with the environment, heritage, and culture. This unique position allows the company to give children a valuable experience of learning through the arts. The ACT 3 drama syllabus is a series of planned, related learning activity modules, in classes for children from ages eighteen months to fifteen years.

Centre Stage School of the Arts (Singapore City)
http://www.centre-stage.com
Offers drama, art, and creative programs for students from eighteen months to adult: parent and toddler, art and craft, and drama classes for children as well as acting, speech and drama, voice, and art classes for adults and tailor-made classes for both teenagers and adults.

Sri Lanka

Lanka Children's and Youth Theatre Organisation (Kotte)
http://www.playhousekotte.org
A training program in drama and theater offered free of charge to youth who are committed to studying drama and theater. The program entails

acting, script writing, directing, movement, and vocal training, as well as training with practical application in designing stage sets and props, costume designing, designing stage lighting, training in stage management, and sound effects.

AUSTRALIA AND NEW ZEALAND

Australia

Australian Theatre for Young People (Walsh Bay, New South Wales)
http://www.atyp.com.au
In collaboration with professional artists, reaches over six thousand young Australians each year through a diverse program of workshops and productions. Programs are offered in remote regions, and scholarships are available. A "Fresh Ink" program identifies, nurtures, and spotlights the next generation of Australian writers.

Canberra Youth Theatre [CYT] (Braddon, Australian Capital Territory)
http://www.cytc.net
Established in 1972, the longest standing youth theater in Australia. Workshops, projects, and productions provide training and performance opportunities for young people aged six to twenty-five years. Working with local and interstate professional artists and arts workers, students explore, extend, and develop their creativity. CYT is committed to supporting emerging artists. Young people unleash their imaginations and create engaging and challenging theater.

The Glenwood Shakespeare Company [GSC] (Casula, New South Wales)
http://www.glenwoodshakespeare.com
A primary and secondary school Shakespeare company specializing in student and amateur film and theatrical productions with current and former students and staff. This company opens up opportunities for young talent to find itself through theater and filmmaking, introducing the excitement and agelessness of Shakespeare to young people by having them perform it. In this enterprise, GSC is associated with a public school. The focus is now on filmmaking, with students writing, shooting, and editing their own productions. Glenwood was instrumental in bringing about a new film festival for young people: Trop Jr., an addition to Tropfest, the world's largest short film festival. The production schedule for Glenwood is remarkably heavy, with at least a half dozen projects of different kinds in various stages of completion at any given time.

Helen O'Grady Children's Drama Academy (Perth, Western Australia)
http://www.helenogrady.com.au
Offers students ages five to seventeen a broad curriculum in drama. Teachers are specially trained in the O'Grady curriculum and teaching methods. Established in Perth, it has organized 150 franchised branches and more than one thousand locations around the world.

Mayte Youth Theatre (Ballarat, Victoria)
http://home.vicnet.net.au/~mayte/
A group run by young people, for young people, to improve their access to and involvement in the performing arts through theater productions and drama workshops.

Point Break Drama Acting School (Dee Why, New South Wales)
http://www.pointbreakdrama.com.au
Offers short courses in acting for the camera and stage. A variety of classes taught by professional actors provide students with the fundamentals of acting in an enjoyable, sociable, and relaxed environment.

The Riverland Youth Theatre (Renmark, South Australia)
http://www.ryt.org.au
Offers workshops for creative expression, workshops in theater sports, and a summer camp.

St Martins Youth Arts Centre (Stonnington, Victoria)
http://www.stmartinsyouth.com.au
Classes offered by leading theater professionals to young performers from beginners to experienced, ages five to twenty-five. Workshops include puppetry, playwriting, and acting techniques for television and film. The "Creative Ensemble" focuses on various areas of playmaking, including writing, clowning, physical theater, movement, and improvisation. The "Performer's Ensemble" is a select group of twelve performers enrolled in intensive technique and production.

Shopfront (Carlton, New South Wales, Australia)
http://www.shopfront.org.au
A youth theater with an international reputation for producing outstanding performances by young and emerging artists up to age twenty-five. Projects embrace hybrid arts, technology, and an immersive approach to performance in community.

SHY (Seen and Heard Youth) Inc. (Perth, Western Australia)
see http://www.geocities.com/shytheatre/

An independent arts organization operated for and by past and present students and staff of John Forrest Senior High School.

Urban Myth Theatre of Youth (Unley, South Australia)
http://www.urbanmyth.asn.au/home.php
Offers a number of workshops and performance groups for children as well as adults. The history of the Workshop Program reflects a commitment to giving young people the opportunity to express their culture to their peers through performance and skills development. Tutors provide professional exchange between artists and the youth membership, as well as an issue-based approach to programming.

Western Australian Youth Theatre Company (Perth, Western Australia)
http://www.wayouththeatre.org.au
Provides young, enthusiastic artists with the opportunity to work with arts industry professionals in theater. Cast and crew members from twelve to twenty-five years of age are encouraged to develop their rehearsal and performance skills through workshop programs and the presentation of major dramatic works to the public.

New Zealand

Calico Young People's Theatre (Napier)
http://www.calicotheatre.org.nz
Aims to produce outstanding professional theater for young audiences and to provide young people aged from five to fifteen with opportunities to participate in theater productions—as performers, behind the scenes and creating their own shows. Calico develops large-cast productions for young performers (suitable for 30 to 250 actors), typically teaming the young participants with professional theater artists. After several years devoted to developing productions in partnership with schools throughout New Zealand, Calico plans to broaden its hometown base with school holiday shows, a children's theater school, and community productions.

National Youth Drama School (Napier)
http://www.nyds.co.nz
An annual program that provides professional tuition of the highest standard in theater, dance/movement, singing, technical, and film disciplines to fifteen- to twenty-year-olds.

National Youth Theatre Company (Auckland)
http://www.nytc.co.nz
Offers young people aged five to twenty-one the opportunity to participate in ongoing performing arts training through workshops, courses, and holi-

day programs. Through the On Stage program, up to 220 children at a time participate in two full-scale musical productions every year.

EUROPE

Armenia

National Centre of Aesthetics (Yerevan)
http://www.pokr-tatron.com/eng/index.html
Offers primary education in dramatic arts to students aged six to fifteen, most of whom have chosen acting as a profession. Subjects studied include acting, stage speech, stage action, and classical dance. This company has participated in several international festivals.

Austria

ICHDUWIR—Theater & Kultur (Vienna)
http://www.ichduwir.at
Introduces individual students to creative expression through theater. Theater courses, workshops, broad cultural activities, and networking expand this mission. The curriculum is structured progressively. The youngest group (three to six years) acts as students play, on impulse; the basic group (seven to ten years) translates impulses into stories for the audience; Basis Aufbau (nine to twelve years) uses drama techniques to find a message and make a story interesting to an audience; Off Off Aufbau (thirteen to seventeen years) begins training with literary plays; and Off Off Theater (fifteen to nineteen years) offers different techniques and puts on a full production. In this process, students learn the value of hard work and collaboration as they discover the fascination of theater. The philosophy and methodology of the company are conveyed in its name, which speaks for children's theater worldwide: "ICH erzahle Dir vom Land der Phantasie" (I will show you something about the wide spaces of imagination); "DU wirst neugierig und kommst naher" (YOU will be nosy and come closer); "WIR erleben gemeinsam die tollsten Abenteur" (WE will undertake great adventures together).

Belgium

BRONKS theater voor kinderen en jongeren (Brussels)
http://www.bronks.be
Founded in 1991 as high-quality theater for youth to produce and perform. Adults are encouraged to serve as mentors, and the educational mission extends to schools to provide education in theater. The company tours, and there is a yearly festival in Brussels, offering a mix of theater productions and multimedia workshops.

Hetpaleis (Antwerp)
http://www.hetpaleis.be
A theater for school children and young people between four and eighteen. Performances are accompanied by theater workshops. An "Ambassador Project" involving people of various nationalities serves as liaison between the theater and the communities of Flanders, addressing the issue of Dutch language and culture for a diverse population. Its Web site is an interactive platform for information and debate on social causes and activities.

Jeugdtoneel Binnenstebuiten (Wetteren)
http://www.toneelbinnenstebuiten.org
Celebrating twenty years, with a dozen productions each year from a cast and crew ages ten to eighteen. Volunteers are encouraged to enlist as crew.

Jonna Toneelschool (Wilsele)
http://www.jonnatoneelschool.be
A group that has grown, over the past three decades, from a small youth club to a creative center of artistic talents. Not only the drama school but also "Crea-atelier" gives younger children the chance to be creative and learn about aesthetics, crafts, and art. In addition, Jonna offers schools and youth clubs a variety of workshops, plays, and projects. Learning is informal, and classes are open to all students, regardless of their experience. Classes are progressive, structured by age. Students nine through eleven learn to be creative with improvised or written texts, movement, music, decor, and costumes. For those who like to learn to sing, dance, and act, there is a special musical group. After age twelve, students are offered an intensified approach to theater, working on attitude, movement, verbal skills, and imagination, experimenting with different kinds of texts and styles. From ages fifteen to seventeen, students work on bigger projects: a longer piece, sometimes newly created especially for the group, is developed entirely by the students. A distinctive feature of the program is street theater for students twelve and older. Jonna has also built an international reputation by participating in festivals and seminars, since 2003 hosting a biannual international theater program.

tekkel attak (Limburg)
http://www.tekkelattak.be
A platform for youth theater including approximately fifteen groups. Sponsored activities include theater camps and workshops.

Czech Republic

Divadelní soubor HOP-HOP (Ostrov)
http://www.zusostrov.cz/hophop/aktualne-cs.html

Part of a Basic School of the Arts, cooperating with other schools throughout Europe. Dramatic play and improvisation stimulate and enhance not only speech and expression skills but imagination, creativity, cultivated movement, communication skills, courage to speak in public, and ability to deal with various interpersonal situations.

Denmark

Dramaverkstadid (Faroe Islands)
http://heima.olivant.fo/~hjck/enindex.htm
Develops and strengthens students through the learning of different skills, giving them insight and experience within the drama/theater environment. Five groups range from age nine to thirty.

Finland

Lokki—Annantalo Arts Centre (Helsinki)
see http://www.finnguide.com/events/events.asp?c=12&p=4496&m=4&y=2009&b=1&o=50
A company of children who begin theater and dance instruction at five to seven years of age and form a goal-oriented youth theater at twelve to fifteen years. The company participates in international training and festivals.

France

Compagnie Légitime Folie (Rennes)
http://www.legitime-folie.fr/
Founded in 1993 as the first children's theater company in the region, launched on the idea of involving the child in the creative process as an artist in full. Its core competencies include acting, choreography, song and voice, and writing. Its hallmark is multidisciplinary exchange and research.

English Children's Theatre (Paris)
http://englishchildrenstheatre.cabanova.com
Offers theater courses in English for children ages four to seventeen. Native and nonnative speakers are welcomed. Classes include theater and musical theater, and individual instruction is offered. Instructors include professional American directors and performers.

Festival International de Théâtre d'Enfants et de Théâtre Jeunes (Toulouse)
http://lefite.free.fr/siteweb/accueilfite.htm
An annual festival that began in 1987. Participants range in age from seven to thirteen; one-third are from the Toulouse region, one-third from

elsewhere in France, and one-third from abroad. Encourages theatrical research and sponsors classes for theater students and teachers not only in theatrical skills but in civic values.

Germany

Children's Theatre Burattino (Stollberg)
http://www.kindertheater-burattino.de
Established in 1962, provides classes and productions mainly for children aged eight to twelve (but also ad hoc instruction for older students and teachers). The basics of instruction include improvisational training, role-playing, stage fighting, and more. Since 1999, a research group has participated annually.

Consol Theater (Gelsenkirchen)
http://www.consoltheater.de
A theater that offers performances for children as well as instruction in theater skills. Children of different ages participate with adults in different plays. Classes include critical reflections on the productions, planned together with local teachers. The company participates in national and international festivals.

Dachtheater (Freital)
http://www.dachtheater-freital.de
A theatrical club that includes members aged ten to fifty years. Many continue in professional theater. Guest performances are offered in nearby theaters and theater festivals.

Die Bluncky-Kids (Berlin)
http://www.bluncky-kids.de
A children's musical theater group for children between six and twelve years of age, founded in 1994. Projects are often based on children's books, with added lyrics and music.

Die Maske—Amateurtheater Wiesloch e. V. (Mühlhausen)
http://www.theater-diemaske.de/portrait/ueber_uns/ueber_uns.shtml
A children's group—"The Little Mask"—with twenty-five boys and girls of primary school age. Theater exercises focus on movement, expression, voice, and speech, and a new play is presented each year.

Die SCHOTTE (Erfurt)
http://www.theater-die-schotte.de
Extensive instruction and experimentation the forms of theater for groups under and over sixteen: a concept of theater that includes street theater,

improvisation, clowning, and Mitspieltheater (audience involvement). The vision is creative potential and individuality without borders.

Düsseldorfer Kinder- und Jugendtheater (Düsseldorf)
http://www.volldastheater.de
An extensive curriculum, from elementary instruction to production. Teachers are involved in the process, and there are independent theater activities for children, including theater laboratories and reviews.

Fundus Theater (Hamburg)
http://www.fundus-theater.de/index.php
Affords children from age four to ten the full scope of drama—puppet, music, film, and visual arts. Cooperates with teachers in partner schools and with visiting productions from Germany and abroad. In collaboration with PROFUND Children's Theater Association of Hamburg, explores the research implications of children's theater.

GRIPS Theater (Berlin)
http://www.grips-theater.de
A children's theater founded in the sixties that challenges young audiences with nontraditional, serious subjects and themes. Includes Banda Agita, a youth club with its own program of productions.

Kinder- und Jugendtheater (Bad Segeberg, Schleswig-Holstein)
http://www.kindertheater-sh.de
Offers a variety of courses to children on elements of theater production and performance. There are special courses in physical rhythm, theater optics (black stage), and spontaneous theater.

Kinder- und Jugendtheater Murkelbühne (Berlin)
http://www.murkelbuehne.de
Offers a broad variety of courses for children of different ages, from four through twenty years old. Performances include classical and original plays. Hosts regional and European workshops.

Kinder- und Jugendtheater Spielwerkstatt (Berlin)
http://www.spielwerkstatt-berlin.de
Theater for, with, and by children, from scenework to reflection on the nature of theater in the schools. Performances involve improvisation and participation of the audience.

Kinder- und Jugendtheater Wuppertal (Wuppertal)
http://www.kinder-jugendtheater.de

A children's and youth theater that offers workshops and productions, featuring classes for children of all ages.

Kolpingjugendtheater (Kempten)
http://www.kolpingjugendtheater.de
A theater specializing in children's musicals and fairy-tale theater. The productions use original music, and members of the company are involved in costuming, stage construction, engineering, advertising, and makeup. The company is made up of children and adolescents, but adults who remain "a bit romantic" are included.

Theater an der Parkaue (Berlin)
http://www.parkaue.de
Contributes to cultural education by offering children and young people opportunities as audiences and actors, including theater clubs, workshops, and a Winter Academy.

Theater Dortmund (Dortmund)
http://www.theaterdo.de/kontakt.php?menu=619
Offers theater and classes to two groups of children, five to twelve and thirteen and older. Workshops include opera and backstage. Classes in applied practice are also provided to teachers.

Theater Stolperdraht (Schwedt)
http://home.arcor.de/stolperdraht/homepage.htm
Includes various children's theater groups: a Kindertheatergruppe (ages seven through fifteen), a Schauspielensemble (fourteen and older), a Karnevalsklub (teenagers and adults), and a Mädchentanzgruppensemble dance group for girls ages fourteen to twenty.

Theatrium Leipzig (Leipzig)
http://www.theatrium-leipzig.de
Offers children ages eight and older the opportunity to participate in the drama and also theater projects and exercises, such as clowning and improvisation. Broad social values are stressed, and disadvantaged students are welcomed.

Italy

Alcantara (Rimini)
http://www.alcantarateatroragazzi.it
Children six to sixteen receive academic instruction and practical training through theater classes and productions. Special laboratories fill out the

curriculum, and opportunities are afforded students who are disabled emotionally and socially.

Casa del Teatro Ragazzi e Giovani (Turín)
http://www.casateatroragazzi.it/corsi/corsi.htm
The historic company of the Teatro Turin-Boys. It includes a circuit regional youth theater, the Children's Theater Project, and Young Piedmont.

Company Teatrale Salamander (Savona)
http://www.salamander.it
Established as part of the International Connections Program, collaborates with the National Theatre of London, the Theatre of the Limonaia of Florence, and the Litta Theatre of Milan in engaging students as actors and extending theater to the schools.

Etoile Centro Teatrale (Reggio Emilia)
http://www.centroetoile.eu/scuolateatro.htm
Includes a children's course (for students age five through twelve) and a school with a particular focus on diction, improvisation, movement, scene design, and text study.

Fondazione Aida (Verona)
http://www.f-aida.it
Offers theater courses and workshops for children of all ages. Associated with many children's theater companies, and has a strong concern about the civic value of theater.

Ortoteatro (Pordenone)
http://www.ortoteatro.it
Offers a variety of beginning and advanced theater laboratories for children.

Quellidigrock (Milan)
http://www.quellidigrock.it
Offers hundreds of students a varied range of courses: acting, singing, diction, and dubbing and theater classes for teens, seminars and workshops theater for the schools.

Teatro Città Murata: L'Alfabeto del Teatro (Lake Como)
http://www.cittamurata.it
A theater school for children and young people divided into two courses, one for children ages six to ten years and the other for ages eleven to fourteen.

Teatro del Sottosuolo (Carbonia, Sardinia)
http://www.teatrodelsottosuolo.it/La_Scuola/la_scuola.html
A theater school aimed at young people who want to study theatrical arts in a serious and professional way, with a view toward a possible career in theater. Two courses are offered, for basic and advanced students.

Terrammare Teatro (Presicce)
http://www.terrammareteatro.com/laboratori/scuolateatro.htm
A company that produces theater productions and offers a theater school for children and youth.

The Netherlands

Kindertheater Kleine Kees (Huissen)
http://www.kleine-kees.nl
Puts on an annual professional-looking production, played by a cast of thirty children from eight to thirteen years of age, complete with singing and dancing.

Kindertheaterschool/Kids with Attitude (Heiloo)
http://www.kidswithattitude.nl
Offers voice, dance, and acting lessons to children ages four to eleven. Participants perform musicals and "movicals" (movie/musicals that include previously recorded footage).

Peeperklips (Rucphen)
http://www.peeperklips.nlrama
Productions by youth from twelve to sixteen years of age.

Theater Spot (Rijswijk)
http://www.theatergroepspot.nl
Theater by older youth, centering on a major musical production each year.

Toneelgroep Jeugdpodium (Bussum)
http://www.jeugdpodium.nl/elckersite/section1.php?sub=Informatie&maandnr=
Provides children and youth between four and eighteen years of age opportunities for personal, social, and artistic development through theater. The groups are formed by ability level in basic classes, advanced courses, and production groups. Children under age four participate in a "Play House" program.

Norway

Den Unge Scenen [DUS] (Oslo)

http://www.dus.as

A project for children age thirteen to nineteen, aimed at strengthening youth theater in Norway. DUS has a network of ten theatrical institutions around the country.

Romania

Andantino (Bucharest)

http://www.andantino.ro

Features performances by children ages seven to twelve, including musical theater.

Switzerland

Junges Schauspielhaus (Zürich)

http://www.schauspielhaus.ch/www/100.asp

Features children, adolescents, and adults performing under professional supervision. They improvise and develop their own stories, training their bodies and voices.

Kinder- und Jugendtheater Metzenthin (Zurich)

http://www.metzenthin.ch

Offers courses for children and young people from age three to eighteen. The primary goal is to provide children with high-quality instruction to stimulate their imaginations and creativity. The company was founded in 1951. Around seven hundred children and adolescents have finished the various courses offered since the company's founding in 1951, and many families are involved for a second generation.

Kinder- und Jugendtheater Turgi (Turgi)

http://www.kjt-turgi.ch

Offers weekly classes for approximately seventy students between the ages of four and twenty-six, divided into three groups. This program offers seminars and workshops as well as theater camp, and regularly hosts an international children's theater festival.

Kinder- und Jugendtheater Zug (Zug)

http://www.kindertheaterzug.ch

Offers professional theater instruction to children and young adults in groups divided by age level.

Ukraine

MACOR Jewish Youth Theater (Vinnitsa)
http://www.vinnitsa.com/vinjew/09Engl/page4.html
A student club that stages theatrical performances about Jewish holidays.

SOUTH AFRICA

National Children's Theatre (Johannesburg)
http://www.jyt.co.za
A registered Public Benefit Organisation that uses theater to enhance children's quality of life, including not only theater performed for children but also workshops that re-create the excitement of the real theater world for young participants. These workshops cover all the disciplines of the performing arts: drama, creative movement, mime, improvisation, singing, and stage and TV techniques.

TRINIDAD AND TOBAGO

Trinidad Children's Theatre Workshop (Belmont)
http://trinidadjunction.wordpress.com/2008/08/31/trinidad-theatre-work-shops
Offers a three-month program that teaches children ages eight to twelve the basic performing and technical skills of theater. Exposes participants to all aspects of theater, not only performing but costume and set design, makeup, lighting and sound, and stage management. The Teen Theatre Studio teaches teenagers the basic skills of theater. In addition to the disciplines of acting, singing, and dancing, teens explore the fundamentals of technical theater and related disciplines, such as theatrical makeup application and costume design. Children develop their imaginations, voices, and bodies by learning theater skills that help them grow as performers and as people.

UNITED KINGDOM AND IRELAND

England

The Academy Theatre School (Cheshire)
http://www.cheshiretheatre.co.uk
Provides professional teaching of complementary theatrical performance disciplines and skills. Pupils are given the opportunity to act, dance, and

sing. They gain experience and knowledge as a result of being taught by professional directors in an atmosphere filled with fun and laughter. All aspects of theater stimulate the student's imagination and expand their creativity: acting, stagecraft, scenery, set design, special effects, makeup, props, script writing, choreography, dance genres, singing, composing, lyric writing, vocal coaching, music, and performance skills.

ACT One (Shepshed)
http://www.act-one.co.uk
An independent youth theater specializing in musicals for ten- to eighteen-year-olds.

Act Too (Haywards Heath)
http://www.acttoo.co.uk
Teaches pupils all three theatrical disciplines—drama, singing, and dance—in equal measure. Also offers a good background in staging, stage sets, design, lighting, sound, props, makeup, and all the behind-the-scenes aspects that give students a good general grounding.

"Act Your Age" Theatre School (Penkridge)
see http://www.penkridge.org.uk/folders/profservices.htm#Music,%20 Dance%20and%20Theatre
A program for children aged eight to sixteen years that teaches about all aspects of acting, from breathing and vocal exercises to performance skills.

Anglia Summer Schools (Colchester)
http://www.inglis-house.demon.co.uk/anglia/index.htm
A summer theater school that provides a theater performance holiday for students aged eight to nineteen.

Arden Theatre Company: Arden Drama School (Stockton-on-Tees)
http://www.arden-theatre.com
Interactive classes for children and teens taught by theater professionals. A Kids Crew offers classes in acting and musical theater. Courses for a Teen Company include playwriting.

Arts Educational Schools (London)
http://www.artsed.co.uk/theschool/theschool.htm
Offers children's productions and includes a school of musical theater for students ages eleven to eighteen as well as a comprehensive range of part-time and short courses for almost every age group, including ballet, jazz, drama classes, and more.

Arts on the Move (Manchester)
http://www.artsonthemove.co.uk
A versatile company specializing in providing quality drama services, resources, and support. Offers courses and workshops to primary and secondary school students.

Aylesbury Vale Youth Theatre (Haddershaw)
http://www.avyt.org
A group of sixteen- to twenty-one-year-olds takes responsibility for every
aspect of production, from proposing the show to acting, directing, musical
production, design, and technical and stage management. Workshops and
theater trips are available to students.

Babbling Vagabonds Storytelling Theatre Company (Bakewell)
http://www.babblingvagabonds.co.uk
Stages theater events that engage and involve all elements of the community, exploring the boundaries of performance and performance space with
our work, and sharing and collaborating with as many people as possible
in both creation and presentation.

Barbara Speake Stage School and Agency (London)
http://www.barbaraspeake.com
A full-time academic and vocational school for students from age four to
sixteen. Offers artistic training in dance, drama, audition technique, and
singing. An in-house agency represents students seeking professional work
in television, theater, and film.

Beck Youth Theatre (West London)
http://www.becktheatre.org.uk/content.asp?CategoryID=1770
A company dedicated to promoting the performing arts to young people
through a mixture of workshops, improvisation, and shows.

Beckenham Theatretrain (Bromley)
http://www.theatretrain.co.uk
Offers combined acting, singing, and dancing classes in groups for children
from six to eighteen years old. Stages large-scale productions in the summer.

Bedfordshire Youth Theatre (Bedford)
http://www.bedsyouththeatre.co.uk
Provides students age sixteen to twenty-one the opportunity to take part
in dramatic productions, both acting and technical. Eleven- to fifteen-year-
olds participate in a one-week summer school program that culminates in
a theater performance.

Belgrade Youth Theatre (Coventry)
http://www.belgrade.co.uk
Runs skills-based workshops, produces performances, and organizes visits to the theater for seven- to twenty-five-year-olds. Also offers outreach groups.

Big Little Theatre School (Bournemouth)
http://www.biglittle.biz
Trains students from five to nineteen years of age in all aspects of the performing arts and boasts an excellent team of directors and qualified staff. Offers specialist training in musical theater and acting, together with regular opportunities to perform in concerts and shows.

Bigfoot Theatre Company (West Norwood)
http://www.bigfoot-theatre.co.uk
Provides drama-based workshops in primary and secondary schools, with community-based programs on weekends and the summer holidays.

The Biz Theatre School (Woking)
http://www.thebizgroup.co.uk
Musical theater arts school for ages eight to sixteen, with classes in drama, singing, and movement. Each term students focus on a different West End musical, with a presentation for family and friends at the end of term.

Bourne Youth Theatre (Bourne)
http://byt.www4.50megs.com/frameset.htm
A nonprofit organization open to children between the ages of eleven to twenty-one, without audition. Aims to provide a professional atmosphere where all can learn and develop their skills regardless of background.

Bradford Youth Players (Bradford)
http://www.bradfordyouthplayers.co.uk
Welcomes any young person between the ages of eight and twenty-three who is interested in the performing arts. Members are given the opportunity to learn and perform drama, music, and dance techniques.

Bright Sparks Theatre Academy (Manchester)
http://www.brightsparksonline.co.uk/
Offers part-time and holiday schools oriented toward professional training, as well as a children's acting agency.

Bristol Old Vic Theatre School (Bristol)
http://www.oldvic.ac.uk/activ8.html

Offers courses and workshops with a broad range of artistic practice, encouraging and developing interest in the arts. Courses and workshops run by professional tutors are available in areas such as acting, voice, role-play, improvisation, singing, dance, and stage combat.

The Brit School (Croydon)
http://www.brit.croydon.sch.uk
An independent, state-funded City College for the Technology of the Arts, the first one of its kind dedicated to education and vocational training for the performing arts, media, art and design, and the technologies that make performance possible. Most of the fourteen- to nineteen-year-old students intend to make a career in the arts, entertainment, and communications industries.

Broadway Youth Theatre (Barking)
http://www.thebroadwaybarking.com
Offers classes in four groups to students between age six and twenty-two. Classes meet weekly, with intensive production projects during the Easter and summer holidays.

Bruvvers Theatre Company (Newcastle upon Tyne)
http://www.bruvvers.co.uk/youth.asp
Bruvvers Theatre Company and The Round, Newcastle's newest theater, are working together to help young people aged eleven to fourteen who want to learn performance skills and take part in shows.

Burnley Youth Theatre Millennium Festival Project (Burnley)
http://www.burnleyyouththeatre.com
A year-round program for students between the ages of five and twenty-five, encompassing all art forms through a range of training workshops and other projects.

Bury St. Edmunds Youth Theatre (Bury St. Edmunds)
http://secure.theatreroyal.org/PEO/site/get%5Finvolved/
Offers drama clubs for children between the ages of five and twelve, along with two youth theater groups for older students. As well as covering a range of work that includes technique and skills building in voice, movement, and acting, the groups also work on scripted pieces, some of which are performed on stage. There is also a group for parents and toddlers in which creative movement is explored.

C&T (Henwick Grove)
http://www.candt.org

Creates original participatory plays that inspire, educate, and empower children through a mix of performance, learning, and digital technologies. C&T uses drama and the arts to help young people make positive changes in their own lives as well as in the communities in which they live. Students are separated by age, with younger students focusing on creative play and drama games while older students research and develop new ideas and practices. Participatory theater projects mix educational drama practices with information and communication technology, creating theater and learning online. Students learn the value of the drama as an applied experience, working with real people in real situations to solve real problems and bring about personal, social, and cultural change.

Calverton Youth Theatre (Calverton)
http://www.telinco.co.uk/throup/cyt/home.html
A group of children aged six through sixteen who perform a wide range of drama, from musicals to pantomime.

Cambridge Drama Centre (Cambridge)
see http://www.wcities.com/en/record/,218427/207/record.html
Offers new and alternative performances, various drama workshops, children's theater, and acting and singing workshops.

Central Youth Theatre (Wolverhampton)
http://www.centralyouththeatre.org
Skills in production drama for people aged eight to twenty-five.

The Centre Stage School of Performing Arts (Southgate)
http://www.centrestageuk.com/home/?area=home
An innovative and independent performing arts school with the objective of delivering high-quality teaching and student development in a warm and friendly learning environment. Offering equal challenges to the experienced, the young professional, and the newcomer. Singing, dance, and drama for four- to eighteen-year-olds.

Centre Stage Theatre Group (Hurstpierpoint)
http://www.centrestagetheatregroup.net
Professional teachers and actors cover all aspects of drama, including mime, improvisation, voice, and script work, with a primary emphasis on building confidence for the students, aged six through seventeen.

The Cheltenham Children's Theatre Association (Cheltenham)
see http://www.cheltenham4u.co.uk/community/community_clubs.asp?
linktype=0062&Type=Clubs+%26+Societies

A theater company run by children. During the year the group gets together to play theatrical games, performing a full-scale play during the summer that is produced and directed by older children.

Chesil Youth Theatre (Winchester)
http://www.chesiltheatre.org.uk/youthworkshops.html
The children's workshops are a key part of the society's activities and from 1995 have been running on a regular basis with access open to all young people for school years five through eight and nine through eleven.

Chichester Festival Theatre (Chichester)
http://www.cft.org.uk
Offers a holiday activities program, aimed at children four to eleven years old, giving participants an opportunity to participate in drama, dance, music, and craft through a series of practical workshops. The ArtsXtra program, aimed at young people from twelve to sixteen years old, offers participants the chance to explore different theater techniques through intensive workshops.

Chicken Shed Theatre Company (Southgate, London)
http://www.chickenshed.org.uk
Offers children's and youth theater workshops for six hundred students, education courses for more than one hundred students, community outreach projects, and a network of satellite "Sheds" across the country (and one in Russia). Its ideals are outreach and also inclusiveness of children out of the mainstream.

Chorley Youth Theatre (Chorley)
http://www.chorleylittletheatre.com/moreinfo/youth/youth.html
Offers weekly sessions on acting on stage, improvisation, and theater games to students with a minimum age of eleven.

Class Act Theatre School (Harlow)
http://www.classacttheatreschool.co.uk/A_Class_Act_Theatre_School.htm
Provides children of all ages with the opportunity to learn skills in acting, singing, and dancing in weekly workshops and in regular public performances. Students are offered opportunities to be selected for professional performing jobs through a children's video and audio company.

Classworks Theatre (Cambridge)
http://www.classworks.org.uk
A well-established professional touring company, which provides theater opportunities and workshops for and with young people, the community,

schools, and venues. The Cambridge base runs two open access youth theater groups and a community theater group.

Cleveland Theatre School (Cleveland)
http://www.ctsonline.co.uk
Includes a dedicated and intense conservatory for students ages ten to adult and the Voice Theatre Company for ages ten to eighteen.

Congleton Amateur Youth Theatre (Congelton)
http://www.danesidetheatre.co.uk/cayt.html
Set up in 1994, has a membership ranging in age from nine to twenty-one, with about fifty members, all from the surrounding area.

Coventry Youth Operetta Group (Coventry)
http://www.dougalswebdesign.co.uk/cyog/default_files/frame.htm
A musical theater group with performers between the ages of nine and nineteen. Auditions are held periodically.

Crucible Youth Theatre [CYT] (Sheffield)
http://www.sheffieldtheatres.co.uk/creativedevelopmentprogramme/youththeatre.asp
Aims to challenge young people to develop confidence, creativity, and consideration for others, in the context of a professional theater. CYT is based in a professional theater, and an important aspect of its work is the teaching and learning of theater skills, aiming for professional standards. In particular the older members aim to work at an advanced level of commitment. Because most CYT members will not go into the professional theater, CYT workshops aim to teach transferable skills as well as theater skills.

Diamond Theatre School (Newport Pagnell)
http://www.diamondtheatreschool.co.uk
A nonfranchised theater school known for successes built up throughout the years. All students have the chance to appear in the Annual Review Show, and all singing and dance students have the opportunity to appear in public performances. While a large number of students have gained leading roles in local productions, many have also have gained professional work in theater, film, television, and radio.

Dinnington Youth Theatre (Sheffield)
http://www.theatre.pits.org.uk
Provides a venue to enable young people to take part in performing arts through a series of workshops and performances.

Donna Maria Company (London)
https://www.donna-marias-world.co.uk
Encourages a level of excellence that is not normally expected of children who are much older. Training is free of charge, encouraging children who would otherwise not be able to pay for performance training, as well as those who could.

Dynamo Youth Theatre (Hampshire)
http://www.dyt.org.uk/aboutus.htm
A performance-based theater group providing drama, music, and dance experience for young people aged between eleven and eighteen. Dynamo was formed to develop the skills in performing arts for the young people of the area, outside of the school environment. Productions include an eclectic mix of well-known musicals, drama, comedy, cabaret and dance reviews, and original dramas and musicals.

East 15 Acting School (Loughton)
http://www.east15.ac.uk
Offers holiday, weekly, and summer workshops for children.

First Act Theatre (Newcastle upon Tyne)
http://www.firstacttheatre.com
Working with a dedicated team, children achieve a professional standard of training in lighting, sound, stage management, marketing, and show direction and production—all the operational aspects of running a professional theater. With more than 250 members, ranging in age from seven to nineteen years, it is one of the largest young people's theater companies in the country.

Flying Ducks Youth Theatre (York)
http://flyingducksyouththeatre.com
Aims to advance the education of young people up to the age of eighteen in the appreciation and practice of drama and the performing arts, and also to support charities local to the York area.

Fowey Funnybone Youth Theatre (Fowey)
http://www.funnybonetheatre.co.uk
A small, independent theater group that works primarily with young people of the area to encourage them to take an interest in the performing arts.

Furness Youth Theatre (Furness)
http://www.furnessyouththeatre.com
Provides a wide range of theatrical activities for young people, including drama games and workshops, drama festival entries, confidence-building

activities, charity performances, singing, movement, speech, improvisation, plays, musicals, and set design and construction. Learning groups are divided by age: under eight, nine to eleven, and eleven to fourteen.

Green Theatre Company (New Malden)
http://www.greentheatre.com/About/AboutGTC.htm
Formed in 1986, the company is open primarily to fourteen- to twenty-five-year-olds and runs on a purely voluntary basis.

Guildhall School of Music and Drama (London)
https://www.gsmd.ac.uk/juniors/drama.html
Open by auditions to students thirteen to eighteen years old. Offerings include drama games, techniques, and skills, ensemble and solo.

The Half Moon Young People's Theatre (East London)
http://www.halfmoon.org.uk
Produces professional theater in youth and school settings and also provides an extensive participatory program including youth theaters as well as school and community projects. The company principally serves London and works exclusively with young people from birth to age seventeen, placing a particular emphasis upon engaging those often excluded in terms of culture (ethnicity) and ability (disability).

The Hampstead Factory (Hampstead)
http://www.thehampsteadfactory.co.uk
Conducts classes in drama, dance, and singing for children and youth from ages four to sixteen. Provides agency and casting for industry professionals.

Harrogate Youth Theatre (Harrogate)
http://www.harrogatetheatre.co.uk/harrogate_youth_theatre_unid5718_page.aspx
Gives more than six hundred members, between the ages of three and eighteen, the opportunity to work with theater professionals in weekly workshops in drama and playwriting, as well as half-term projects, specialist workshops, and an annual summer production.

Hazlitt Youth Theatre (Maidstone)
http://www.hazlittartscentre.co.uk/pages/hazlittyouththeatre.html
Boasts more than 160 members aged between six and eighteen. Weekly workshops give young people a chance to learn about all aspects of the theatrical world—improvisation, acting techniques, performing arts, mime, text work, singing, lighting, sound, design, and much more.

Holybourne Youth Theatre (Alton)

http://www.holybournetheatre.co.uk

An established youth theatre with thirty years of experience providing an opportunity for children to do drama in Alton and the surrounding area.

The Italia Conti Academy of Performing Arts (London)

http://www.italiaconti.com

A full-scale, accredited academic and theater arts school for students aged ten to sixteen. Pupils are afforded the chance to gain professional experience in a huge range of productions, from film to the West End. Students are trained as "thinking performers," and their careers can be expected to break new ground in an industry that is continually changing and forever seeking new media outlets.

Jigsaw Music Theatre Company (Chester)

http://www.jigsaw-music.co.uk/jigsaw.htm

Draws young people between seven and sixteen years from Chester and the wider area. It provides members with a unique experience of being involved in the creation and performance of innovative musical theater. Members are encouraged to play instruments live on stage as well as to act, and some of the older members develop directing and workshop leadership skills.

Kent Youth Theatre (Canterbury)

http://www.kentyouththeatre.co.uk

Dedicated to young people age three and up who want to sing, dance, and act. Provides quality training and opportunities for performance to young people of all abilities and ages, throughout Kent, and promotes ambitious individuals in show business.

Kidz R Us (St. Ives)

http://www.kidzrus.net

Aims to give young people in the local area a chance to express themselves within a dramatic medium and develop their artistic talents in musical theater. Children audition to join, and the company performs widely.

Lafour Theatre Schools (Crowthorne)

http://www.lafourtheatre.co.uk

A chain of schools throughout the South of England that teach children into their late teens a variety of dance and drama disciplines. Aims to provide a nurturing environment in which every student acquires a foundation of training in the performing arts and gains confidence through performance.

Lakeside Youth Theatre (Nottingham, England)
http://www.lakesidearts.org.uk/ChildrenYoungPeople/Youth_Theatre.html
Runs three youth theater groups for children and young people aged eight
to ten, eleven to thirteen, and fourteen to seventeen, covering the broadest range of theater skills including devising and improvising, text, mask,
mime, dance, and music. Also offers the opportunity to learn more about
behind-the-scenes work, with sessions on staging, lighting, and sound.

Lancaster Drama Group (Lancaster)
http://www.dramafactory.co.uk/junior.html
Weekly after-school classes aim to introduce pupils to performance skills.
Improvisation, movement, mime, voice, and speech work help build confidence and communication skills in many areas of life as well as drama.

Laxfield Children's Drama Club (Halesworth)
http://www.lcdcuk.org.uk
Offers classes for children between the ages of six and fifteen, divided into
five age groups, as well as weekly improvisation sessions and summer
camp.

Leeds Children's Theatre (Leeds)
http://www.leeds-childrens-theatre.co.uk
Dedicated to the principle of quality, affordable children's entertainment,
in order to encourage the introduction of the theatrical experience for
young children. The group is staffed entirely by volunteers who offer their
vast range of experience to the younger members, covering most aspects of
theatrical production. Membership is open to all young people interested
in theater.

Lights, Music, Action (Suffolk)
http://www.lma-online.co.uk
A stage school offering classes in audiovisual, band, dance, drama, and
musical theater, as well as a residential summer school for youth ten to
nineteen years old.

London Bubble Theatre Company Youth Theatre Groups (London)
http://www.londonbubble.org.uk/do_stuff/youth_theatre_groups
Offers theater groups for children aged six to eighteen. The program includes a wide variety of theater and storytelling techniques, as well as movement, voice work, and improvisation, sometimes with scripts.

Lyric Young Company [Lyric Theatre Hammersmith] (London)
http://www.lyric.co.uk/p558.html

An educational program that develops social abilities and creativity in young children and performance skills in students aged fourteen to twenty-one.

M.A.O.D.S.—Next Generation Youth Theatre (Ashton-under-Lyne)
http://www.mossleynextgeneration.co.uk
Provides a safe, open, and inclusive environment where young people aged five to eighteen years are encouraged to express themselves through performing arts.

The Mill Youth Theatre (Banbury)
http://www.themillartscentre.co.uk/wps/wcm/connect/MillArts/Youth+
Arts/MillArts+-+aYouth+theatre
Presents original productions under the direction of professional artists. Classes are organized by ages and are coordinated with the Cheswell Theatre Company.

Mountview Academy of Theatre Arts (London)
http://www.mountview.org.uk
Offers theater training classes for young people (ages six through eighteen) throughout the year, a teenage musical theater course, and a summer school.

Mu-Lan Youth-Theatre (London)
http://www.mu-lan.org/youth.html
The first award-winning British–East Asian youth theater company, founded in 1988. Productions are devised by company members, and the adult company offers drama workshops in local schools.

National Youth Theatre (London)
http://www.nyt.org.uk
Established in 1956 to offer young people the chance to develop their creative and social skills through acting and technical disciplines. Provides opportunities to all young people aged thirteen to twenty-one in the UK, regardless of background.

Nichola Rees Youth Academy (Watford)
http://www.nrya.co.uk
A children's theater company that specializes in drama workshops and performance. Classes are structured as workshops, including devised drama or improvisation and games. When preparing for a production, the lessons turn into rehearsals.

Oxford Playhouse Young Company (Oxford)
http://www.oxfordplayhouse.com/takingpart/1622.spx
Creates out-of-school opportunities for young people to engage in arts, such as summer theater residencies, a half-term workshop program, and a Youth Theatre.

Performers Stage School (South Tyneside)
http://www.performersclass.biz
A facility that encompasses the three main performance disciplines: drama, dance, and music. The approach is modern, informative, and practical. More important than talent is commitment. Enjoyment matters most.

Pleasance Theatre Islington—Young Pleasance (Islington)
http://www.pleasance.co.uk/yp
A collaboration of award-winning theater practitioners, choreographers, composers, and designers who share the aim of introducing and developing performance and technical skills in young people. Workshops, holiday courses, and special performance projects give children and young people the chance to develop an awareness of their own abilities and to improve and enhance aptitude, expectations, and potential as part of a vibrant, focused, and motivated team. Four Summer Junior Workshop courses are offered to local children.

The Pollyanna Children's Training Theatre (Wapping)
http://www.pollyannatheatre.org
A training theater offering that encourages students' interest in professional recruitment. Courses are offered in drama and musical theater, with two full productions per year and a summer program.

Rabble Youth Theatre (Coventry)
http://rabbletheatre.tripod.com
A nonprofit independent youth theater group consisting of up to thirty young people aged between eight and sixteen. Besides actors, the theater invites music and drama tutors, technical crew, stage crew, costume coordinators, and scenery painters.

The Rage Ensemble (Birmingham)
http://ragearts.org.uk/JM153/index.php/the-rage-ensemble.html
A group for young people ages sixteen to nineteen who cannot or do not want to attend college, run by Rage, a professional acting company.

Rainbow Theatre (Worthing)
http://www.rainbow-theatre.com

An adult company that works with young audiences and offers workshops for children aged four to thirteen.

Rare Productions (Hatfield)
http://www.rareproductions.co.uk
A youth musical theater group dedicated to giving children and young adults ages eight to eighteen from all backgrounds the chance to perform.

Ravenscourt Theatre School (Hammersmith)
http://www.ravenscourt.net/aboutus.cfm
Couples a general education program with instruction in the techniques of dramatics, dance, and singing. The aim is to help each child to develop talents and abilities and to cultivate practical and creative skills, so that they gain the experience they need to follow a career in the theatrical profession. This, coupled with an efficient theatrical agency, enables the pupils to gain practical experience in professional theater, television, and film productions.

Redroofs Theatre Company (Maidenhead)
http://www.redroofs.co.uk/about.html
A co-educational independent day school for students ages nine to sixteen years old, providing a performing arts curriculum combined with a sound academic education. Also offers part-time courses in dance, musical theater, and drama, and an agency, placing students in West End shows, feature films, television programs, and commercials.

Riding Lights Theatre Company (York)
http://www.ridinglights.org/education/ytheatre.php
Engages children in theater in an atmosphere where Christian faith and art can be explored side by side, but membership is open to all, irrespective of religious beliefs. During the year, a program of projects consists of a series of weekly workshops aimed at developing performance skills and giving participants the opportunity to create original work as well as working with existing scripts. Offers weeklong theater courses in the summer.

Shakespeare Schools Festival [SSF] (London)
http://www.ssf.uk.com
An arts education initiative that enables children eleven to eighteen years old to perform a half-hour production of Shakespeare's most famous plays in their local professional theater. Taking care of the production side of each performance, SSF also provides specialist drama training for both directors and casts. Teacher/directors receive a training day with the Map Consortium, while the casts have a half-day workshop in their performance

theater with one of the four National Youth Theatres. SSF is open to every secondary school and youth theater in Great Britain and runs for one week in February in one hundred theaters across the UK, on a biennial basis.

Shakespeare's Globe (Bankside)
http://www.shakespeares-globe.org/globeeducation/
Offers workshops for schools, universities and colleges, distance learning, events and continuing education, community outreach, and summer schools.

Sixth Sense Theatre for Young People (Swindon)
http://www.sixthsensetheatrecompany.co.uk
Provides a safe environment in which young people are encouraged to develop performance and theater-making skills, grow in confidence, work as a team, and develop an appreciation for and enjoyment of theater. The tutors are all experienced workshop leaders who have a wide breadth of knowledge and skills.

South London Theatre (London)
http://www.southlondontheatre.co.uk/youth.php
A junior class for seven- to nine-year-olds, an intermediate class for ten- to twelve-year-olds, and a youth class for teenagers, thirteen to eighteen, involved in backstage work. The two younger groups together and the older group produce shows of their own at the end of the season.

Spotlites Theatre Co. Ltd. (Kent)
https://spotlites.co.uk
Specializes in providing innovative drama and performance arts for young people aged five and up in the form of productions, workshops, and training in all areas of theater and at all levels.

Stage 2 Theatre Company (Birmingham)
http://www.stage2.org
Produces high-quality shows in all genres using actors from ages ten to twenty, appealing to audiences who want to see original and professional performances, not just children's theater. Offers skills workshops and opportunities for children to develop their acting, technical, and personal skills as well as being a friendly, supportive, exciting environment.

Stagecoach Theatre Arts Schools (London)
http://www.stagecoach.co.uk
Offers both nonprofessional and professional theater training for children four to sixteen. Founded in 1988, it now serves four thousand students at

seven hundred schools worldwide. Locations are in London, across the UK, and around the world.

Stagefright Drama (London)
http://www.stagefrightdrama.com/home.htm
A drama group and small community theater, founded in 1990 and consisting entirely of teenagers. Two productions are performed each year, generally achieved in twenty rehearsals or fewer.

Sylvia Young Theatre School (Marylebone)
http://www.sylviayoungtheatreschool.co.uk
Offers a full-time school as well as part-time acting courses. Classes are based on scripted work, where students work on speeches and scenes. The teachers have been or are currently involved in professional performance. The emphasis is on development with good training, aiming to build confidence and communication skills. The atmosphere of the school is friendly, informal, and very busy.

Theatre Royal and Drum Theatre Plymouth (Plymouth)
http://www.theatreroyal.com/content.asp?CategoryID=968
Offers summer workshops for young people, a Young Company for students five to twenty-five, and Playhouse, for primary teachers who want the experience of directing. In this way, Playhouse takes the drama to the heart of the primary school curriculum. A Summer Stakeout program offers master classes and workshops.

Theatre Royal Stratford East (East London)
https://www.stratfordeast.com/our_work/youth_arts_and_education.shtml
Offers youth arts and education programs that include playwriting as well as acting for participants between eleven and twenty-one years old, with an emphasis on musical theater.

Theatre Studio West (Acton)
http://www.theatrestudiowest.co.uk
Provides a vibrant, all-inclusive environment, enabling young people to participate in all aspects of theatre and to fulfill their technical and artistic potential working toward performances.

Theatre Venture (Newham)
http://www.theatre-venture.org/youth-programmes.aspx?nav=whatwedo
Offers weekly classes and training workshops, holiday schools, showcase festivals, performances, and professional development for children of all

ages. Theater-in-education projects reach across the curriculum, incorporating drama, live performance, visual arts, and media.

Theatre4Kids (Camberley)
http://www.theatre4kids.co.uk
A theater school managed and run by experienced drama professionals delivering the very best children's theater training and drama workshops in the disciplines of drama, movement, and singing for six- to sixteen-year-olds. As well as participating in drama workshops and training in the primary disciplines of theater, students are encouraged to create their own pieces of theater.

Theatrecraft (Walton-on-Thames)
http://www.theatrecraft.co.uk/theatrecraft/aboutus.htm
Teaches young people from age six to eighteen about theater through performance of stage productions, including musicals, plays, and dance shows. Children are given the opportunity to learn about theater and all of the many skills that make theatrical adventures happen: lighting design, costume design, sound, set design, the way in which performance spaces vary and can be used, and all of the myriad parts that make up theater.

Theatretrain (Epping, with centers across England)
http://www.theatretrain.co.uk
Provides professional training in the performing arts for young people. Classes in acting, singing, and dancing are taught in age groups six to nine, nine to twelve, and thirteen to eighteen. Offers the prospect of local, regional, and West End shows, as well as opportunities for international travel. Teachers are trained, and new centers are supported.

Travelling Light Theatre (Bristol)
http://www.travellinglighttheatre.org.uk/
Runs three youth theater groups that feature dance/physical theater, music, design, and writing for performance. Youth theatre sessions encourage exploration and imagination. This creative approach has led to the presentation of a number of devised performances in various venues.

The Turrets [Castle Players] (Barnard Castle)
http://www.castleplayers.co.uk/index.php?option=com_content&view=article&id=139&Itemid=70
A thriving, professionally run youth theater, first established in 1995. There are now seven groups for children ages nine to eighteen.

UK Theatre School (London, England, and Glasgow, Scotland)
http://uktheatreschool.com
Provides professional tutoring and training for applicants who audition successfully. Four main age groups range from four to nineteen years old. Academy students age fifteen and older can apply to be part of a Musical Theatre Masterclass. The school has its own casting department that takes care of any students wishing to audition for professional work.

VictoryLand Children's Theatre School (Portsmouth)
see http://www.geocities.com/victorylandtc/
Offers acting, dancing, and singing lessons for children aged four to eighteen, with shows ranging from serious drama to comedy and musicals. In these classes, age groups are split and are tutored in mime, mask work, physical theater, forum theater, and a variety of other methods. The older age ranges are taught directly, but with the younger students, these skills are passed on through games. At the highest end, other possibilities open up, such as crew, stage fight direction, and direction and/or writing of their own productions.

Warwick Arts Centre (Warwick)
http://www.warwickartscentre.co.uk/education/
Offers sessions for four age groups covering a wide range of skills, including text, improvisation, mime, Shakespeare, mask, and music and lots of games. Children are given the opportunity to increase confidence, make new friends, and improve teamwork.

Watford Palace Young People's Theatre (Watford)
http://www.watfordtheatre.co.uk
For all young people regardless of ability, led by professional theater directors. Weekly workshops take place in the rehearsal spaces of the Palace Theatre with productions on the main stage and venues around Hertfordshire and beyond. Three groups are divided by age: Junior Youth Theatre (ages ten to twelve), Middle Youth Theatre (ages thirteen and fourteen), and Senior Youth Theatre (ages fifteen to twenty-one). A backstage youth theater is available for children fourteen and older.

Worthing Youth Media (Worthing)
http://www.worthingyouththeatre.org.uk
Offers children instruction in various media techniques as well as theater. Drama workshops for ages eight to thirteen lead to small-scale theater productions. Project work for the thirteen-and-up age group includes camera techniques, animation, editing, and acting for film.

Young REP (Birmingham)
http://www.young-rep.org.uk/participate/young-people/young-rep
Based at the Birmingham Repertory Theatre, works with young people aged between eight and eighteen across Birmingham and the West Midlands. Professional staff create and produce a broad range of high-quality theatrical experiences.

Young Theatre (Beaconsfield)
http://www.youngtheatre.org.uk
For young people, aged ten and above, who have an interest in theater production, whether as actor or technician. The company currently mounts three main productions a year and enters local and national one-act play competitions.

Youth Action Theatre (London)
http://www.yat.org.uk/backstage/history/index.htm
Dedicated to stimulating the love of drama and theater in sixteen- to twenty-five-year-olds. Students participate in drama workshops and performances. Membership is voluntary and requires no prior experience.

Youth Theatre Yorkshire (York)
http://www.communigate.co.uk/ne/youththeatreyorkshire
Offers ten workshops in different age ranges for young people from five to twenty-five; also runs annual residential drama courses, summer workshops, theater trips, and specialist workshops. Stages three main productions each year as well as smaller performances by the various groups. The workshops explore issues that concern young people today.

Zenith Youth Theatre Company (Bath)
http://www.zenithytc.co.uk
A theatrical society for all young people aged between thirteen and twenty-one who demonstrate an enthusiasm and commitment to the group's aim of presenting musical theater of the highest standard. The group has an "access for everyone" policy, so anyone within the age range can be actively involved in any aspect of theater production and presentation. Members have two things in common—commitment and enthusiasm—enabling many different types of young people to enjoy a creative and social experience together, forging friendships and gaining experience outside their normal social circle.

Ireland

Barnstorm Theatre Company (Kilkenny)
http://www.barnstorm.ie

Includes children's theater, community theater, and the Kilkenny Youth Theatre. Works with young people in the community through outreach and education projects in schools, clubs, and community groups.

Centre Stage (Limerick)
http://centrestageireland.com/index.html
Offers weekly classes for children and adults in acting, singing, dance, television, and film. Classes are designed for people interested in developing their skills and confidence in the performing arts, and to enhance life skills through teamwork and personal development. Pupils have become very prominent contributors to the theatrical landscape of Limerick City and county and on the national and international stage.

Griese Players Drama Group (Ballitore)
http://www.grieseplayers.com/index.html
A drama group for children and teenagers that offers programs divided into age groups. It started in 1999 as a social inclusion project with emphasis being placed on the provision of a community-based alternative learning experience through the medium of the arts by way of staged drama productions.

Irish Academy of Dramatic Arts (Dublin)
http://www.irishacad.com
A fresh and innovative approach to drama, music, and dance that is student centered and aims to develop creativity and self-confidence. Courses are designed to suit students of all ages from six to adult, from beginners through to advanced level. Throughout the year, regular showcase performances are staged, in addition to performances in professional theaters, to give students genuine performing experience.

Jack Drum Arts (Baldersdale)
http://www.jackdrum.co.uk
Provides a wide variety of workshops and participatory arts activities, including music making, drama, and digital media as well as a small touring theater.

Stagewise Residential Youth Theatre Course (Ballinasloe)
http://www.stagewise.ie
Provides hundreds of young people with an experience of the performing arts and drama, in addition to building individual confidence and creativity. An annual event with a well-earned reputation as a well-organized and thoroughly enjoyable week.

Northern Ireland

Centre Stage Summer Drama Holidays (Belfast)
http://www.summerdrama.co.uk
Summer drama activities for children ages eight to eighteen, including improvisation, mime, dance, and choral speaking.

Scotland

4WORD Maryhill Youth Theatre (Glasgow)
http://www.4wordcreative.com
Performance and production skills for young people aged twelve to eighteen. Recent work includes stage plays, film projects, and a podplay for iTunes.

Aberdour Players Youth Theatre (Aberdour)
see http://www.bebo.com/Profile.jsp?MemberId=4358046417
A group of thirty actors aged ten to sixteen, with three youth leaders. Authors some of its own productions. Welcomes everyone to join.

Ankur Productions (Glasgow)
http://www.ankurproductions.org.uk/Education.htm
Includes an education and outreach program to address the lack of participation in the arts by people from Scotland's ethnic minority communities as well as the lack of cultural and creative diversity. Offers drama workshops for children nine and older.

Brunton Youth Theatre (East Lothian)
http://www.bruntontheatre.co.uk/webpages/community_youththeatre.php
Offers young people aged eight through eighteen an opportunity to learn a huge range of theater skills through workshops, rehearsals, and performances, supported by experienced drama tutors. Visiting drama tutors develop acting techniques, circus skills, stage makeup, stage fighting, and production skills.

Carnegie Youth Theatre (Dunfermline)
http://www.carnegieyouththeatre.org.uk
Provides the youth of Dunfermline and the surrounding area the chance to gain skills in performing arts. The group performs twice a year, concentrating on musical theatre.

Clax Youth Theatre (Clackmannanshire)
http://www.clacksweb.org.uk/culture/claxyouththeatre/

A theater program that allows young people to run their own group. Includes dance, drama, costume making, music, stage crews, directing, singing, script writing, art, filming, photography, and computing.

Collusion Theatre (Glasgow)
http://www.collusiontheatre.co.uk
Offers drama sessions and productions known for their quality, imagination, and professionalism, employing first-class tutors. The group has had opportunities to participate in workshops with international theater directors and to work with Polish, German, Irish, Czech, and Romanian young people.

Cumbernauld Youth Theatre (Kildrum)
http://www.cumbernauldtheatre.co.uk/outreach.html
Includes a variety of programs organized by age for children five to ten and eleven to twenty-one. Works in conjunction with several education departments, Scottish Enterprise, and the Scottish Executive to support and develop creativity in the classroom and in lifelong learning.

Dramarama 2000 (Aberdeen)
http://www.dramarama2000.com
Provides enjoyment while developing confidence through drama activities such as games, mime and movement, improvisation, script work, and acting. Special classes prepare students for entrance exams to professional training schools.

Dundee Rep Youth Theatre (Dundee)
http://www.dundeereptheatre.co.uk/p53.html
A group of fourteen- to eighteen-year-olds who meet to develop drama skills and work toward productions, sometimes in collaboration with the award-winning Dundee Rep Ensemble.

Forth Children's Theatre (Edinburgh)
http://forthchildrenstheatre.wordpress.com/
An amateur group that offers young people a chance to experience all of the aspects of theater. Two or three productions every year give participants a chance to take part with no financial outlay to them or their parents, giving them all equal status and affording opportunities that some of them would not otherwise have. They learn about discipline, commitment, and teamwork; they also gain in self-confidence and form friendships that will last a lifetime.

Largs Youth Theatre (Largs)
http://largsyouththeatre.moonfruit.com/#

Produces films, videos, music, and theater performances, including original scripts written by company members. Includes a company of senior class students.

Lyceum Youth Theatre [LYT] (Edinburgh)
http://www.lyceum.org.uk/webpages/youth_theatre.php
Actively involves young people between the ages of five and eighteen years old in drama every week. By pushing boundaries, LYT has established a name for itself as a producer of contemporary professional theater for young people, by young people. LYT works with five basic principles of drama—discipline, respect, attitude, motivation, and application—and is regularly approached by British and international film, television, and theatrical casting agencies and is recognized as a reliable source of young Scottish-based talent.

Moffat Youth Theatre in Education (Moffat)
http://www.moffat-youth-arts.co.uk
Offers after-school classes in art, drama, photography, film, dance, and music, all specially designed to help young people develop self-confidence, self-esteem, and life coping skills. No auditions, no high fees or need for talent in any artistic area, but a commitment to enhancing personal development and acting respectfully is required.

North Lanarkshire Children's Theatre (North Lanarkshire)
see http://www.northlanarkshire.gov.uk/index.aspx?articleid=6033
Open to all young people aged five to fifteen years. Members have the opportunity to participate in weekly drama workshops.

RSAMD YouthWorks (Glasgow)
http://www.rsamd.ac.uk/academyworks/dramaworks/young/
Offers courses with open access to students and a premium on diversity: opportunities for people to grow and develop regardless of background, ability, or culture. Classes for young people include television presenting, screenwriting, audition preparation, fight choreography, and radio presenting. There is an acting masterclass.

Scottish Youth Theatre (Edinburgh and Glasgow)
http://www.scottishyouththeatre.org
A children's theater that is especially broad in scope. Students range in age from three to twenty-five, and there are tens of thousands of participants annually, from weekly classes to productions of professional caliber. The program is year-round: weekly classes are offered in Glasgow, Edinburgh, and Aberdeen; a summer festival in various locations through Scotland; an

autumn tour with drama workshops; and a winter festival that celebrates the work of the year. In addition, special projects for young people of all ages, abilities, and skill levels are delivered locally, nationally, and internationally. Many students have graduated into success in the theater profession, but its broad purpose is to create confident, culturally aware citizens.

Solar Bear UNITED & Deaf Youth Theatre (Glasgow)
http://www.solarbear.org.uk
An innovative, multidisciplinary theater with a strong social commitment. Aims to make progress in areas of accessibility, inclusion, and integration and to develop and deliver a wide range of education, outreach, and training programs. In addition, offers Scotland's first deaf theater school, for students aged twelve to twenty-one.

Theatre École (Glasgow)
http://www.theatre-ecole.org/uk
Offers training through workshops in all aspects of the performing arts, including dance, music, acting, and stage management. Workshops also address such topics as drug education, bullying, health, and the environment.

Toonspeak Young People's Theatre (Glasgow)
http://www.toonspeak.co.uk
Provides drama and theater opportunities and training for young people aged eleven to twenty-five. Young people are at the heart of Toonspeak and make most of the decisions about the company and the artistic work. Toonspeak's work supports the regeneration of the local area and addresses problems of economic and social exclusion.

Tread the Boards Youth Music Theatre (Dundee)
http://www.treadtheboardsymt.co.uk
Encourages participation in musical theater productions among children aged eight and older in the region. Develops the creative skills of young people through the craft of theater and encourages them to work together as a community and, in so doing, experience the practical workings of theater while respecting its skills and disciplines.

Tron Theatre: Skillshops (Glasgow)
http://www.tron.co.uk/education/workshops/
Each year delivers workshops to participants between the ages of three and seventy-eight. The program presents openings to explore creativity and learning both as artist and audience.

UK Theatre School (London, England, and Glasgow, Scotland)
http://uktheatreschool.com
Provides professional tutoring and training for applicants who audition
successfully. Four main age groups range from four to nineteen years old.
Academy students age fifteen and older can apply to be part of a Musical
Theatre Masterclass. The school has its own casting department that takes
care of any students wishing to pursue professional work.

West Lothian Youth Theatre (West Lothian)
see http://www.scottisharts.org.uk/1/artsinscotland/lotteryandthearts/capital
projects/archive/westlothianyouththeatre.aspx
Aims to enhance and enrich the lives of young people through a range of
drama and theater-related workshops and high-quality performance projects of a professional standard. Delivers fifty-five weekly drama workshops,
"Play in a Week," annual festivals, international exchanges, and productions to young people.

Wales

Class Act Youth Theatre (Cardiff)
http://www.classact.org.uk/1.html
Provides an opportunity for young people to participate in the performing
arts. Workshops cover such topics as improvisation (drama and dance), use
of the voice (projection, diction, emphasis, etc.), singing, and dancing.

Dolman Youth Theatre (Newport)
http://www.sadoldgoth.co.uk/dolman/YouthTheatre.asp
Children offered opportunities to participate in large and small stage productions. The program is set up to encourage them in all areas of the theater:
in addition to acting, sound, lights, set design and building, stage combat,
stage make-up, front-of-house work, and even writing for the theater.

Gwent Young People's Theatre (Abergavenny)
http://www.gwenttheatre.com/gypt
Since 1956, has offered opportunities for young people aged ten to twenty
to participate in a wide range of theater activities under the direction of
professional theater practitioners. Members participate in workshops with
a professional drama-in-education company, Gwent Theatre, which in turn
is part of a network of eight professional Theatre in Education companies
across Wales. The policy of the company is "open door," inviting all young
people to participate irrespective of social, ethnic, and educational background or ability. Many graduates continue in the performing arts in higher

education and the profession. The company stages at least six productions a year. Young people are involved in the selection of plays for production and then function as a production team. A stage management course includes technical skills, such as sound, lighting, and video. The company also goes out to schools, working with students and teachers.

National Youth Theatre of Wales (Cardiff)
http://www.nyaw.co.uk/e_nytw.html
A competitive six-week summer program made up of members of children's theater companies across Wales. During a residency, the company works alongside professional directors, choreographers, musicians, designers, and technicians to create and rehearse their production. After auditions, the company is divided into actors and crew (set design and construction, costume and makeup, lighting and sound, and stage management). The program then culminates in a performance tour. The Youth Theatre also offers a program of workshops, master classes, and training courses throughout the year across Wales, and it is considering tours abroad.

PACE Youth Theatre (Ayr and Paisley)
http://www.pacetheatre.co.uk/YouthTheatre/default.asp
Offered to youth ages three to eighteen, with no auditions required. Weekly workshops take place during the school term, run by a full team of drama, technical, and musical staff. Workshops follow a unique new youth theater syllabus, devised to increase confidence, communication, self-expression, and performance skills. Although PACE is a workshop-based youth theater, members have the opportunity to participate in large-scale productions.

Perth Youth Theatre (Perth)
http://www.horsecross.co.uk/community/perth-youth-theatre/
A theater company for young people aged between twelve and twenty-one from Perth and Kinross. Students apply at any time of the year and attend competitive recruitment workshops.

PROPS Theatre School (Glan Conwy)
http://www.propstheatreschool.co.uk
Offers opportunities to perform in regular, professionally produced shows alongside experienced theater practitioners and to develop self-confidence and team-building skills. The full-time Vocational Theatre Course is available to students aged sixteen and over and is designed to offer practical experience that will lead to professional status.

West Glamorgan Youth Theatre (Swansea)
http://www.wgytc.co.uk

Open to young people aged thirteen to twenty one who are interested in performance or production. The company is residential, recruited through yearly nominations and auditions that involve group and solo workshops. Members of the company are invited to return. In the company, students learn and perform under the guidance of specialist tutors experienced in arts education.

Selected Bibliography

A complete bibliography of resources is available online at http://www.childrens theaterinfo.com. If you wish to suggest additional resources, please contact us at ctsurvey2@aol.com.

BOOKS, ESSAYS, AND JOURNALS

Ackroyd, Judith, ed. *Research Methodologies for Drama Education.* Stoke-on-Trent, England: Trentham Books, 2006.

Addams, Jane. *The Spirit of Youth and the City Streets.* New York: Macmillan, 1909.

Adler, Stella. *The Technique of Acting.* New York: Bantam Books, 1988.

Aimes, Raina S. *A High School Theatre Teacher's Survival Guide.* New York: Routledge, 2005.

American Alliance for Theatre and Education (AATE). *A Model Drama/Theatre Curriculum: Philosophy, Goals and Objectives.* Anchorage, AK: Anchorage Press, 1987.

———. *Youth Theatre Journal,* 1986–.

Bailey, Sally Dorothy. *Wings to Fly: Bringing Theatre Arts to Students with Special Needs.* Rockville, MD: Woodbine House, 1993.

Bailin, Sharon. "In the Spaces between the Words: Play Production as an Interpretive Enterprise." *Journal of Aesthetic Education* 35 (2001): 67–75.

Baldwin, Patrice. *Teaching Literacy through Drama: Creative Approaches.* London: RoutledgeFalmer, 2003.

Ball, Christopher. *Taking Time to Act: A Guide to Cross-Curricular Drama.* Portsmouth, NH: Heinemann, 1995.

Barnfield, Gabriel. *Creative Drama in Schools.* London: Macmillan, 1968; New York: Hart, 1969.

Bauer, Karl W. *Emanzipatorisches Kindertheater: Entstehungszusammenhänge, Zielsetzungen, dramaturgische Modelle.* Munich: Fink, 1980.

Bedard, Roger L., ed. *Dramatic Literature for Children: A Century in Review*. 2nd ed. Louisville, KY: Anchorage Press Plays, 2005.

Bedard, Roger L., and C. John Tolch, eds. *Spotlight on the Child: Studies in the History of American Children's Theatre*. New York: Greenwood, 1989.

Beneventi, Paolo. *Introduzione alla storia del theatro ragazzi*. Firenze: la Casa Usher, 1994.

Benjamin, Walter. "Program for a Proletarian Children's Theater" (1928). In *The Weimar Republic Sourcebook*, ed. Anton Laes, Martin Jay, and Edward Dimendberg. Berkeley and Los Angeles: University of California Press, 1994.

Blatner, Adam, and Daniel Wiener, eds. *Interactive & Improvisational Drama: Varieties of Applied Theatre and Performance*. Lincoln, NE: iUniverse, 2007.

Bolton, Gavin M. *Acting in Classroom Drama: A Critical Analysis*. Portland, ME: Calendar Islands, 1999.

——. *Dorothy Heathcote's Story: Biography of a Remarkable Drama Teacher*. Stoke-on-Trent, England and Sterling, VA: Trentham Books, 2003.

——. "A History of Drama Education—A Search for Substance." In *International Handbook of Research in Arts Education*, edited by Liora Bresler. Springer International Handbooks of Education, volume 16. New York: Springer, 2007.

——. *New Perspectives on Classroom Drama*. Hempstead, England: Simon & Shuster Education, 1998.

Booth, David, and Kathleen Gallagher, eds. *How Theatre Educates: Convergences and Counterpoints with Artists, Scholars and Advocates*. Toronto and Buffalo, NY: University of Toronto Press, 2003.

Bray, Errol. *Playbuilding: A Guide for Group Creation of Plays with Young People*. Portsmouth, NH: Heinemann, 1994.

Burger, Isabel B. *Creative Play Acting: Learning through Drama*. New York: A. S. Barnes, 1950.

Burns, Michael. *First You Sit on the Floor: A Guide to Developing a Youth Theatre Troupe*. Portsmouth, NH: Heinemann, 2002.

Camilleri, Vanessa A., ed. *Healing the Inner City Child: Creative Arts Therapies with At-Risk Children*. London and Philadelphia: Jessica Kingsley, 2007.

Centre for Public Culture and Ideas (Griffith University). *Applied Theatre Researcher/ Idea Journal*. 2000–.

Cerny, Gabriele. *Theaterpädagogik*. Augsburg: Wissner, 2004.

Chorpenning, Charlotte Barrows. *Twenty-one Years with Children's Theatre*. Anchorage, KY: Children's Theatre Press, 1954.

Clifford, Sara, Alec Davison, and Anna Herrmann. *Making a Leap: Theatre of Empowerment: A Practical Handbook for Drama and Theatre Work with Young People*. London and Philadelphia: Jessica Kingsley, 1999.

Combs, Charles E. "Theatre and Drama in Education: A Laboratory for Actual, Virtual or Vicarious Experience." *Youth Theatre Journal* 2 (1988).

Croteau, Jan Helling. *Perform It! A Complete Guide to Young People's Theatre*. Portsmouth, NH: Heinemann, 2000.

Davis, David, ed. *Interactive Research in Drama in Education*. Stoke-on-Trent, England: Trentham Books, 1997.

Dodd, Nigel, and Winifred Hickson. *Drama and Theatre in Education*. London: Heinemann, 1971.

Donclan, Kate, and H. Cahill, eds. "Drama and Learning" [special issue]. *Melbourne Studies in Education* 43 (2002).

Doyle, Rex. *Staging Youth Theatre: A Practical Guide*. Wiltshire, England: Crowood, 2003.

Drama Australia: The National Association of Drama Education. *ADEM: Australian Drama Education Magazine*. 1995–2008.

———. *NJ: Drama Australia Journal*. 1976–.

Educational Theatre Journal, 1949–1978; *Theatre Journal* 1978–.

Fleming, Michael. *Starting Drama Teaching*. 2nd ed. London: David Fulton, 2003.

Freeman, Gregory D., Katherine Sullivan, and C. Ray Fulton. "Effects of Creative Drama on Self-Concept, Social Skills, and Problem Behavior." *Journal of Educational Research* 96 (2003): 131–39.

Friedman, Lise. *Break a Leg! The Kids' Book of Acting and Stagecraft*. New York: Workman, 2002.

Gallagher, Kathleen. "Conceptions of Creativity in Drama Education." In *International Handbook of Research in Arts Education*, ed. Liora Bresler. Springer International Handbooks of Education, volume 16. New York: Springer, 2007.

Gandini, Lella, Lynn Hill, Louise Caldwell, and Charles Schwall, eds. *In the Spirit of the Studio: Learning from the Atelier of Reggio Emilia*. New York: Teacher's College Press, 2005.

Gillespie, Patti P. "Theater Education and Hirsch's Contextualism: How Do We Get There, and Do We Want to Go?" *Journal of Aesthetic Education* 24 (1990): 31–47.

Goldberg, Moses. *Children's Theatre: A Philosophy and a Method*. Englewood Cliffs, NJ: Prentice Hall, 1974.

Gonzalez, Jo Beth. *Temporary Stages: Departing from Tradition in High School Theatre Education*. Portsmouth, NH: Heinemann, 2006.

Granville-Barker, Harley. "Drama in Education." In *The Use of the Drama*. Princeton, NJ: Princeton University Press, 1945.

Guide to Curriculum Planning in Classroom Drama and Theatre. Madison: Wisconsin Department of Public Instruction, 1992.

Hackbarth, Judith A. *Plays, Players, and Playing: How to Start Your Own Children's Theater Company*. Colorado Springs: Piccadilly Books, 1994.

Haydon, Andrew. *Raw Talent: Fifty Years of the National Student Drama Festival*. London: Oberon Books, 2006.

Heathcote, Dorothy, and G. Bolton. *Drama for Learning: Dorothy Heathcote's Mantle of the Expert Approach to Education*. Portsmouth, NH: Heinemann, 1995.

Henry, Mallika. "Drama's Ways of Learning." *Research in Drama Education* 5 (2000): 45–62.

Herts, Alice Minnie. *The Children's Educational Theatre*. New York and London: Harper & Brothers, 1911.

Hornbrook, David. *Education and Dramatic Art*. Oxford: Blackwell, 1989.

Hughes, Jenny, and Karen Wilson. "Playing a Part: The Impact of Youth Theatre on Young People's Personal and Social Development." *Research in Drama Education* 9 (2004): 57–72.

Hulson, Maggie. *Schemes for Classroom Drama*. Stoke-on-Trent, England and Sterling, Virginia: Trentham Books, 2006.

Hume, Samuel J., and Lois M. Foster. *Theater and School*. New York and Los Angeles: S. French, 1932.

International Journal for Education through Art. 2005–.

Jackson, Anthony. "Anecdotes Are No Longer Enough—Academic Research and the Evaluation of Theatre in Education." In *Drama and Theatre in Education: Contemporary Research*, ed. John Somers. Concord, ON: Captus University Publications, 1996.

———, ed. *Learning through Theatre: Essays and Casebooks on Theatre in Education*. Manchester: Manchester University Press, 1980.

———, ed. *Learning through Theatre: New Perspectives on Theatre in Education*. London: Routledge, 1992.

Jacobs, Paul DuBois, and Jennifer Swender. *Putting on a Play: Drama Activities for Kids*. Salt Lake City, UT: Gibbs Smith, 2005.

JEDA: Journal of the Educational Drama Association of New South Wales. 1993–.

Johnson, Margaret F. *The Drama Teacher's Survival Guide: A Complete Toolkit for Theatre Arts*. Colorado Springs, CO: Meriwether, 2007.

Kaick, Barbara von. *Theater in der Schule*. Hamburg: Körber-Stiftung und Bundesarbeitsgemeinschaft Darstellendes Spiel, 2000.

Kase-Polisini, Judith, ed. *Drama as Meaning Maker*. Lanham, MD: University Press of America, 1989.

Kempe, Andy, ed. *Drama Education and Special Needs: A Handbook for Teachers in Mainstream and Special Schools*. Cheltenham, England: Stanley Thornes, 1996.

Little, Ruth. *The Young Vic Book: Theatre Work and Play*. London: Methuen, 2004.

McCammon, Laura, and Debra McLauchlan. *Universal Mosaic of Drama and Theatre: The IDEA 2004 Dialogues*. City East, QLD, Australia: IDEA Publications, 2006.

McCaslin, Nellie. ed. *Children and Drama*. 3rd ed. Studio City, CA: Players Press, 1999.

———. *Creative Drama in the Classroom and Beyond*. 8th ed. New York: Longman, 2006.

———. *Historical Guide to Children's Theatre in America*. New York: Greenwood Press, 1987.

———. "Seeking the Aesthetic in Creative Drama and Theatre for Young Audiences." *Journal of Aesthetic Education* 39 (2005): 12–19.

———. *Shows on a Shoestring: An Easy Guide to Amateur Productions*. New York: David McKay, 1979.

———. *Theatre for Children in the United States: A History*. Norman: University of Oklahoma Press, 1971.

Merrill, John, and Martha Fleming. *Play-Making and Plays: The Dramatic Impulse and Its Educative Use in the Elementary and Secondary School*. New York: Macmillan, 1930.

Moses, J. Garfield. "The Children's Theatre." *Charities and the Commons* 18 (1907): 23-34.

Munier, Asif, and Michael Etherton. "Child Rights Theatre for Development in Rural Bangladesh: A Case Study." *Research in Drama Education* 11 (2006): 175–83.

National Association for Youth Drama (NAYD). *Youth Drama Ireland*. 2000–.

National Association of Youth Theatres (NAYT). *State of the Sector*. 2009–.

———. *Youth Theatre Now*. 2009–.

Neelands, Jonothan, and Tony Goode, eds. *Structuring Drama Work: A Handbook of Available Forms in Theatre and Drama*. Cambridge: Cambridge University Press, 1991.

Nicholson, Helen. *Applied Drama: The Gift of Theater*. New York: Palgrave Macmillan, 2005.

Norris, Joe, Laura A. McCammon, and Carole S. Miller, eds. *Learning to Teach Drama: A Case Narrative Approach*. Portsmouth, NH: Heinemann Drama, 2000.

O'Regan, Ted, and John O'Regan. *A Sense of Wonder: A Short Introduction to Drama in Education*. Dublin, Ireland: Liffey, 2005.

O'Toole, John. *Doing Drama Research: Stepping into Enquiry in Drama, Theatre and Education*. City East, QLD: Drama Australia, 2006.

———. *The Process of Drama*. New York: Routledge, 1992.

O'Toole, John, and Kate Donelan, eds. *Drama, Culture and Empowerment: The IDEA 95 Dialogues*. Brisbane: IDEA Publications, 1996.

Overton, Grace Sloan. *Drama in Education, Theory and Technique*. New York and London: Century, 1926.

Peterson, Lenka, and Dan O'Connor. *Kids Take the Stage: Helping Young People Discover the Creative Outlet of Theater*. New York: Back Stage Books, 1997.

Philips, Sarah. *Drama with Children*. New York: Oxford University Press, 1999.

Poston-Anderson, Barbara. *Drama: Learning Connections in Primary Schools*. New York: Oxford University Press, 2007.

Rainer, John. *Teaching Drama and Theatre*. London: Taylor & Francis, 2007.

Roberts, Vera Mowry. "Theatre Education in the United States." *Educational Theatre Journal* 20 (1968): 308–10.

Saxton, Juliana, and Carole Miller, eds. *Drama and Theatre in Education: International Conversations*. Victoria, BC: American Educational Research Association, Arts and Learning Special Interest Group, 1999.

———. *Drama and Theatre in Education: The Research of Practice, the Practice of Research*. Victoria, BC: IDEA Publications, 1998.

Schonmann, Shifra. "'Master' versus 'Servant': Contradictions in Drama and Theatre Education." *Journal of Aesthetic Education* 39 (2005): 31–39.

Shapiro, Michael. *Children of the Revels: The Boy Companies of Shakespeare's Time and Their Plays*. New York: Columbia University Press, 1977.

Siks, Geraldine Brain. "Theatre for Youth: An International Report." *Educational Theatre Journal* 7 (1955): 306–14.

Siks, Geraldine Brain, and Hazel Brain Dunnington, eds. *Children's Theatre and Creative Dramatics*. Seattle: University of Washington Press, 1961.

Somers, John, ed. *Drama and Theatre in Education: Contemporary Research*. Concord, ON: Captus University Publications, 1996.

Spolin, Viola. *Improvisation for the Theater: A Handbook of Teaching and Directing Techniques*. Evanston, IL: Northwestern University Press, 1999.

Swortzell, Lowell. *International Guide to Children's Theatre and Educational Theatre: A Historical and Geographical Source Book*. New York: Greenwood, 1990.

Taylor, Philip. *The Drama Classroom: Action, Reflection, Transformation*. London and New York: Routledge Falmer, 2000.

——, ed. *Researching Drama and Arts Education: Paradigms and Possibilities*. London and Washington, DC: Falmer, 1996.

Taylor, Philip, and Christine Hoepper, eds. *Selected Readings in Drama and Theatre Education: The IDEA '95 Papers*. NADIE Research Monograph Series, 3. Brisbane, Australia: IDEA Publications, 1995.

Thomas, Charles. *The Theatre of Youth: Being a Brief Introduction to the Art of the Stage for Those Who Are Not Too Old to Learn*. London: Chapman & Hall, 1933.

Urion, Dan, ed. *Drama in Education: Case Studies*. Newark, NJ: Harwood Academic Publishers, 2001.

Ward, Winifred. *Creative Dramatics*. New York and London: D. Appleton, 1930.

——. *Theatre for Children*. Anchorage, KY: Children's Theatre Press, 1958.

Way, Brian. *Development through Drama*. Amherst, NY: Humanity Books, 1998.

Winston, Joe. *Drama and English at the Heart of the Curriculum: Primary and Secondary Years*. London: David Fulton, 1998.

Wright, Lin. "Preparing Teachers to Put Drama in the Classroom." *Theory into Practice* 24 (1985): 205–11.

WEB SITES AND ONLINE MAGAZINES

Amateur Dramatics and Operatics. http://www.amateurdramatics.info.

American Theatre Association. *Educational Theatre Journal* (1949–1978). http://fsearch-sandbox.jstor.org/journals/00131989.html.

——. *Theatre Journal* (1979–1995): http://fsearch-sandbox.jstor.org/journals/01922882.html; (1996–present): http://muse.jhu.edu/journals/theatre_journal.

Arts Education Policy Review. http://www.heldref.org/pubs/search/about.html.

ARTSEDGE: The National Arts and Education Network. http://artsedge.kennedy-center.org/aboutus.

Association for Drama in Education in Ireland. http://www.ict.mic.ul.ie/adei.

British Theatre Guide: Youth Theatre News and Youth Theatre Reviews. http://www.britishtheatreguide.info/amateurtheatre/ytreviews.htm.

Creative Drama & Theatre for Youth WebRing. http://www.amergin.net/cdytmain.html.

D4LC: Drama for Learning and Creativity. http://d4lc.org.uk.

Drama Queensland. http://www.dramaqueensland.org.au.

Drama Resource. http://www.dramaresource.com.

Drama-Education: learning in, with and through drama. http://www.drama-education.com.

Dramatool. http://www.dramatool.org.

Educational Theatre Association. *Dramatics: The Magazine for Students and Teachers of Theatre*. http://www.edta.org/publications/dramatics/default.aspx.

——. *Teaching Theatre*. http://www.edta.org/publications/teaching.aspx.

Interactive Drama for Education and Awareness in the Schools (IDEAS). http://www.ideasdrama.org.

International Journal of Education and the Arts. http://www.ijea.org.

Journal of Aesthetic Education (JAE). http://www.ijea.org

National Drama. *Drama: One Forum Many Voices.* http://www.dramamagazine.co .uk.

National Endowment for the Humanities. EDSITEment! The Best of Humanities on the Web. Drama Lesson Plans: http://edsitement.neh.gov/tab_lesson.asp; Drama Web Sites: http://edsitement.neh.gov/tab_websites.asp.

New Hampshire Public Television Knowledge Network. Drama Curriculum Resources. http://www.nhptv.org/kn/vs/drama4.htm.

New Zealand Journal of Research in Performing Arts and Education: Nga Mahi a Rehia. http://www.drama.org.nz/ejournal.asp?ID=2#contents.

onstage: The Monthly Newsletter of the National Association of Youth Theatres. http://www .nayt.org.uk/old/onstage.

Plays: The Drama Magazine for Young People. http://www.playsmag.com.

Research in Drama Education. http://www.tandf.co.uk/journals/titles/13569783.asp.

Stage Directions. http://stage-directions.com/index.php?option=com_frontpage& Itemid=1.

Theatre Research International. http://journals.cambridge.org/action/display Journal?jid=TRI.

Zeitschrift für Theaterpädagogik. http://www.bag-online.de/start.html.

Index

About the Authors

Kelly Eggers was the cofounder of Oyster River Players in 1995. She teaches, trains, and directs more than forty children in three terms a year and three or four productions a season. Her career includes acting, singing, and dancing on television and the professional stage.

Walter Eggers teaches Shakespeare and other literature courses at the University of New Hampshire. His career includes writing about literature and academic administration.